IMS PROGRAMMING TECHNIQUES

A Guide to Using DL/I

DAN KAPP
Cybernetic Resources Management, Inc.

JOSEPH F. LEBEN
DELTAK, Inc.

VNR VAN NOSTRAND REINHOLD COMPANY
NEW YORK CINCINNATI TORONTO LONDON MELBOURNE

FOR PAT AND CAROL

Copyright © 1978⟩ by Van Nostrand Reinhold Company Inc.

Library of Congress Catalog Card Number: 77-13233
ISBN: 0-442-80505-5

Manufactured in the United States of America

Published by Van Nostrand Reinhold Company Inc.
135 West 50th Street, New York, N.Y. 10020

Van Nostrand Reinhold Publishing
1410 Birchmount Road
Scarborough, Ontario M1P 2E7, Canada

Van Nostrand Reinhold
480 Latrobe Street
Melbourne, Victoria 3000, Australia

Van Nostrand Reinhold Company Limited
Molly Millars Lane
Wokingham, Berkshire, England

15 14 13 12 11

Library of Congress Cataloging in Publication Data
Kapp, Dan.
　　IMS programming techniques.

　　Bibliography: p.
　　Includes index.
　　1. Data base management. 2. Electronic digital computers—Programming. I. Leben, Joseph F., joint author. II. Title.
QA76.9.D3K36　　　　001.6'42　　　　77-13233
ISBN 0-442-80505-5

PREFACE

One of the most important topics currently of interest to people in the computing industry is the topic of data base technology, and new titles in this area are appearing at a faster and faster rate. Most publications in the data base field try to be all things to all people and to present information which has wide application to many different software implementations of data base techniques.

This book deals specifically with techniques that can be used in writing application programs in ANS COBOL, PL/I, or Assembler Language in an IMS DL/I data base environment. While some of the techniques may apply to other data base management systems, we decided to focus specifically on the IMS family of data base manager systems supplied by IBM. We feel that there is a real need in the industry for such a book. The subject of application programming in an IMS DL/I environment has long been made to seem a lot more difficult than it really is because the manufacturer's documentation is ill suited for use as training material.

This book starts from scratch and assumes no prior knowledge of IMS or any other data base management system. However, a basic knowledge of one of the IBM operating systems that supports IMS is assumed. This basic knowledge includes concepts and terminology used in describing the IBM access methods: QSAM, BSAM, ISAM, and VSAM.

We use a central case study, a data base for a hospital system, to present key concepts and programming techniques. While the main orientation of the book is toward the application programmer, it may be used by anyone who will be exposed to one of the IBM data base management systems. Analysts, designers, operators, and managers can use this book to learn what IMS is all about, and how application programs interface with it.

Exercises follow each of the chapters and answers are provided in the appendices. Some of the exercises consist of assignments to write entire programs. The organization of the book allows it to be used by individuals in a self-study environment, as a supplement to an in-house training program, or as a text in a college level data base programming course.

CONTENTS

3
Describing the Data Base to DL/I

4
Random Retrieval

5
Sequential Retrieval

6
Loading and Inserting Segments

7
Deleting and Updating Segments

8
Using Command Codes

9
Advanced Data Base Features

10
IMS Data Communications Concepts

11
Data Communications Programming Techniques

12
Access Methods

1

IMS Systems and DL/I

Introduction

In this book, we'll deal mainly with programming techniques that can be used to write application programs for the IMS family of IBM data base management systems. Most of the book will focus on the data base interface of these systems.

In this chapter, we'll look at some of the main purposes and objectives of data base management systems, particularly the three IBM products that this book applies to: IMS/VS, IMS/360 and DL/I DOS/VS. IMS/VS and IMS/360 contain a data communications interface as well as a data base interface. DL/I DOS/VS contains a data base interface only.

We'll look at the major parts of IMS and the functions each one performs in a data base management environment.

The Objectives of Data Base Management Systems

The main objectives of most data base management systems are to *increase data independence, reduce data redundancy,* and *provide data communications* facilities. You'll learn more about these and other objectives throughout this book. Here, we'll talk about these three main objectives briefly.

Data Independence

One of the objectives that data base systems attempt to accomplish is to reduce your program's dependence on the format of the data it processes. Data independence allows application programs to be written with little regard to how data is physically stored. You'll see later that the IBM data base management systems accomplish data independence by handling the requests that programs make for data. This allows application programs to request specific pieces of data by name, so they don't have to be aware of the actual stored format of data.

Data Redundancy

In a traditional data processing installation, the same information tends to be repeated in many different places. For example, customer information might be contained in several files, and if each file is keyed on customer number, the customer number would be carried in every file. Data base systems attempt to reduce the need for data redundancy by providing you with facilities that make it easy to retrieve information that's stored in a single place. This will become more clear when we compare a traditional file structure to a DL/I data base structure.

Data Communications

In addition to giving you new ways of organizing and accessing data, a third main objective of IMS/360 and IMS/VS is to provide you with facilities for accessing that data via remote terminals. DOS/VS DL/I systems do not supply data communications services. However, many installations use CICS for this purpose. If you choose, you can implement only the data base manipulation portion of the IMS systems. This allows application programs to access data bases in a batch environment. Optionally, you can implement both the data base facilities and the data communications portion. The data communications facilities provide programmers with an easy-to-use method for transferring data between the data base and remote terminals.

The Main Variations of IBM Data Base Systems

IBM supplies three data base systems. Each one is a program product, available from IBM for a fee. These three products are IMS/VS, IMS/360, and DL/I DOS/VS. The one that's selected by your installation depends heavily on the operating system that you use.

IMS/VS and IMS/360 consist of a DL/I component, which is the interface with the data base, and a data communications component, which is the user's interface with remote terminals. An individual installation may choose to use either the DL/I component, the data communications component, or both. DL/I DOS/VS systems consist of only the DL/I component.

Most of this book deals with DL/I, the data base component of the IBM data base management systems, but later chapters will provide an introduction into IMS data communications facilities.

IMS/VS

IMS/VS is the latest variation of IMS. In order to use IMS/VS, your installation must use one of IBM's virtual storage operating systems, OS/VS1 or OS/VS2. IMS/VS is the most comprehensive of the IMS variations. The other two, IMS/360 and DL/I DOS/VS, provide only subsets of the facilities provided by IMS/VS.

IMS/360

IMS/360 is the predecessor of IMS/VS. Although IMS/VS is a much more comprehensive software system than IMS/360, IMS/360 is still widely used. IMS/360 requires the use of either OS/MFT or OS/MVT. If your installation uses one of the virtual storage operating systems, IMS/VS will probably be selected because of its advanced functions. However, it is possible to run IMS/360 under the control of OS/VS1 or OS/VS2. In this book we'll refer to IMS/VS and IMS/360 collectively as IMS. The version of IMS/360 that this book applies to is IMS/360 Version 2. There is a Version 1 of IMS/360 that is now obsolete, and this book does not apply to that version.

DL/I DOS/VS

DL/I DOS/VS is an even more limited subset of IMS/VS. It is designed to be used only with DOS/VS systems. Since this data base management system implements only the data base interface portion of the IMS systems, it is named after that interface.

The Systems Covered in this Book

Since IMS/VS is the most comprehensive of the IMS systems, this book will be oriented to IMS/VS. However, features that are not available in IMS/360 will be clearly labeled "IMS/VS Only." Most of the data base facilities available in IMS/360 are also available in DL/I DOS/VS so you can use this book if you work with any of these three IBM data base management systems. In this book, we'll use the generic term *DL/I* to refer to the data base interface of either of the three systems. And we'll use the term *IMS* to refer to either IMS/VS or IMS/360.

The Five Components of the IMS
Software Environment

There are a number of ways that we can look at IMS. For the purposes of this introductory chapter, we'll break the IMS software environment into five main parts, the *application program,* the *data base,* the *DL/I control blocks,* the portion of the system known as *DL/I,* and the *data communications component.* Supporting IMS is an essential software component, the operating system. (See figure 1.1)

For DL/I DOS/VS, just remove the data communications component.

The Application Program

The application programs are those parts of the system that are designed and coded by the people at your installation. A DL/I application program uses a standard interface between it and the other components of the system. Those interfaces will be described in detail in this book. In general, DL/I application

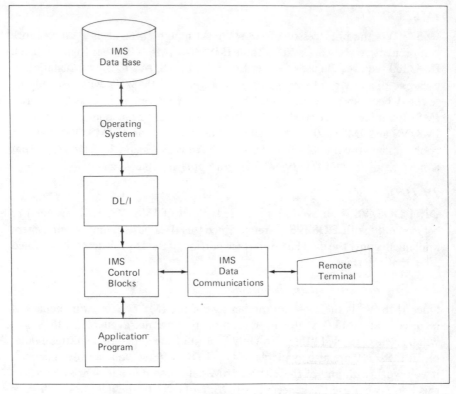

Figure 1.1 The IMS software environment

programs use standard CALL statements and parameter lists to communicate with DL/I. Because DL/I uses standard operating system interfaces, application programs may be written in either COBOL, PL/I, or Assembler Language.

The Data Base

The data base itself is the heart of any system using DL/I. We'll be talking a lot about the structure of DL/I data bases in this book. In general, a DL/I data base is organized differently from a traditional file or data set. A file is generally used by one or a small number of programs. A data base is generally shared by many programs.

DL/I data bases are normally stored in direct access storage, but in certain circumstances, tape can be used. One important thing to remember is that in a data base system, the data base is not accessed directly by application programs using standard operating system access methods. Application programs make calls to DL/I to request data. DL/I performs the actual manipulation of data in the data base.

The DL/I Component

DL/I is a set of program modules that sits between the data base and the application program. These DL/I program modules use standard operating system access methods and a set of specialized access methods to handle data transfer to and from the data base.

The way that we're using the term, DL/I stands for Data Language/I. While DL/I is not actually a programming language, DL/I does provide a set of programming standards for interfacing with DL/I modules. This set of programming standards forms what is sometimes called an *interface language*. The main purpose of most of this book is to describe, in detail, this interface language.

The DL/I Control Blocks

The application program uses the DL/I interface language in communicating with the system. The person who sets up DL/I data bases uses two main DL/I control blocks in describing the data base structure and identifying how the data base may be accessed. These two control blocks are called the *Data Base Description,* or DBD, and the *Program Specification Block* or PSB. These control blocks are normally maintained by your *data base administration group,* and we'll talk more about their function later.

The DBD is generally used to describe the physical nature of a DL/I data base. This includes the way in which it's stored on the storage device and the way in which the data will be accessed.

The PSB, on the other hand, describes the data base as a particular application program views it. The PSB identifies which pieces of data a program is allowed to access and the kinds of functions it can perform on each collection of data, such as read only, update, or delete.

The Data Communications Component

The data communications component of IMS is a set of program modules that allow your program to communicate with remote terminals. These data communications modules allow application programs to communicate with remote terminals through a standard interface language using CALL statements and parameter lists. The way in which you communicate with remote terminals is very similar to the way you communicate with DL/I.

CHAPTER 1 EXERCISES

1. List the three main purposes and objectives of IBM data base management systems.

2. From a knowledge of the operating system that's used by your installation, select the IBM program product that is most appropriate for your shop.

3. Following is a list of the five main components of IMS systems. Following that are five statements. Match each component with the statement that best describes it.

Components:

1. The Application Program
2. The DL/I Data Base
3. The DL/I Component
4. The DL/I Control Blocks
5. The Data Communications Component

Statements:

a. Written by your installation.
b. Communicates with remote terminals.
c. Handles data base access.
d. Pool of data shared by one or more programs.
e. Maintained by the data base administration group.

2

Basic DL/I Terminology

Introduction

The main purpose of this chapter is to define a series of terms. Many of these terms may be new to you because they're all used in describing DL/I data bases. If you've had any experience with other data base management systems, some of them may be familiar. To make it easy to define these DL/I terms, we're going to use a fictitious data base as an example. This data base will be used to keep track of information about a group of hospitals. Much of this chapter will describe the characteristics of this hospital data base, and we'll show how DL/I terminology relates to this example.

The HOSPITAL Data Base

Our sample data base is used by a series of applications to keep track of patients, hospital beds, and special facilities in a group of hospitals. Before we go any further, an explanation is in order if you happen to be familiar with medical applications. Our sample data base is not meant to be a solution to any real problem. Any data base which might actually be used in the real world for a similar purpose would be a lot more complex. Keep in mind, as you read on, that our data base is designed to illustrate key concepts about DL/I, and is not designed to be used in any real application.

The Information in the Data Base

Following is the general kind of information that we're going to store in the
HOSPITAL data base.

I. Hospital General Information
   A. Wards and Rooms in Each Hospital
      1. Patients in Each Ward
         a. Symptons
         b. Treatments
         c. Doctors
   B. Special Facilities Available at Each Hospital

First, we'll want general information about each hospital, such as name,
address, and phone number. Then, for each hospital, there are two types of
information that we'll store. First, we'll keep track of the wards and rooms in
each hospital. (Our example assumes that each hospital is divided into a series
of wards each having several rooms.) This information will include ward
number, total number of rooms, total number of beds, and the number of
available beds. The second type of information we'll store for each hospital will
be information about each special facility available at the hospital, such as a
pump-oxygenator.

For each ward in each hospital, we'll store information about each
patient in that ward. First, we'll store general information about each patient,
such as name, address, and date admitted. We'll also store more detailed
information about each patient's symptoms, treatments, and the doctors in
attendance. Keep in mind that each patient can have more than one symptom,
treatment, and doctor.

COBOL DATA DIVISION Coding

Rather than show the detailed information that we'll store in the data base in
a tabular form, such as in a traditional record layout, we'll show the format
of each piece of information in the form of COBOL DATA DIVISION coding.
You'll see that this will come in handy later. Figure 2.1 shows this coding.
Look it over just to familiarize yourself with it, and we'll describe this information in more detail as we go along. As an exercise, look at Figure 2.1 and try
to organize this information into a traditional file, or a series of traditional files.

Did you notice that there is very little redundant information in the
COBOL coding that you looked at? Any attempt to organize this information
into a series of interrelated files would probably require some data redundancy.
For example, to construct a file of patient records, you might have to carry
the patient's ward number and hospital identification in each record. Notice
that the COBOL coding for general patient information (under the 01 level
name PATIENT) does not contain that information.

Also note that if you were organizing this information into a set of
interrelated files, programmers attempting to use the information would have

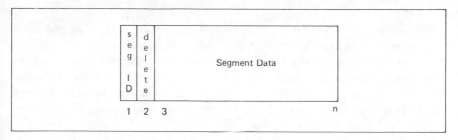

```
01   HOSPITAL.
     03   HOSPNAME          PIC X(20).
     03   HOSP-ADDRESS      PIC X(30).
     03   HOSP-PHONE        PIC X(10).
01   WARD.
     03   WARDNO            PIC XX.
     03   TOT-ROOMS         PIC XXX.
     03   TOT-BEDS          PIC XXX.
     03   BEDAVAIL          PIC XXX.
     03   WARDTYPE          PIC X(20).
01   PATIENT.
     03   PATNAME           PIC X(20).
     03   PAT-ADDRESS       PIC X(30).
     03   PAT-PHONE         PIC X(10).
     03   BEDIDENT          PIC X(4).
     03   DAILADMT          PIC X(6).
     03   PREV-STAY-FLAG    PIC X.
     03   PREV-HOSP         PIC X(20).
     03   PREV-DATE         PIC X(4).
     03   PREV-REASON       PIC X(30).
01   SYMPTOM.
     03   DIAGNOSE          PIC X(20).
     03   SYMPDATE          PIC X(6).
     03   PREV-TREAT-FLAG   PIC X.
     03   TREAT-DESC        PIC X(20).
     03   SYMP-DOCTOR       PIC X(20).
     03   SYMP-DOCT-PHONE   PIC X(10).
01   TREATMNT.
     03   TRTYPE            PIC X(20).
     03   TRDATE            PIC X(6).
     03   MEDICATION-TYPE   PIC X(20).
     03   DIET-COMMENT      PIC X(30).
     03   SURGERY-FLAG      PIC X.
     03   SURGERY-DATE      PIC X(6).
     03   SURGERY-COMMENT   PIC X(30).
01   DOCTOR.
     03   DOCTNAME          PIC X(20).
     03   DOCT-ADDRESS      PIC X(30).
     03   DOCT-PHONE        PIC X(10).
     03   SPECIALT          PIC X(20).
01   FACILITY.
     03   FACTYPE           PIC X(20).
     03   TOT-FACIL         PIC XXX.
     03   FACAVAIL          PIC XXX.
```

Figure 2.1 COBOL DATA DIVISION coding for the HOSPITAL data base

to be aware of the interrelationships, know the structure of the files, and know the formats of all the records that they would be working with.

In the worst case, suppose you had organized all the information into one big file containing many kinds of records. Programmers would have to be told how they could distinguish the records *they* required from all the other records. They would also have to know the general structure of the file, and how the records related to one another.

Problems of this kind are, of course, not impossible to solve. If you spent some time at it, you could probably come up with any number of solutions. The point is that data base management systems can help you with problems like these. At this point, we'll show you how DL/I can handle the hospital information and achieve two key objectives. We'll keep redundant information to a minimum, and at the same time make it very easy for programmers to access the information they're interested in without having to know anything about the information they don't need. At the same time, we'll introduce some key DL/I concepts and define some terms.

DL/I Terminology

The first concept that we'll introduce is that of *hierarchical structure*. This is a very key concept, and you'll run across the word "hierarchical" a lot in DL/I literature. If you'll look at the information that we're going to store in the data base, you'll notice that the information is already laid out in the form of a hierarchy. An outline is always in the form of a hierarchical structure. At the top of the outline is general information about hospitals. Under hospitals, at the second level of the outline, are two categories of information: information about wards and information about special facilities. Under wards, at the third level, is patient information. And finally, at the fourth level, under patient information, is specific symptom, treatment, and doctor information about each patient.

DL/I Hierarchical Structure

As you might expect, the fact that the information is laid out in a hierarchy is no accident. As we were designing the hospital data base, we had a hierarchical structure in mind. So we organized the information in that way on purpose. As with any hierarchical type of structure, such as a traditional company's organization chart, our hospital information can be laid out in the form of a series of boxes arranged in an inverted *tree structure.* The HOSPITAL data base tree structure is shown in figure 2.2. (TREATMNT isn't misspelled; you'll see later that most DL/I names are limited to eight characters.)

THE DATA BASE HIERARCHY CHART. Figure 2.2 shows one of the ways that you can represent the information in a DL/I data base. It's known as a *data base hierarchy chart.* Now let's use that figure to define some terms. Each box

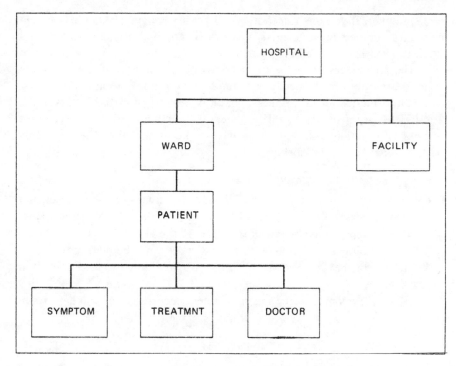

Figure 2.2 HOSPITAL data base hierarchy chart

in the chart represents a *segment,* and in each box is that segment's name. A segment is the smallest unit of information that DL/I handles when it's working with information in the data base. Within each segment are one or more data *fields.* You may not have known it when you first looked at the COBOL coding for the hospital information, but each 01 level data name defines one of the *segments* in the HOSPITAL data base. Each 03 level data name defines one of the *fields* within a segment.

It is possible to construct a DL/I data base in which each segment consists of only a single field. This would give you data independence at the data field level. By that we mean that programmers could be given access to only those data fields required by their applications, without having to be concerned about any other fields. In the HOSPITAL data base, the overhead generated by that level of data independence would be quite prohibitive.

On the other hand, we could have defined only a single segment containing all the information. In the HOSPITAL data base, that would require a great deal of data redundancy, and would completely eliminate any data independence. As in most data base applications, we looked for a reasonable compromise. We tried to group items of information that would normally be required at the same time and by the same application. For example, if you need a patient's address, the chances are good that you also need that patient's phone number. If you don't need it, you'll get it anyway. That's the compromise. Programmers must normally be made aware of all the information in a segment, even if they need only part of it.

The advantages of the segment approach are obvious if the segment's contents are carefully planned. For example, if your application requires only general information about hospitals, you only need to know the format of the HOSPITAL segment. As you'll see later, if your application only requires hospital information, you don't even have to know that the other segments exist, or what their relationships are.

Segment Types and Segment Occurrences

There is a very important distinction, in DL/I, between *segment types* and *segment occurrences*. In the HOSPITAL data base there are seven segment types. Each is represented by one of the boxes in the hierarchy chart. A DL/I data base is limited to 255 different segment types, and the hierarchy can go only fifteen segments deep. In other words, you are limited to fifteen *levels* in your hierarchy.

However, you may store as many segment occurrences as you have room

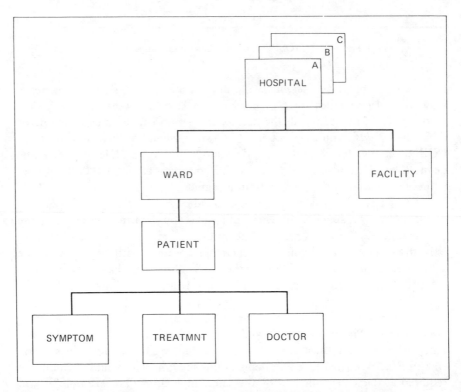

Figure 2.3 Three occurrences of the HOSPITAL segment type

for on your storage device. For example, if you're storing information about three hospitals, you'll have three occurrences of the hospital segment type in your data base. Figure 2.3 shows how you can represent three occurrences of the HOSPITAL segment type in a modified hierarchy chart.

The term *segment* is used to mean either segment type or segment occurrence depending on the context in which it's used. Notice that the segments under the second and third occurrences of the HOSPITAL segment are not shown. That would make the chart hopelessly complicated. We'll usually show multiple occurrences only for selected segments in the chart. You can, of course, show multiple occurrences at any level in the hierarchy. There's only a single PATIENT segment type, but there's an occurrence of the PATIENT segment for each patient, in each ward, in each hospital. (See figure 2.4.)

As you can probably imagine, in any data base of normal size, it would be impossible to show, in a diagram, all the occurrences of all the segment types. That's why we usually use a simple hierarchy chart, as in figure 2.2, to represent the structure of the data base. The fact that multiple occurrences may generally exist for each segment is taken for granted.

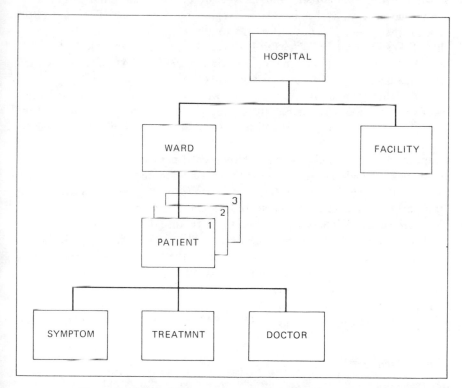

Figure 2.4 Three occurrences of the PATIENT segment type

The Relationships Between Segments

The terms *parent* and *child* are used to describe the relationships between segments in DL/I data bases. Any segment that has one or more segments directly below it in the hierarchy is called a *parent*. Any segment that has a segment directly above it in the hierarchy is called a *child*. For example, the PATIENT segment is a parent, and the SYMPTOM, TREATMNT, and DOCTOR segments are its children. However, the PATIENT segment is also a child of its parent, the WARD segment. *Parent* and *child* are relative terms and whether a segment is a parent or a child depends upon which portion of the data base you're looking at. A segment that is a child of some other segment is also known as a *dependent segment*. For example, the DOCTOR segment is a *dependent* of the PATIENT segment.

A particular DOCTOR segment cannot exist unless there is a PATIENT segment above it in the data base. The converse is not true. It is valid to have a PATIENT segment without SYMPTOM, TREATMNT, or DOCTOR segments below it, although it's possible that an application may not allow this.

The term *dependent* is often used to describe all those segments below a particular segment in the data base. For example, all the occurrences of SYMPTOM, TREATMNT, and DOCTOR below a particular PATIENT segment are known as that PATIENT segment's *dependents*. The concept of dependent segments extends more than one level in the hierarchy. For example, all occurrences of WARD, PATIENT, SYMPTOM, TREATMNT, DOCTOR, and FACILITY below a particular HOSPITAL segment occurrence are known as its *dependent* segments.

Another term to introduce here is *twin*. All occurrences of a particular segment type under a single parent segment occurrence are called *twins*. For example, if a particular patient had five symptoms, there would be five occurrences of the SYMPTOM segment under that PATIENT segment. Those five symptom segments would be twins. However, if patient A had one symptom and patient B had another, those two SYMPTOM segments would not be twins because they don't have the same parent. The set of all twins dependent on a particular parent is often referred to as a *twin chain*.

In order to maintain the inverted tree structure that is required by DL/I, no segment can have more than one parent. That means that any DL/I data base must have a single segment at the top of the hierarchy: this segment is only a parent segment; it's not a child of any other segment. This segment has special significance and is called the *root segment*. It's the segment through which all dependent segments are accessed. For example, to locate a particular PATIENT segment, the proper HOSPITAL root segment must be located first.

Hierarchical Paths

Segments are always retrieved along *hierarchical paths*. A path is a line that starts at the root segment, passes through segments at intermediate levels in the hierarchy, and ends at a segment at the bottom of the hierarchy. There are four paths in the HOSPITAL data base. You can construct the four paths by drawing a line through the segment types in each list in figure 2.5. Hierarchical paths govern the types of retrievals that you can specify. You'll learn more about this in later chapters when you learn how to retrieve segments.

The Data Base and Data Base Records

There are two more important terms to define. A *data base record* consists of a single occurrence of the root segment and all of its dependent segments. In our example, a single data base record consists of all the segments that belong to a particular hospital. This would include a single occurrence of the HOSPITAL segment, and all of the segment occurrences below it in the hierarchy. The *data base* consists of all the root segments and all of their dependents.

We've now defined most of the terms that you'll use in talking about

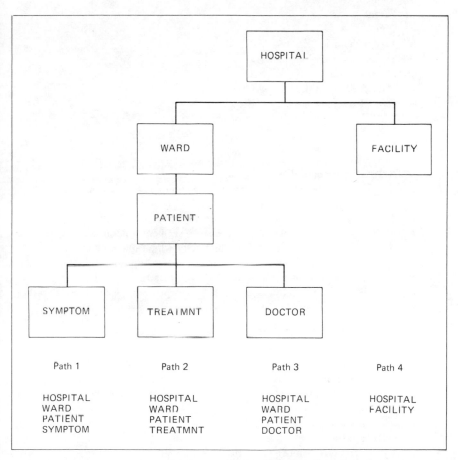

Path 1

HOSPITAL
WARD
PATIENT
SYMPTOM

Path 2

HOSPITAL
WARD
PATIENT
TREATMNT

Path 3

HOSPITAL
WARD
PATIENT
DOCTOR

Path 4

HOSPITAL
FACILITY

Figure 2.5 The four hierarchical paths

DL/I data bases. It's possible that some of them aren't completely clear to you at this point. Don't worry about it for now. They'll become a lot more clear after the next chapter where you'll learn how to work with the data in the data base.

CHAPTER 2 EXERCISES

1. Below are twelve terms that are used in describing DL/I data bases and twelve statements. Match each term with the statement that best describes it.

Terms

1. Hierarchy Chart
2. Dependent Segments
3. Field
4. Segment Type
5. Segment Occurrence
6. Parent
7. Child
8. Tree Structure
9. Twins
10. Root Segment
11. Data Base Record
12. Data Base

Statements

a. The collection of all root segment occurrences and all of their dependents.
b. A segment directly below some other segment in the hierarchy.
c. An individual data item.
d. A structure in which no segment can have more than one parent.
e. One occurrence of the root segment and all of its dependents.
f. All occurrences of a particular segment type under a single parent.
g. A chart showing the relationships between segment types in a DL/I data base.
h. A segment type at the top of the hierarchy which has no parent.
i. A segment directly above some other segment in the hierarchy.
j. A collection of related data items retrieved as a unit by DL/I.
k. All those segments below a particular segment occurrence in the hierarchy.
l. A generic term used to describe collections of related data items.

2. Figure 2.6 is a hierarchy chart for a data base. Answer the following questions about it.

a. What are the names of all the segment types in the data base?
b. What is the name of the root segment?
c. Identify the hierarchical paths in the data base by listing the segments along each path.
d. What is the name of segment F's parent?
e. What are the names of segment B's children?
f. How many levels are there in the hierarchy?
g. How many segment types are there in the data base?

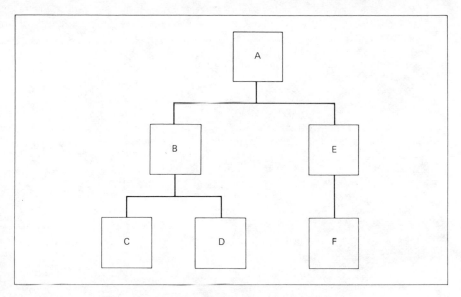

Figure 2.6 Exercise 2 hierarchy chart

3. Answer the following questions.
   a. What is the maximum allowable number of segment types in a DL/I data base?
   b. What is the maximum allowable number of levels in the hierarchy of a DL/I data base?

3

Describing the Data Base to DL/I

Introduction

Now that you've seen what an IMS hierarchical structure looks like, and you've learned most of the terms that we're going to use, let's see how the various people at your installation view a DL/I data base. After that, you'll see how the structure of a data base is defined. You'll learn a few more terms useful in describing data bases and DL/I application programs. We'll also introduce important control blocks used by IMS, and you'll see how your program operates in the DL/I environment.

At the end of this chapter, you'll learn some of the rules that you have to follow in writing DL/I programs. That will serve as a good introduction to the next chapter, where you'll learn how to retrieve information from a data base.

The Designer's View of the Data Base

A data base is normally used by multiple applications. Therefore, the data must be organized so it will serve the varied needs of all the applications that will work with it, and the organization of the data base often represents many compromises. Because the tasks involved in designing a data base require a variety of highly specialized skills, most installations that use data base systems have a group called the *Data Base Administration* group.

You can think of this group as being in total charge of what goes into the data base, who can access it, and its overall organization. This function is normally performed by a number of people, but for simplicity we'll refer to this group as though the function were performed by a single person. We'll call this person the *Data Base Administrator* or *DBA* for short.

Some shops separate the job of installing and maintaining the IMS system into a group called *IMS systems programming.* In other shops the system programming tasks are performed by data base administration. For simplicity, we'll assume these tasks are all performed by the data base administration group.

Factors in Designing Data Bases

When the DBA designs a data base, a number of factors must be considered. A few of these factors are important to the programming function. Some questions that programmers may ask about the data base include:

What are the names of the segments that I may access?

What are the formats of the various fields within those segments?

What are the names and formats of the fields that I can search on?

What are the hierarchical relationships of the segments that I may access?

What kind of processing can I perform on the segments that I'm allowed to access?

There are a number of additional questions that the DBA may ask that are not of as much concern to the individual programmer. These include:

What are the hierarchical relationships that will best fit the needs of the applications that will access the data base?

Which DL/I access method will provide the best level of efficiency and storage economy for the data base?

How often should the data base be reorganized?

What kinds of data security should be built into the system?

These lists are by no means complete, but they illustrate the kinds of decisions that the DBA must make in designing a data base. And they illustrate the kinds of questions that must be answered for the application programmer.

So far, you've seen the hierarchical structure of the HOSPITAL data base as it's viewed by the DBA, and you've seen the names of the segments. As you can probably already guess, we haven't yet provided all the information that you and DL/I need to know about the data base. So far, you have no way of asking DL/I to search for information within the data base. For example, if you wanted to retrieve a particular occurrence of the HOSPITAL segment, how would you ask for it? Would you provide DL/I with the hospital's name, or its address, or its phone number? All three of those pieces of information are stored in the HOSPITAL segment.

Key and Search Fields

When we performed the DBA's role in designing the HOSPITAL data base, we had to decide not only what should be stored in each segment, but also which of the fields within each segment would be known to DL/I as *key fields* and *search fields*. For example, when we decided that the HOSPITAL segment should contain the hospital's name, its address, and its phone number, we also decided that no application would ever need to ask DL/I to search for a segment based on the address or phone number field. The only field that DL/I will be interested in is the hospital name field. Figure 3.1 shows what the HOSPITAL segment will look like to an application program that retrieves it. But as far as DL/I is concerned, it will look like figure 3.2 when DL/I manipulates it.

DL/I does not know that the remaining fields contain an address and phone number; anything beyond the hospital name is meaningless to DL/I. When the DBA designs a data base, any data item, part of a data item, or combination of contiguous data items can be designated as a field on which DL/I can search. The DBA assigns a one to eight character symbolic name to each field identified to DL/I. You'll see how this is done in a minute.

KEY OR SEQUENCE FIELDS. One type of field that DL/I works with is called a *key field* or *sequence field*. These terms mean the same thing and they're used interchangeably. A key or sequence field is a field that DL/I uses to maintain segments in ascending sequence. In the HOSPITAL segment, we've designated the hospital name field as a key field, so DL/I will maintain HOSPITAL segments in ascending alphabetic sequence by hospital name. Only a single field within each segment may be designated as a key or sequence field. However, segments are generally *not required* to have a key or sequence field.

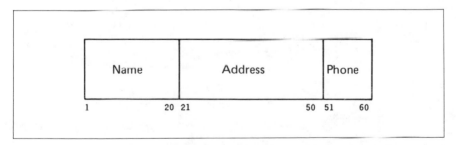

Figure 3.1 The HOSPITAL segment to the program

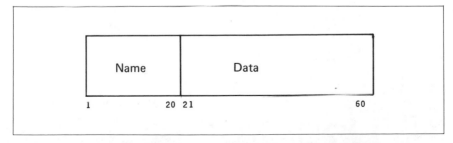

Figure 3.2 The HOSPITAL segment to DL/I

Sequence fields may be designated as unique or nonunique. If the HOS-
PITAL segment sequence field were designated as unique, DL/I would not
allow a program to place two HOSPITAL segments with the same hospital
name into the data base.

```
01  HOSPITAL.
    03  HOSPNAME          PIC  X(20).  ← unique key
    03  HOSP-ADDRESS      PIC  X(30).
    03  HOSP-PHONE        PIC  X(10).
01  WARD.
    03  WARDNO            PIC  XX.      ← unique key
    03  TOT-ROOMS         PIC  XXX.
    03  TOT-BEDS          PIC  XXX.
    03  BEDAVAIL          PIC  XXX.     ← search
    03  WARDTYPE          PIC  X(20).   ← search
01  PATIENT.
    03  PATNAME           PIC  X(20).   ← search
    03  PAT-ADDRESS       PIC  X(30).
    03  PAT-PHONE         PIC  X(10).
    03  BEDIDENT          PIC  X(4).    ← unique key
    03  DATEADMT          PIC  X(6).    ← search
    03  PREV-STAY-FLAG    PIC  X.
    03  PREV-HOSP         PIC  X(20).
    03  PREV-DATE         PIC  X(4).
    03  PREV-REASON       PIC  X(30).
01  SYMPTOM.
    03  DIAGNOSE          PIC  X(20).   ← search
    03  SYMPDATE          PIC  X(6).    ← non-unique key
    03  PREV-TREAT-FLAG   PIC  X.
    03  TREAT-DESC        PIC  X(20).
    03  SYMP-DOCTOR       PIC  X(20).
    03  SYMP-DOCT-PHONE   PIC  X(10).
01  TREATMNT.
    03  TRTYPE            PIC  X(20).   ← search
    03  TRDATE            PIC  X(6).    ← non-unique key
    03  MEDICATION-TYPE   PIC  X(20).
    03  DIET-COMMENT      PIC  X(30).
    03  SURGERY-FLAG      PIC  X.
    03  SURGERY-DATE      PIC  X(6).
    03  SURGERY-COMMENT   PIC  X(30).
01  DOCTOR.
    03  DOCTNAME          PIC  X(20).   ← search
    03  DOCT-ADDRESS      PIC  X(30).
    03  DOCT-PHONE        PIC  X(10).
    03  SPECIALT          PIC  X(20).   ← search
01  FACILITY.
    03  FACTYPE           PIC  X(20).   ← search
    03  TOT-FACIL         PIC  XXX.
    03  FACAVAIL          PIC  XXX.     ← search
```

Figure 3.3 The HOSPITAL data base key and search fields

ADDITIONAL SEARCH FIELDS. If the DBA decides that it will be useful to perform a search for a segment based on the contents of some field, but that the segments should not be sequenced on that field, that field can be designated as a *search field*. The DBA can identify up to 255 search fields in a segment, but the total number of key and search fields cannot exceed 255 for any segment. So if the DBA has already specified a key field, only 254 additional search fields can be defined. It's not likely, however, that you'll ever see a data base that uses this many search fields in a single segment.

The HOSPITAL Data Base Key and Search Fields

Figure 3.3 shows another listing of the COBOL DATA DIVISION coding for the HOSPITAL data base segments. This time we've identified the key fields and search fields in each segment.

Each key field and search field that the DBA defines generates more overhead for DL/I. We've probably specified more key and search fields than would normally be considered efficient, but as we mentioned earlier, the HOSPITAL data base was designed with teaching in mind, and not efficiency.

The HOSPITAL Segment

Normally, a root segment, such as the HOSPITAL segment is required to have a unique key field. We've chosen the hospital name field. (See figure 3.4.) We didn't think that it would ever be useful to search for a HOSPITAL segment based on a hospital's address or phone number, so we haven't specified any additional search fields for the HOSPITAL segment.

The WARD Segment

We'll be able to search for a WARD segment based on the contents of up to three fields. (See figure 3.5.) The key field, which we will require to be unique, is the ward number field. We also want to search for a WARD segment based

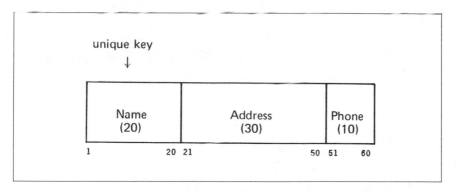

Figure 3.4 The HOSPITAL segment

on the number of beds available, and/or the contents of a twenty-character description of the type of ward the segment describes. So we've designated those two fields as additional search fields.

The PATIENT Segment

We'll also allow programs to search for PATIENT segments based on three different fields. (See figure 3.6.) The unique key field for the PATIENT segment will be the four-character bed identifier. It consists of a two-character room number and a two-character bed number. We didn't use the patient's name for the key field, because we might have two patients with the same name, and we wanted to guarantee that this segment would have a unique key. We did want to allow programs to search for PATIENT segments based on a patient's name and also on the date that a patient was admitted to the hospital, so we've designated those fields as additional search fields.

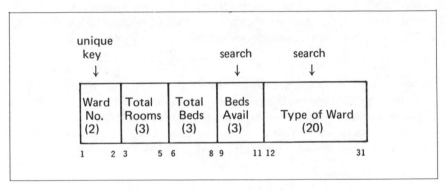

Figure 3.5 The WARD segment

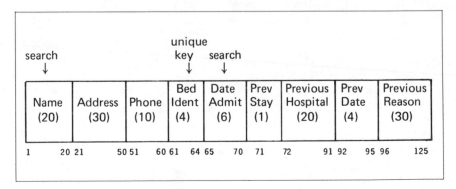

Figure 3.6 The PATIENT segment

The SYMPTOM and TREATMNT Segments

The SYMPTOM and TREATMNT segments are sequenced on the date that the segments are stored in the data base. (See figure 3.7.) The date fields were chosen as the key fields because having the segments in date sequence will provide some useful historical information. For example, if the first SYMPTOM segment is stored in the data base at the time of a patient's admittance, and the last TREATMNT segment is entered at the time of the patient's release, we'll always be able to figure out a patient's length of stay. We've designated a twenty-character description field in each segment as an additional search field as well. Notice that in these two segments, the key fields are not unique. This is because many segments of each type might be stored in the data base under a single PATIENT segment in any given day.

The DOCTOR Segment

The DOCTOR segment is very straightforward. We've designated two fields as search fields, the doctor's name, and a description of the doctor's specialty. (See figure 3.8.) The sequence of the DOCTOR segments is not important, so the DOCTOR segments will not have key fields.

The FACILITY Segment

The FACILITY segment is equally straightforward. We'll allow a search based on a description of the facility, or on the number of facilities of that type available. (See figure 3.9.) Again, we didn't feel that the sequence of the segments would be important, so both will be search fields and there will be no key field.

In the HOSPITAL data base, each segment has at least one field defined as a key or search field. DL/I does, however, allow the data base administrator to define a segment that has no key or search fields. For example, a program might always need to access all occurrences of a particular segment type under one parent. In that case, key or search fields would not be necessary.

Defining the Data Base

Once segments have been defined, the hierarchical structure decided upon, and key and search fields chosen, the DBA can communicate this information to DL/I. To do this, a *control block* is created in a DL/I library, called a *data base description,* or *DBD* for short. It describes the physical nature of a data base to DL/I. A process called *DBD generation,* or *DBDGEN,* is used to create a DBD. The DBA creates a DBD by coding a series of DBDGEN control statements. We'll go over the coding for the HOSPITAL data base DBD later in this chapter, but remember that performing

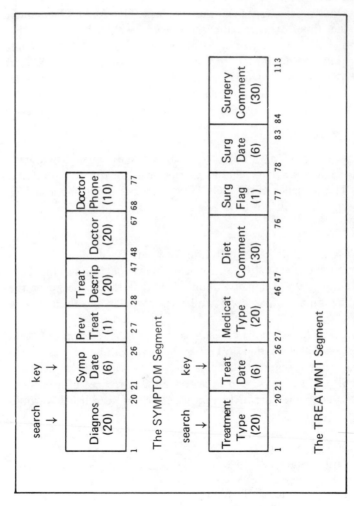

Figure 3.7 The SYMPTOM and TREATMNT segments

The SYMPTOM Segment

search →	key →				
Diagnos (20)	Symp Date (6)	Prev Treat (1)	Treat Descrip (20)	Doctor (20)	Doctor Phone (10)
1 20 21	26 27	28	47 48	67 68	77

The TREATMNT Segment

search →	key →					
Treatment Type (20)	Treat Date (6)	Medicat Type (20)	Diet Comment (30)	Surg Flag (1)	Surg Date (6)	Surgery Comment (30)
1 20 21	26 27	46 47	76 77	78	83 84	113

26

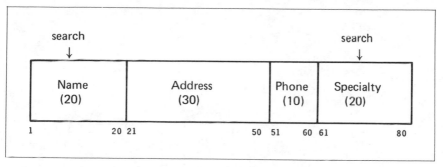

Figure 3.8 The DOCTOR segment

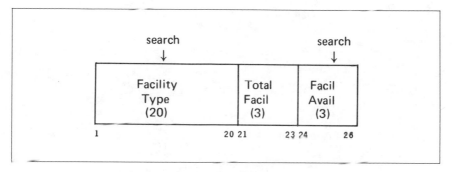

Figure 3.9 The FACILITY segment

the DBDGEN for a data base is normally the job of the data base administrator. It's not normally done by the analyst or programmer.

The DBDGEN Process

Before we look at DBDGEN control statements, let's look at the DBDGEN process itself. (See figure 3.10.) DGDGEN control statements are actually Assembler Language macro statements. The macros are supplied by IBM in a library named something like IMS2.MACLIB or IMSVS.MACLIB. DBDGEN control statements are normally coded by the DBA and submitted to the system with JCL that invokes a cataloged procedure usually called DBDGEN. The DBDGEN procedure causes the DBDGEN control statements to be processed by the assembler, producing an *object module*. The object module is then passed to the linkage editor which, in turn, stores a load module in another IMS library, usually called something like IMS2.DBDLIB or IMSVS.DBDLIB. We'll refer to this library as DBDLIB. The load module that's stored in DBDLIB by the DBDGEN procedure is the DBD itself, ready to be loaded into storage.

The DBD process is normally performed only once for a data base. Then all applications can use that DBD in accessing the information in the data base.

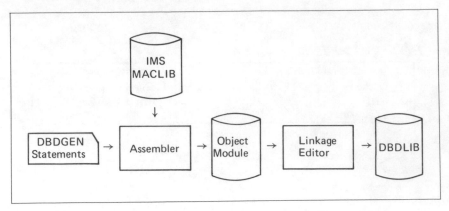

Figure 3.10 The DBDGEN process

```
PRINT    NOGEN
DBD      NAME=HOSPDBD,ACCESS=HISAM
DATASET  DD1=PRIME,OVFLW=OVERFLW,DEVICE=3330
SEGM     NAME=HOSPITAL,PARENT=0,BYTES=60
FIELD    NAME=(HOSPNAME,SEQ,U),BYTES=20,START=1,TYPE=C
SEGM     NAME=WARD,PARENT=HOSPITAL,BYTES=31
FIELD    NAME=(WARDNO,SEQ,U),BYTES=2,START=1,TYPE=C
FIELD    NAME=BEDAVAIL,BYTES=3,START=9,TYPE=C
FIELD    NAME=WARDTYPE,BYTES=20,START=12,TYPE=C
SEGM     NAME=PATIENT,PARENT=WARD,BYTES=125
FIELD    NAME=(BEDIDENT,SEQ,U),BYTES=4,START=61,TYPE=C
FIELD    NAME=PATNAME,BYTES=20,START=1,TYPE=C
FIELD    NAME=DATEADMT,BYTES=6,START=65,TYPE=C
SEGM     NAME=SYMPTOM,PARENT=PATIENT,BYTES=77
FIELD    NAME=(SYMPDATE,SEQ),BYTES=6,START=21,TYPE=C
FIELD    NAME=DIAGNOSE,BYTES=20,START=1,TYPE=C
SEGM     NAME=TREATMNT,PARENT=PATIENT,BYTES=113
FIELD    NAME=(TRDATE,SEQ),BYTES=6,START=21,TYPE=C
FIELD    NAME=TRTYPE,BYTES=20,START=1,TYPE=C
SEGM     NAME=DOCTOR,PARENT=PATIENT,BYTES=80
FIELD    NAME=DOCTNAME,BYTES=20,START=1,TYPE=C
FIELD    NAME=SPECIALT,BYTES=20,START=61,TYPE=C
SEGM     NAME=FACILITY,PARENT=HOSPITAL,BYTES=26
FIELD    NAME=FACTYPE,BYTES=20,START=1,TYPE=C
FIELD    NAME=FACAVAIL,BYTES=3,START=24,TYPE=C
DBDGEN
FINISH
END
```

Figure 3.11 The HOSPITAL data base DBD

A new DBD is normally created only if the physical nature of the data base changes in some way.

The HOSPITAL Data Base DBDGEN

Figure 3.11 is a listing of the DBDGEN control statements that the DBA would use to describe the HOSPITAL data base. PRINT NOGEN is an Assembler Language control statement that causes the assembler to suppress the listing of the machine instructions that are generated by each DBDGEN macro. You won't normally be interested in those.

THE DBD MACRO. The second card is the DBD macro. It communicates general information about the physical nature of the data base. In this case, it gives the DBD a name, HOSPDBD, and it tells which of the DL/I access methods will be used to manipulate the data. There are several access methods that the DBA can choose from, each having its own unique advantages and disadvantages. You'll learn more about these in a later chapter. Here we're using an access method called HISAM. It has a lot in common with the standard ISAM access method, and stands for *Hierarchical Indexed Sequential Access Method.*

THE DATASET MACRO. This card gives information about the data sets that will be used to store the data. A HISAM data base requires two data sets. In the example, the DD names that we chose for these two data sets are PRIME and OVERFLW. DD statements with these names must be included in the execution JCL for any programs that access this data base. The DEVICE operand tells DL/I what kind of device will be used to store the segments, in this case an IBM 3330 direct access storage device.

DEFINING THE HIERARCHICAL STRUCTURE. Following the DBD and DATASET macros are a series of SEGM and FIELD statements. Each SEGM statement names and describes one of the segment types that will make up the HOSPITAL data base. Following each SEGM statement are one or more FIELD statements that name and describe sequence fields or search fields that have been chosen for the segment.

THE SEGM MACROS. In each SEGM statement, the NAME operand gives a name to the segment and the PARENT operand identifies its parent. The operand PARENT=0, or the absence of the PARENT operand, identifies the root segment. The PARENT operands define the hierarchical structure of the data base. As an exercise, try to construct a hierarchy chart by using the PARENT operands in the SEGM statements.

The SEGM statements are coded in *hierarchical sequence.* You'll learn more about hierarchical sequence when you see how DL/I reads sequentially through a data base. For now, notice that when you compare the sequence of the SEGM statements to the HOSPITAL data base hierarchy chart, hierarchical sequence of the segment types is *top to bottom, left to right.*

The only other operand in the SEGM statement is the BYTES operand. It gives the length of the segment in bytes.

THE FIELD MACROS. In FIELD statements, NAME operands contain from one to three positional subparameters. The first subparameter gives a name to the key or search field. If it's the only subparameter coded, the field is a *search field.* If the characters SEQ are coded in the second position, the field is a *key* or *sequence field.* Only one of these is allowed per SEGM statement. If a U is coded in the third position, the field is a *unique* sequence field.

The START operand tells the starting byte location of the key or search field, relative to the beginning of the segment. The BYTES operand tells its length in bytes. TYPE=C says that the field consists of character (alphanumeric) data.

If you check back to the DATA DIVISION coding in figure 3.3, you'll notice that the names of the segments, key fields, and search fields in the SEGM and FIELD statements correspond to the data names used in the COBOL coding. This is not a requirement, however, since DL/I has no knowledge of the data names that you code in your program. All communication between your program and DL/I is done by means of parameter lists. Using the same names, however, is a useful convention. It can cut down on the communication problems that occur when many people are using the same data base or working on the same project.

DBDGEN CONTROL MACROS. The last three statements in figure 3.11 are used for control purposes. The DBDGEN statement signifies the end of the SEGM and FIELD statements for this DBD. The FINISH statement causes the assembler to set a nonzero condition code if errors are caught during the assembly, and the END statement signals end-of-data to the assembler. These three statements are almost always used at the end of a DBDGEN.

Take some time at this point to review the hierarchical structure of the HOSPITAL data base, and the information that you just read about the various key fields and search fields that we described at the beginning of this chapter. Make sure that you understand how all of this information is communicated to DL/I through the information in the DBDGEN control statements.

Physical and Logical Data Bases

In the DBDGEN that you just looked at, we defined what is called a *physical data base.* The term *physical data base* is used to describe the physical nature of a data base and the hierarchical relationships between the segment types. We won't go into very much detail here, but the DBDGEN process can also be used to define a *logical data base*. A logical data base is normally used to combine segments from more than one physical data base into a new hierarchical structure. This is done through the use of *logical relationships*. Logical relationships allow the DBA to define new hierarchical relationships without actually having to create a new physical data base. It's a powerful way of relating the data stored in more than one physical data base so that it may be accessed in a single hierarchical structure. This can often reduce the need for redundant information. You'll learn more about logical relationships later in this chapter.

It's important to remember at this point that physical and logical data bases are normally only of interest to the DBA. Individual programs do not access physical or logical data bases directly. Let's see how this works.

Logical and Application Data Structures

Logical data structure is a term that we'll use to refer to the group of segments that an individual application program may access. To the application program, *the logical data structure is the data base*. Let's look at a possible logical data structure that would be useful to a program accessing the HOSPITAL data base. Suppose a program will do nothing but retrieve PATIENT segments. Figure 3.12 shows the portion of the HOSPITAL data base that this program would be required to know about.

The program will retrieve only PATIENT segments, but the hierarchical structure must include the HOSPITAL and WARD segments because the PATIENT segments are dependent on them. We'll be using this retrieval program as an example throughout the rest of this chapter and into the first part of the next. In the next chapter, you'll see the specifications for this program and a complete listing of it.

To be more accurate, we can also represent the hierarchical structure of the portion of the data base that the program will access, as in figure 3.13. The DBA can let a program access the HOSPITAL and WARD segments to locate a dependent PATIENT segment, but prevent that program from accessing the data stored in those segments. That would make sense for our retrieval program since it only needs access to the information in the PATIENT segment. Now let's see what the DBA would have to do before you could run the retrieval program.

Defining a Logical Data Structure

The DBA communicates the hierarchical structure that the application will use in much the same way as the hierarchical structure of the physical data base is communicated. The DBA sets up a logical data structure by creating a control block called a *program specification block* or *PSB*. This is done with a process called *PSB generation* or *PSBGEN* which is very similar to the DBDGEN process. Before we look at the PSB statements

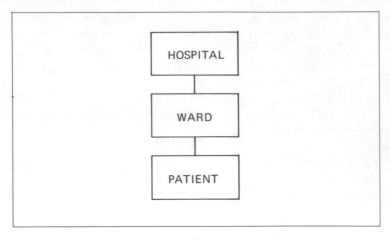

Figure 3.12 Retrieval program logical data structure

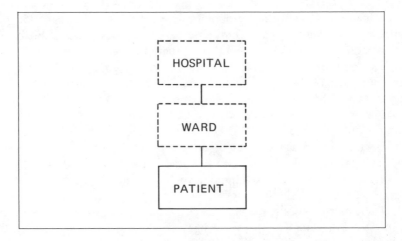

Figure 3.13 Retrieval program logical data structure

for our retrieval program logical data structure, let's look at the PSBGEN process itself.

The PSBGEN Process

The PSBGEN process is very similar to DBDGEN. The PSBGEN statements are processed by the assembler and the linkage editor to produce a load module, or PSB, that is stored in a library usually called PSBLIB. (See figure 3.14.) Each PSB consists of one or more control blocks called *program communication blocks* or *PCBs*. Our example will contain only a single PCB. Each PCB within a PSB defines one logical data structure. All the PCB's within a single PSB are collectively known as an *application data structure*.

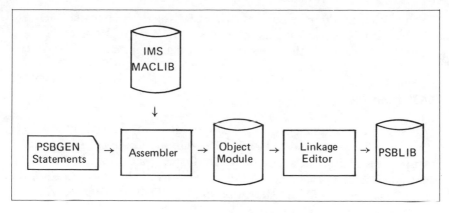

Figure 3.14 The PSBGEN process

```
PCB      TYPE=DB,NAME=HOSPDBD
SENSEG   NAME=HOSPITAL,PARENT=0,PROCOPT=K
SENSEG   NAME=WARD,PARENT=HOSPITAL,PROCOPT=K
SENSEG   NAME=PATIENT,PARENT=WARD,PROCOPT=G
PSBGEN   LANG=COBOL,PSBNAME=PATGET
END
```

Figure 3.15 Retrieval program PSB

DL/I allows a PSB to define more than one logical data structure because each DL/I application program in an installation has its own PSB stored in PSBLIB. Although it is possible that more than one program may share a single PSB, no program can use more than one PSB in a single execution. Individual programs may require access to more than one physical or logical data base, however, and it is also possible that a single program may require separate access to different parts of the same data base. So DL/I allows the DBA to define any number of logical data structures in a single PSB. These logical data structures define all the segments that an individual application program may access.

The PSBGEN for the Retrieval Program

Let's look at the PSB coding for the retrieval program and see what each of the control statements means. (See figure 3.15.)

THE PCB MACRO. The first statement is the PCB macro. It begins the coding for one program communication block or PCB. It tells the type of PCB that is being defined, in this case a data base PCB. You'll see later that there are other types of PCBs, such as data communication PCBs. It also gives the name of the DBD that defines the segments that are named in this PCB. A PSB can only identify segments that have already been defined in a DBD. In the example, the segments are defined in HOSPDBD, the DBD for the HOSPITAL data base.

THE SENSEG MACROS. Following the PCB statement is a series of SENSEG statements. These statements identify the segments in the HOSPITAL data base that this application is *sensitive* to. The first operand in each is the NAME operand. The name coded here must be the same as the name coded in the NAME operand in a SEGM statement in the DBD for the HOSPITAL data base.

The PARENT operands identify the hierarchical structure of this logical data structure. The PARENT operands work the same way here as they do in the DBD. One difference is that the hierarchical structure may not be chosen arbitrarily. The PSB may not define hierarchical relationships that do not exist in the DBD.

The PROCOPT operands are optional. PROCOPT stands for *processing options;* these operands identify the type of processing that may be performed on each segment. PROCOPT=K means that the segment is *key sensitive* only. That means that the application may use the segment to gain access to segments below it in the hierarchy, but that the application may not access the data within it. If a sensitive segment is not key sensitive, it is *data sensitive.* PROCOPT=G means that the segment is data sensitive, but that the application may only retrieve the segment. The application may not delete the segment or replace it in the data base. We'll go over the other possible PROCOPT values in later chapters.

THE PSBGEN MACRO. The PSBGEN statement is always the last statement, other than the END statement, in the PSBGEN. It identifies the language the program that will use this PSB is coded in, and gives the name of this PSB. If more than one data base PCB is defined in a single PSB, there will be two or more PCB statements, each followed by a group of SENSEG statements for the segments making up each logical data structure. All those statements would then be followed by a single PSBGEN statement.

If the need for more than one PCB for a single program is not completely clear to you at this point, don't worry about it. You'll see plenty of examples later on when we cover the topic of multiple PCBs.

Logical Relationships

Earlier, we said that the DBA can write DBDGEN control statements to define either physical or logical data bases. An example of a physical data base is the HOSPITAL data base we've been looking at. Now let's look at an example of a logical data base.

Suppose we wanted to write a PSB to give us access to the logical data structure in figure 3.16. The last segment type, called BILLING, contains information that allows the hospital to send bills to patients. We could provide access to the BILLING segment by adding it to the hierarchical structure of the HOSPITAL data base, performing a new DBDGEN, and loading the data base, including the new BILLING segment occurrences. Then our physical data base would contain the billing information. This is shown in figure 3.17. But suppose that billing information already existed in some other physical data base. Figure 3.18 shows a HISTORY data base that contains the BILL-ING information that we need access to.

If the billing information already exists, it would be redundant to store it again in the hospital data base. What we actually need is a combination of the information in the two physical data bases.

One way that we can gain access to both data bases is to code a PSB that contains two PCBs, one for each physical data base. That would provide us access to the two data bases. But we'd have to provide the ties between the two data bases through our own programming. We wouldn't get a logical data structure as shown in figure 3.16. We'd actually get two separate logical data structures, one with segments from the HOSPITAL data base, and one with segments from the HISTORY data base.

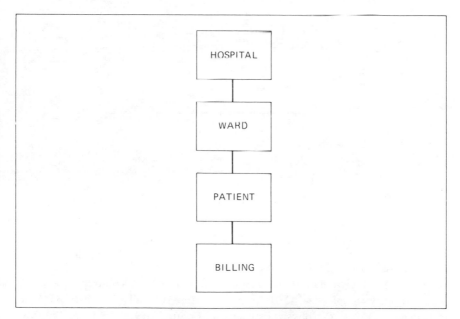

Figure 3.16 Accessing billing information

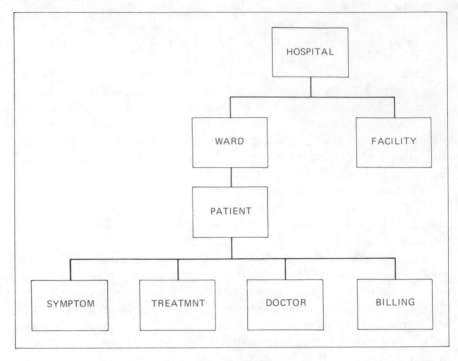

Figure 3.17 Adding a BILLING segment

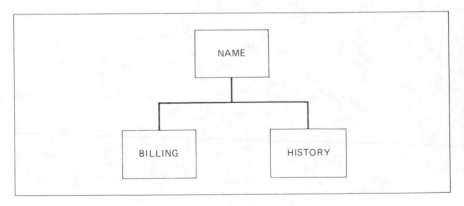

Figure 3.18 The HISTORY data base

There is a way to hook the data bases together so that our program can work with the logical data structure shown in figure 3.16. To do this the DBA would modify the physical DBD coding for the HOSPITAL and HISTORY data bases to create the physical structure in figure 3.19. Here logical path is created from the HOSPITAL data base to the HISTORY data base. Instead of duplicating the BILLING segment in the HOSPITAL data base, we're creating a new segment type called the PBILL segment. Each occurrence of it points to the appropriate occurrence of the BILLING segment in the HISTORY data base.

The DBA would then code up a logical DBD which maps against our two new physical DBDs. This logical DBD would define the logical structure shown in figure 3.16. PSBs requiring access to that logical structure would reference the logical DBD rather than either one of the physical DBDs.

In logical relationships terminology, the PBILL segment in the HOSPITAL physical data base is called a *logical child* segment. The segment it points to, the BILLING segment, is *called a logical parent.*

The advantage to this logical relationship is that the BILLING information exists in only one place. But your program has access to it as if it were a part of the HOSPITAL data base. When the BILLING data base is updated, the logical child segments will point to the updated information. This is much better than trying to repeat the billing information in two places.

The example we just looked at is an example of the simplest kind of logical relationship. It's called a *unidirectional logical relationship.* There are more complex types of logical relationships that allow you to hook data bases together in two directions. This would allow you to access certain segments in the HOSPITAL data base via the HISTORY data base, as well as allowing you to access certain segments in the HISTORY data base via the HOSPITAL

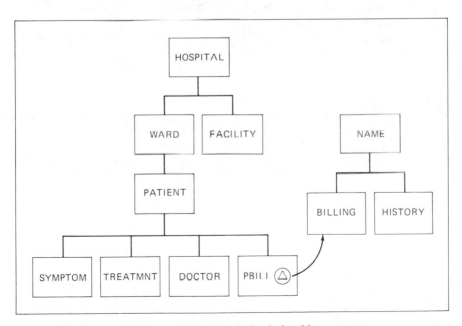

Figure 3.19 A logical relationship

data base. Since logical relationships are of concern mainly to the DBA, we won't go into any more detail on them here.

How the Control Blocks Hook Together

Let's take a look now, at how the DBD, the PSB, the PCBs, and the application program work together to access the data in the data base. We'll use the retrieval program as an example. The DBD and PSB help your program communicate with DL/I. Let's begin our investigation of how your program communicates with DL/I by looking at how a DL/I program gets into execution. Figure 3.20 shows the JCL for a job step to execute our retrieval program.

Executing a DL/I Program

As in any job step, the EXEC statement gives the name of the program that you want to execute. When you execute a DL/I batch program, you give the name of a DL/I load module called the *region controller.* Now, how does DL/I know which application program to run? A programming standard will make this clear. A convention which is required for data communications programs, and optional for batch programs, is that your load module name and the name of your PSB should be the same. In the PARM parameter of the EXEC statement, you code the name of your PSB. This tells DL/I the name of your program and the name of your PSB. (If your program name is different for a batch program, DL/I allows you to specify both names in the PARM parameter.)

From the NAME operand in the PCB statement in your PSB, the system

```
//RETRIEVE   EXEC   PGM=DFSRRC00,PARM='DLI,PATGET'
//STEPLIB    DD     DSN=IMSVS.RESLIB,DISP=SHR
//           DD     DSN=IMSVS.PGMLIB,DISP=SHR
//IMS        DD     DSN=IMSVS.PSBLIB,DISP=SHR
//           DD     DSN=IMSVS.DBDLIB,DISP=SHR
//SYSUDUMP   DD     SYSOUT=A
//PRIME      DD     DSN=IMS.VSAM.PRIME,DISP=OLD
//OVERFLW    DD     DSN=IMS.VSAM.OVERFLOW,DISP=OLD
//OUTPUT     DD     SYSOUT=A
//INPUT      DD     *
              ---
       input transactions
              ---
```

Figure 3.20 Retrieval program JCL

is able to load into memory the DBD for the physical or logical data base that will be required. The DBD contains the DD names of the DD statements that describe the data base. Your execution JCL, in addition to naming the program that will be executed, contains the DD statements for the data base.

Notice that there are other DD statements in the job step besides the ones for the data base. The PRIME and OVERFLW DD statements describe the HISAM data base. The INPUT DD statement is for the input file, and the OUTPUT DD statement is for the output report. The other DD statements are required by DL/I, and you'll see more about them later.

DL/I Programming Standards

In order for your program to communicate correctly with DL/I, certain programming standards must be followed in any DL/I application program that you write. Your application program is treated as a subroutine of DL/I, and standard subroutine linkages and parameter lists are used to hook your program to the DL/I module that passes control to it. When DL/I links to your program, it passes you a parameter list containing a list of addresses of the PCBs in your PSB. Each PCB contains a series of data items that will be useful to your program during execution. For example, one of the fields within the PCB tells your program whether or not a retrieval was successful.

DL/I ENTRY LINKAGE. It's necessary for you to establish a linkage between your program and the PCBs that DL/I passes to you. Figure 3.21 shows the coding, in COBOL, that will accomplish this linkage for you. This entry linkage coding accomplishes three things. First, it gives the standard DL/I name to the entry point of the program. The entry point of any COBOL DL/I program must be DLITCBL. Second, it hooks your program to the PCB through the USING clause of the ENTRY statement. Third, the data names in the LINKAGE SECTION describe the data areas in the PCB passed to you by DL/I. These data names make up what's called the *PCB mask*. This entry coding, or something similar to it, must be a part of any DL/I program that you write.

Figure 3.22 shows graphically the relationships that exist between your program and DL/I. Each programming language has linkage statements that let you accomplish these same functions. You can look at the coding examples in appendices F and G to see how this works in PL/I and Assembler Language.

REQUESTING DL/I SERVICES. Just as your program is treated as a subroutine of a DL/I module, other DL/I modules are treated as subroutines of your program. Once your program has received control from DL/I, your program can request DL/I services. In the program that will retrieve PATIENT segments, you'll ask DL/I to retrieve selected segments for you by making calls to DL/I. Your CALL statement parameter list will point

```
            .
            .
            .
LINKAGE SECTION.
01  PCB-MASK.
       03  DBDNAME                  PIC X(8).
       03  LEVEL-NUMBER             PIC XX.
       03  STATUS-CODE              PIC XX.
       03  PROC-OPTIONS             PIC XXXX.
       03  JCB-ADDRESS              PIC XXXX.
       03  SEGMENT-NAME             PIC X(8).
       03  KEY-LENGTH               PIC S9(5)  COMP.
       03  NUMBER-SEGS              PIC S9(5)  COMP.
       03  KEY-FEEDBACK.
           05  HOSPNAME-KEY         PIC X(20).
           05  WARDNO-KEY           PIC XX.
           05  BEDIDENT-KEY         PIC XXXX.
            .
            .
            .
PROCEDURE DIVISION.
    ENTRY  'DLITCBL'  USING  PCB-MASK.
            .
            .
            .
```

Figure 3.21 COBOL entry linkage coding

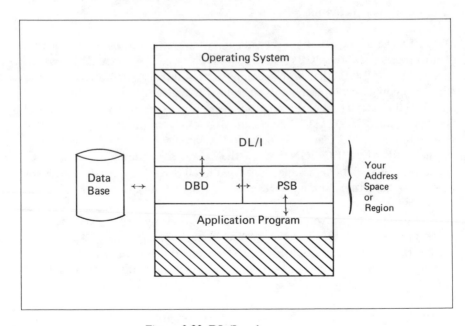

Figure 3.22 DL/I and your program

to information that spells out for DL/I what kind of retrieval you'd like to make.

The information that you include in your CALL statement parameter lists is determined by a series of rules that make up much of the DL/I interface language. You'll learn these basic rules in the next chapter. There you'll learn how to use the DL/I interface language in performing the various types of retrievals that you can make from a DL/I data base.

CHAPTER 3 EXERCISES

1. Below are twelve terms that are used in describing DL/I data bases. Below them is a series of twelve statements. Match each statement with the term that matches it best. A statement may match more than one term.

   Terms

   1. Physical Data Base
   2. Key Field
   3. Application Data Structure
   4. DBD
   5. Sequence Field
   6. Logical Data Base
   7. Search Field
   8. PSB
   9. Key Sensitive
   10. Logical Data Structure
   11. Sensitive Segment
   12. PCB

   Statements

   a. A segment that your application is allowed to access.
   b. The collection of all segments that your application is allowed to access.
   c. A group of segments and the hierarchical relationships between them as they reside on a physical storage device.
   d. A data item within a segment, known to DL/I, on which a set of segments is sequenced.
   e. A segment that you may use only to gain access to segments below it in the hierarchy. You may not access the segment's data.
   f. A control block which describes one logical data structure.
   g. A set of control blocks that describes your program's application data structure.
   h. The program's view of a data base. One set of segments and their hierarchical relationships.
   i. A field on which DL/I can search for a segment, but on which segments are not sequenced.
   j. A control block that defines a physical or logical data base.
   k. Segments combined from one or more physical data bases into a new hierarchical structure.

2. The listing in figure 3.23 shows the DBD statements for a physical data base.

   Answer the following questions about that listing.

   a. What are the names and lengths of each of the segments described in the DBD?
   b. What are the names, lengths, and starting locations of each of the key fields? Indicate which of the key fields are unique keys.
   c. What are the names, lengths, and starting locations of each of the search fields?
   d. What is the name of the DBD?
   e. Construct a hierarchy chart showing the hierarchical relationships in this physical data base.

```
PRINT     NOGEN
DBD       NAME=PAYROLL,ACCESS=HISAM
DATASET   DD1=KSDS,OVFLW=ESDS,DEVICE=3330
SEGM      NAME=EMPLOYEE,PARENT=0,BYTES=100
FIELD     NAME=(EMPNO,SEQ,U),BYTES=8,START=1,TYPE=C
FIELD     NAME=EMPNAME,BYTES=25,START=30
SEGM      NAME=TASK,PARENT=EMPLOYEE,BYTES=42
FIELD     NAME=(TASKNO,SEQ,U),BYTES=6,START=1,TYPE=C
FIELD     NAME=TASKNAME,BYTES=25,START=7
SEGM      NAME=TIME,PARENT=TASK,BYTES=20
FIELD     NAME=(DATE,SEQ),BYTES=6,START=15
SEGM      NAME=PERSONNL,PARENT=EMPLOYEE,BYTES=56
DBDGEN
FINISH
END
```

Figure 3.23 Exercise 2 DBD listing

```
PRINT     NOGEN
PCB       TYPE=DB,NAME=PAYROLL
SENSEG    NAME=EMPLOYEE,PARENT=0,PROCOPT=K
SENSEG    NAME=TASK,PARENT=EMPLOYEE,PROCOPT=G
SENSEG    NAME=TIME,PARENT=TASK,PROCOPT=G
PSBGEN    LANG=COBOL,PSBNAME=HOURCALC
END
```

Figure 3.24 Exercise 3 PSB listing

3. The listing in figure 3.24 shows the PSB statements for an application program.

Answer the following questions about that listing:

a. What are the names of the segments that the application using this PSB is sensitive to?

b. Construct a hierarchy chart to show the application data structure represented by this PSB.

c. How many PCBs are in this application data structure?

d. What is the name of this PSB?

e. What is the name of the DBD that defines the segments named in this logical data structure?

f. In which segments can this application access the data?

4

Random Retrieval

Introduction

In this chapter, we'll look at a complete DL/I batch application program. You'll see a listing of the PATIENT segment retrieval program that we talked about in the last chapter, and we'll use this program to point out some differences between a DL/I program and a traditional file-oriented program. You'll also learn the basic rules for communicating with DL/I when retrieving segments.

In addition to studying the basic rules, you'll learn the format of DL/I calls, how to write segment search arguments to qualify DL/I calls, and how to use the Get-Unique call to retrieve segments randomly. You'll also learn how to code simple status code logic for random retrieval calls.

The Retrieval Program

Figure 4.1 is a complete COBOL listing of the retrieval program that you read about in chapter 3. Before you go any further, look the program over carefully. After you look it over, we'll discuss each part of it, especially those parts that are unique to DL/I. If you write programs in languages other than COBOL, appendices F and G contain listings of this program in PL/I and Assembler Language. The sections that follow refer to the COBOL example, but you should have no trouble following the discussion if you refer to one of the other listings.

Entry Coding and the PCB

Notice that the entry coding and the PCB mask coding correspond to what you learned in chapter 3. The entry point name is DLITCBL, and the program expects to be passed a single parameter, the address of the PCB. We're using the PSB that you saw in the last chapter, so this program is key sensitive to the HOSPITAL and WARD segments and data sensitive to the PATIENT

Figure 4.1 The PATIENT segment retrieval program

```
000100 ID DIVISION.
000200 PROGRAM-ID. CHAP4C.
000300 AUTHOR. JOSEPH F. LEBEN.
000400 DATE-COMPILED.
000500 REMARKS: THIS IS A VERY SIMPLE LIST PROGRAM.  IT DOES VERY
000600         LITTLE ERROR CHECKING.  IT READS AN INPUT CARD
000700         IMAGE DATA SET WHOSE RECORDS HAVE THE FOLLOWING
000800         FORMAT.
000900
001000         COLUMNS   1 - 20  HOSPITAL NAME
001100                  21 - 22  WARD NUMBER
001200                  23 - 42  PATIENT NAME
001300
001400         FOR EACH CARD READ, THE PROGRAM ISSUES A DL/I CALL
001500         FOR THE PATIENT SEGMENT IDENTIFIED IN THAT CARD.
001600         IT THEN PRINTS OUT THAT PATIENT SEGMENT.
001700
001800 ENVIRONMENT DIVISION.
001900 CONFIGURATION SECTION.
002000 SOURCE-COMPUTER. IBM-370-168.
002100 OBJECT-COMPUTER. IBM-370-168.
002200 INPUT-OUTPUT SECTION.
002300
002400 FILE-CONTROL.
002500     SELECT  CARDFILE      ASSIGN TO   UT-S-INPUT.
002600     SELECT  OUTFILE       ASSIGN TO   UT-S-OUTPUT.
002700
002800 DATA DIVISION.
002900 FILE SECTION.
003000
003100 FD  CARDFILE
003200     LABEL RECORDS ARE STANDARD
003300     RECORDING MODE IS F
003400     BLOCK CONTAINS 0 RECORDS
003500     DATA RECORD IS CARD-DATA.
003600
```

```
003700  01  CARD-DATA.
003800      03  HOSPNAME-CARD         PIC X(20).
003900      03  WARDNO-CARD           PIC X(2).
004000      03  PATNAME-CARD          PIC X(20).
004010      03  FILLER                PIC X(38).
004100
004200  FD  OUTFILE
004300      LABEL RECORDS ARE STANDARD
004400      RECORDING MODE IS F
004500      BLOCK CONTAINS 0 RECORDS
004600      DATA RECORD IS PRINT-LINE.
004700
004800  01  PRINT-LINE.
004900      03  CARR-CNTL            PIC X.
005000      03  PATIENT-INFO         PIC X(125).
005100      03  FILLER               PIC X(7).
005200  WORKING-STORAGE SECTION.
005400
005500  77  TOP-PAGE                 PIC X     VALUE '1'.
005600  77  SINGLE-SPACE             PIC X     VALUE ' '.
005700  77  GET-UNIQUE               PIC X(4)  VALUE 'GU  '.
005500  77  LINE-COUNT               PIC S99   VALUE 50   COMP-3.
005900
006000  01  HOSPITAL-SSA.
006100      03  FILLER               PIC X(19)  VALUE 'HOSPITAL(HOSPNAME ='.
006200      03  HOSPNAME-SSA         PIC X(20).
006300      03  FILLER               PIC X      VALUE ')'.
006400
006500  01  WARD-SSA.
006600      03  FILLER               PIC X(19)  VALUE 'WARD    (WARDNO    ='.
006700      03  WARDNO-SSA           PIC X(2).
006800      03  FILLER               PIC X      VALUE ')'.
006900
007000  01  PATIENT-SSA.
007100      03  FILLER               PIC X(19)  VALUE 'PATIENT (PATNAME   ='.
007200      03  PATNAME-SSA          PIC X(20).
007300      03  FILLER               PIC X      VALUE ')'.
007400
```

```
007500 01  I-O-AREA COPY PATIENT.
007600
007700 LINKAGE SECTION.
007800 01  PCB-MASK COPY MASKC.
008000 PROCEDURE DIVISION.
008100 START-OF-PROGRAM.
008200
008300     ENTRY 'DLITCBL' USING   PCB-MASK.
008400
008500 BEGIN-HERE.
008510
008600     OPEN INPUT CARDFILE.
008700     OPEN OUTPUT OUTFILE.
008800
008900 READ-CARD.
008910
009000     READ CARDFILE  AT END GO TO  END-OF-JOB.
009100     MOVE HOSPNAME-CARD TO HOSPNAME-SSA.
009200     MOVE WARDNO-CARD  TO WARDNO-SSA.
009300     MOVE PATNAME-CARD  TO PATNAME-SSA.
009400
009500     CALL 'CBLTDLI' USING GET-UNIQUE
009600                         PCB-MASK
009700                         I-O-AREA
009800                         HOSPITAL-SSA
009900                         WARD-SSA
010000                         PATIENT-SSA.
010100
010200     IF  STATUS-CODE  NOT EQUAL   SPACE
010300         PERFORM BAD-STATUS
010400         GO TO READ-CARD.
010500
010600     PERFORM PRINT-ROUTINE.
010800
010900     GO TO READ-CARD.
011000
011100 BAD-STATUS.
011110
```

```
011200.        MOVE PCB-MASK TO I-O-AREA.
011300         PERFORM PRINT-ROUTINE.
011400
011500  PRINT-ROUTINE.
011510
011600     IF LINE-COUNT = 50
011700        MOVE ZERO TO LINE-COUNT
011800        MOVE '          P A T I E N T   L I S T' TO PATIENT-INFO
011900        WRITE PRINT-LINE AFTER POSITIONING TOP-PAGE
012000        MOVE SPACE TO PRINT-LINE
012100        WRITE PRINT-LINE AFTER POSITIONING SINGLE-SPACE.
012200
012300     MOVE I-O-AREA TO PATIENT-INFO.
012400     WRITE PRINT-LINE AFTER POSITIONING SINGLE-SPACE.
012500     ADD 1 TO LINE-COUNT.
012600
012700  END-OF-JOB.
012900
012310     CLOSE CARDFILE.
012900     CLOSE OUTFILE.
013000     GOBACK.
013100
```

49

segment. Remember, however, that the PROCOPT=G parameter for the PATIENT segment says that this program may only *retrieve* PATIENT segments; it may not *replace* or *delete* them.

Notice that there are two COPY statements in this program. These statements copy predefined COBOL source coding that has been stored in a library. Figure 4.2 shows what will be copied in as a result of the COPY statements.

```
000010 01   HOSPITAL.
000020      03   HOSPNAME              PIC X(20).
000030      03   HOSP-ADDRESS          PIC X(30).
000040      03   HOSP-PHONE            PIC X(10).

000010 01   WARD.
000020      03   WARDNO                PIC XX.
000030      03   TOT-ROOMS             PIC XXX.
000040      03   TOT-BEDS              PIC XXX.
000050      03   BEDAVAIL              PIC XXX.
000060      03   WARDTYPE              PIC X(20).

000010 01   PATIENT.
000020      03   PATNAME               PIC X(20).
000030      03   PAT-ADDRESS           PIC X(30).
000040      03   PAT-PHONE             PIC X(10).
000050      03   BEDIDENT              PIC X(4).
000060      03   DATEADMT              PIC X(6).
000070      03   PREV-STAY-FLAG        PIC X.
000080      03   PREV-HOSP             PIC X(20).
000090      03   PREV-DATE             PIC X(4).
000100      03   PREV-REASON           PIC X(30).

000010 01   SYMPTOM.
000020      03   DIAGNOSE              PIC X(20).
000030      03   SYMPDATE              PIC X(6).
000040      03   PREV-TREAT-FLAG       PIC X.
000050      03   TREAT-DESC            PIC X(20).
000060      03   SYMP-DOCTOR           PIC X(20).
000070      03   SYMP-DOCT-PHONE       PIC X(10).

000010 01   TREATMNT.
000020      03   TRTYPE                PIC X(20).
000030      03   TRDATE                PIC X(6).
000040      03   MEDICATION-TYPE       PIC X(20).
000050      03   DIET-COMMENT          PIC X(30).
000060      03   SURGERY-FLAG          PIC X.
000070      03   SURGERY-DATE          PIC X(6).
000080      03   SURGERY-COMMENT       PIC X(30).

000010 01   DOCTOR.
000020      03   DOCTNAME              PIC X(20).
000030      03   DOCT-ADDRESS          PIC X(30).
000040      03   DOCT-PHONE            PIC X(10).
000050      03   SPECIALT              PIC X(20).

000010 01   FACILITY.
000020      03   FACTYPE               PIC X(20).
000030      03   TOT-FACIL             PIC XXX.
000040      03   FACAVAIL              PIC XXX.
```

Figure 4.2 COPY statements

DL/I does not require you to use COPY statements for segment descriptions or PCB masks, but this is good programming practice. It's very useful in reducing communication problems, especially on large projects.

File Description Coding

One of the differences between DL/I programs and traditional file-oriented programs is the absence of file description coding for what would normally be the master file. Our retrieval program has file description coding for an input card image file and an output report file. There is no file description coding for the data base. That's because you don't access the data base with standard data management coding. Access to the data base will be made through calls to DL/I, rather than with READ statements.

The Input Records

The data description coding for the input record shows the format of the input file. Each card image will supply the information required to locate a particular occurrence of PATIENT segment type. The cards will contain the name of the hospital, the number of the ward, and the name of the patient. (We'll assume for this simple example that we don't have to worry about two patients with the same name, in the same ward and hospital.)

The WORKING-STORAGE SECTION

Much of the coding in the WORKING-STORAGE SECTION is probably strange to you because it's all unique to DL/I programs. The coding you see there is for the *function code* and *segment search arguments,* or *SSAs* for short, that will be used when the program asks DL/I to retrieve a segment. Basically, the function code and SSAs describe to DL/I the type of retrieval you'd like to make.

The PROCEDURE DIVISION

The PROCEDURE DIVISION coding at the beginning of the program is an example of the type of coding that DL/I programs use to retrieve segments randomly. The program reads an input record, stores the information contained in the card into data areas used as SSAs, and then executes a call to DL/I. After that call, the program checks a field in the PCB to see if the retrieval was successful. After printing a line on the report, it loops back to read another card. These elements are present in most DL/I random retrieval programs. The rest of the PROCEDURE DIVISION is similar to what you'd find in a traditional program.

Notice that execution of the program terminates with a GOBACK statement. This is because all DL/I programs are subroutines of DL/I. Don't terminate a DL/I program with a STOP-RUN. Your program won't return control to DL/I properly.

Now let's see how the call to DL/I works, and what the various entries in the parameter list mean.

The DL/I Call

The CALL statement parameter list, and the formats of the data items identified in that list, make up the DL/I interface language. Standard CALL statements and parameter lists make DL/I language independent, so you can write programs in COBOL, PL/I, or Assembler Language. (Each language has a few individual rules, and we'll go into those in the appendices F and G.)

Notice that the entry point name in the CALL statement is CBLTDLI. This is the name that you use whenever you request a DL/I service in a COBOL program. PL/I and Assembler Language use the names PLITDLI and ASMTDLI respectively. (Assembler programs may also use CBLTDLI.)

The Parameter List

The parameter list names data items in your program that supply information about your call. Let's look at the parameter list and see what each item means.

THE FUNCTION CODE. The first parameter names a four-byte *function code* that describes the type of service that you are requesting. In the retrieval program, the function code that we're using is GU. (See figure 4.3.) GU, or Get-Unique, tells DL/I that we are requesting a random retrieval of a segment. Figure 4.4 shows the various function codes that can be used to retrieve and manipulate segments. You'll learn how to use all of them in later chapters.

THE PCB MASK. The second parameter names the PCB that you're going to use in this call. (See figure 4.5.) This parameter is included in the call parameter list as well as in the entry coding, because many DL/I programs use more than one PCB. By including it in the parameter list, you have a way of indicating which PCB you're using. This parameter is required even if your program uses only a single PCB.

THE I/O AREA. The third parameter gives the address of the data area into which you would like DL/I to place the segment you're retrieving. (See figure 4.6.) We know that we're going to retrieve a PATIENT Segment, so we've coded the name of a data area that describes the PATIENT Segment. In other

```
77   GET-UNIQUE     PIC X(4)  VALUE 'GU'.
     .
     .
     .
     CALL  'CBLTDLI'  USING  GET-UNIQUE
                             PCB-MASK
                             PATIENT-SEG
                             HOSPITAL-SSA
                             WARD-SSA
                             PATIENT-SSA.
```

Figure 4.3 The GU function code

GU	Get-Unique
GN	Get-Next
GNP	Get-Next-Within-Parent
GHU	Get-Hold-Unique
GHN	Get-Hold-Next
GHNP	Get-Hold-Next-Within-Parent
DLET	Delete
REPL	Replace
ISRT	Insert

Figure 4.4 Data base function codes

```
LINKAGE SECTION.

01  PCB-MASK        COPY   HOSPPCB.
        .
        .
        .
    CALL  'CBLTDLI'  USING  GET-UNIQUE
                           PCB-MASK
                           PATIENT-SEG
                           HOSPITAL-SSA
                           WARD-SSA
                           PATIENT-SSA.
```

Figure 4.5 The PCB mask

retrieval programs, you may not know which segment you have until after the retrieval has been made, so you would use an I/O area big enough to contain the largest segment type. After you've determined which segment you have, you could move the segment to an area describing it. Another option is to use the REDEFINES clause to describe the I/O area for each segment type.

The I/O area identified in the third item in the parameter list must be big enough to contain the largest segment that you'll be retrieving. You'll find out, in a later chapter, that some retrievals can return more than one segment at a time, so the length of the I/O area must be planned carefully.

THE SEGMENT SEARCH ARGUMENTS. The first three parameters are the same for any DL/I retrieval call. The function code, PCB address, and I/O area address are required when retrieving a segment. Optionally, you can specify

```
01  PATIENT-SEG  COPY  PATIENT.
         .
         .
         .
     CALL  'CBLTDLI'  USING  GET-UNIQUE
                             PCB-MASK
                             PATIENT-SEG
                             HOSPITAL-SSA
                             WARD-SSA
                             PATIENT-SSA.
```

Figure 4.6 The I/O area

```
01  HOSPITAL-SSA.
    03  FILLER    PIC X(19)   VALUE 'HOSPITAL(HOSPNAME ='.
    03  HOSPNAME  PIC X(20).
    03  FILLER    PIC X       VALUE ')'.

01  WARD-SSA.
    03  FILLER    PIC X(19)   VALUE 'WARD      (WARDNO   ='.
    03  WARDNO    PIC XX.
    03  FILLER    PIC X       VALUE ')'.

01  PATIENT-SSA.
    03  FILLER    PIC X(19)   VALUE 'PATIENT (PATNAME  ='.
    03  PATNAME   PIC X(20).
    03  FILLER    PIC X       VALUE ')'.
         .
         .
         .
     CALL  'CBLTDLI'  USING  GET-UNIQUE
                             PCB-MASK
                             PATIENT-SEG
                             HOSPITAL-SSA
                             WARD-SSA
                             PATIENT-SSA.
```

Figure 4.7 Segment search arguments

from one to fifteen additional items called *segment search arguments,* or *SSAs,* to further describe your retrieval. In the retrieval program, we're using three SSAs. (See figure 4.7.)

It's easier to understand SSAs when you can look at them as they appear in memory, rather than in the form of COBOL coding. Figure 4.8 shows the card just read by the READ statement. Figure 4.9 shows what the SSAs would look like after the card in figure 4.8 was read, and just before the call was executed. We'll be looking at SSAs in this form most of the time. They're easy to understand, and they'll make our discussion more language independent. When we show the SSAs associated with DL/I calls in this way, we'll usually put the four-byte function code we're using to the left of the SSAs, as in figure 4.9.

We'll look at the rules for setting up SSAs in a minute. But first, let's look at the information in these three SSAs. The first one starts with a segment name, HOSPITAL. Following that is a left parenthesis followed by the name of the key field for the HOSPITAL segment. Next is an equal sign followed

```
GU       HOSPITAL(HOSPNAME =RIVEREDGE                      )
^^^^     ^^^^^^^^^^^^^^^^^^^^^^^^^^^^^^^^^^^^^^^^^^^^^^^^^^^^^
         WARD    (WARDNO   =02)
         ^^^^^^^^^^^^^^^^^^^^^^^^^
         PATIENT (PATNAME  =BROWN                          )
         ^^^^^^^^^^^^^^^^^^^^^^^^^^^^^^^^^^^^^^^^^^^^^^^^^^^^^
```

Figure 4.9 SSAs in memory

Figure 4.8 Retrieval program input card

```
HOSPITAL(HOSPNAME =RIVEREDGE                      )
^^^^^^^^^^^^^^^^^^^^^^^^^^^^^^^^^^^^^^^^^^^^^^^^^^^^^
1         9 10       18 20

WARD    (WARDNO   =02)
^^^^^^^^^^^^^^^^^^^^^^^^^
1         9 10       18 20

PATIENT (PATNAME  =BROWN                          )
^^^^^^^^^^^^^^^^^^^^^^^^^^^^^^^^^^^^^^^^^^^^^^^^^^^^^
1         9 10       18 20
```

Figure 4.10 Retrieval program SSAs

by the name of a hospital. Notice that this SSA uniquely identifies a particular occurrence of the HOSPITAL segment.

The second SSA identifies a unique occurrence of the WARD segment under the *Riveredge* HOSPITAL segment, and the third SSA identifies the particular PATIENT Segment that we want. Can you see how these three SSAs work together to identify a PATIENT segment? They give DL/I all the information that it needs in order to efficiently find the segment.

Using SSAs

The SSAs that you've just been looking at are examples of *fully qualified* SSAs. They're called fully qualified because they give complete information about a segment occurrence. Let's look at the specific format of a fully qualified SSA.

Fully Qualified SSAs

Figure 4.10 below is a repeat of the fully qualified SSAs for the retrieval program. The first field in each SSA is eight characters long, and identifies the segment type that each SSA describes. If your segment name is less than eight characters long, you must pad this field to the right with blanks. In fully qualified SSAs, the ninth position normally contains a left parenthesis.

The ninth position in the SSA tells DL/I what kind of SSA this is. A left parenthesis indicates a qualified SSA, a blank indicates an unqualified SSA. We'll look at unqualified SSAs shortly. An asterisk in position nine tells DL/I that the SSA includes one or more command codes. Command codes are one character codes in the SSA that request special options to be performed. We'll talk about command codes in a later chapter.

Following the left parenthesis is another eight-character name. This must be the name of either the key field or one of the search fields for this segment type. Again, this field must be padded to the right with blanks if your key or search field name contains less than eight characters.

Following the key or search field name, beginning in position 18, is a two-position relational operator. This tells DL/I what kind of comparison to make when it performs the search. Figure 4.11 shows the valid relational operators and their meanings. If your relational operator consists of only a single character, like the equal sign, you may place the operator in either position 18 or 19. The other position must be blank. (See figure 4.12.)

Following the relational operator is a variable-length field that contains the value against which DL/I is to compare when it searches for the segment. For example, the HOSPITAL SSA tells DL/I to search for a HOSPITAL segment whose HOSPNAME key field contains a value that is equal to *River-edge*. (See figure 4.13.) The length of this field must correspond to the length of the key or search field that you're searching on. For example, in the HOSPITAL and PATIENT SSAs, this field is twenty bytes in length. The field is two bytes in length for the WARD SSA. You can find these lengths by looking at the segment description coding or in the DBDGEN for the HOSPITAL data base.

Following the field that DL/I compares against is a right parenthesis. It marks the end of the SSA. All qualified SSAs must be coded following this rather rigid format. DL/I will indicate an error condition if the correct format is not followed.

Unqualified SSAs

In addition to qualified SSAs, you are also able to use *unqualified* ones. Figure 4.14 shows an example of an unqualified SSA for the HOSPITAL segment. Notice that the ninth position contains a blank, rather than a left parenthesis. The blank tells DL/I that this is an unqualified SSA. You use unqualified SSAs when you don't want to indicate a particular occurrence of a segment, for example, when you don't care which occurrence of a segment you get.

Unqualified SSAs are treated differently depending upon which function code you're using. You'll learn how DL/I handles unqualified SSAs with Get-Unique calls in this chapter.

Calls without SSAs

In addition to using qualified and unqualified SSAs in your parameter lists, you can also issue calls *without* SSAs. Again, the way that DL/I handles calls without SSAs depends upon the function code you're using. Let's take a more detailed look at DL/I calls with the GU function code and see how the various combinations of SSA types work with random retrievals. To do this, we'll use a diagram that shows actual segment occurrences within the HOSPITAL data base.

Random Retrievals

In figure 4.15 we're showing segments from the HOSPITAL data base in an indented form that simulates the way in which segments would be retrieved sequentially from the data base. The indentations show the hierarchical levels

Operator	Meaning
= or EQ	equal
> = or GE	greater than or equal to
< = or LE	less than or equal to
> or GT	greater than
< or LT	less than
¬= or NE	not equal to

Figure 4.11 Relational operators

```
HOSPITAL(HOSPNAME =RIVEREDGE              )
```

```
HOSPITAL(HOSPNAME= RIVEREDGE              )
```

Figure 4.12 One position relational operator

```
HOSPITAL(HOSPNAME =RIVEREDGE              )
```

Figure 4.13 The HOSPITAL SSA

```
HOSPITAL
```

Figure 4.14 An unqualified SSA

of the segment types. Since our retrieval program is only interested in HOSPI-TAL, WARD, and PATIENT segments, these are the only segment types shown in the chart. For the examples coming up, assume that these are the only segments in the data base that our retrieval program can access.

Each box in the diagram represents a segment occurrence in the HOSPITAL data base. The first line of each box identifies the segment type, and the second line shows the values of key and search fields. To make it easy to read, we've left out all the other information in each segment, and we're showing only the first ten positions of each twenty-position key or search field. We've also numbered each segment in the upper left-hand corner. We'll use these numbers to refer to segment occurrences, but the numbers are not stored in the data base.

The key and search fields are in the same order as they are coded in the data descriptions for each segment. So, in segment 3, *Moriarty* is the value stored in that PATIENT segment's PATNAME search field, *0003* is the value in the BEDIDENT key field, and *082377* is the value in the DATEADMT search field. Notice that the PATIENT segments under each WARD segment are sequenced on the BEDIDENT key field.

SSA Combinations.

We'll use this chart to show which segments are retrieved from the data base when different combinations of SSAs are used with Get-Unique calls. We'll suppose, for these examples, that our PSB specified that we are data sensitive to all three segment types, so we'll be able to retrieve any of the segments shown in the chart. That will allow us to show all the variations of SSAs that you can use. Let's start with some examples of fully qualified SSAs.

FULLY QUALIFIED CALLS. You normally use sets of fully qualified SSAs when you know exactly which segment you want, and you have all the information available that will allow DL/I to find it for you with a minimum of searching. To fully qualify a call for a particular PATIENT segment occurrence, you must supply a fully qualified SSA for the PATIENT segment, and one for each level above it. The SSAs must be coded in hierarchical sequence, starting with the one for the root segment. The call in the retrieval program is an example of this kind of call.

One thing to keep in mind is that in any retrieval call, except in a special case involving SSAs using the D command code, you will only retrieve the segment identified in the last SSA in the list. The others above it are used only to further qualify your call. (You'll learn how to use the D command code in chapter 8.)

Let's suppose you wanted to make a fully-qualified call for a WARD segment. It's at the second level of the hierarchy, so two SSAs are required. (See figure 4.16.) Using a GU function code with the SSAs in figure 4.16 will cause segment 9 to be retrieved from the data base. Notice that the second SSA used a search field rather than the key field for the WARD segment. Any

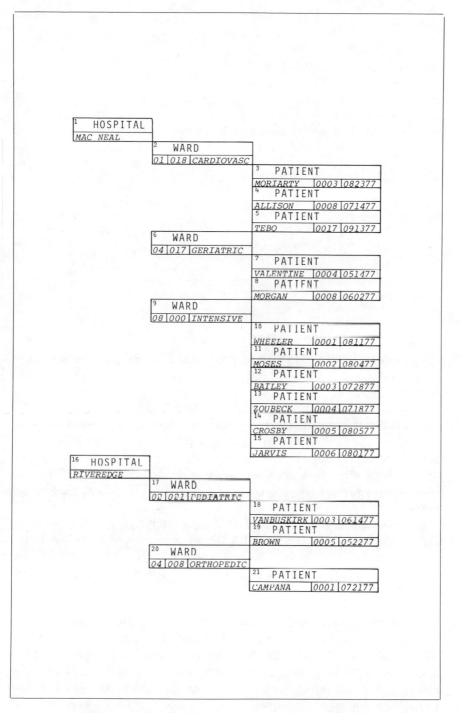

Figure 4.15 **HOSPITAL** data base segment occurrence chart

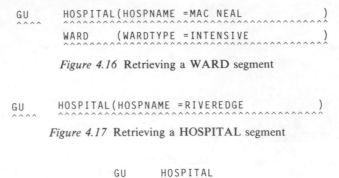

Figure 4.16 Retrieving a WARD segment

GU   HOSPITAL(HOSPNAME =RIVEREDGE   )

Figure 4.17 Retrieving a HOSPITAL segment

GU   HOSPITAL

Figure 4.18 Get-Unique with an unqualified SSA

GU   HOSPITAL

WARD

PATIENT

Figure 4.19 Get-Unique with three unqualified SSAs

search field or the key field may be referenced in an SSA. If you wanted to make a fully qualified call for a HOSPITAL segment, you'd need only one SSA. (See figure 4.17.)

CALLS USING UNQUALIFIED SSAs. Whenever you use an unqualified SSA with the GU function code, you tell DL/I to locate the *first occurrence* of that segment type. For example, suppose you issued the Get-Unique call with the SSA in figure 4.18. That call would get you the first occurrence of the root segment, so you'd get segment 1, the *Mac Neal* HOSPITAL segment occurrence.

Let's suppose you issued the Get-Unique call in figure 4.19. That would get you the first occurrence of the PATIENT segment, under the first occurrence of the WARD segment, under the first occurrence of the HOSPITAL segment. The segment that you'd get would be segment 3, the *Moriarty* PATIENT segment.

COMBINATIONS OF QUALIFIED AND UNQUALIFIED SSAs. In making Get-Unique calls, you can use any combination of qualified and unqualified SSAs. The way DL/I handles these depends upon the level at which the unqualified SSAs are coded. Let's suppose that you issued the Get-Unique call in figure 4.20. Since there are fully qualified SSAs at levels one and two, DL/I will use the information in those SSAs to locate segment 17. It will then retrieve the first occurrence of the PATIENT segment under segment 17. In this case, you'll get segment 18, the *Vanbuskirk* PATIENT segment.

Now let's suppose you issued the call in figure 4.21. The two unqualified SSAs tell DL/I to locate segment 2, and search from there. DL/I will then search all the way through the data base until it reaches segment 21, the PATIENT segment for *Campana*. As you might guess, this is not the most efficient way to retrieve the *Campana* segment. DL/I allows you to do it, however, and it might be the only way to locate the *Campana* segment if you don't know which hospital and ward that patient is in.

Notice that DL/I does not limit its search to only those PATIENT segment occurrences under the first occurrence of the WARD segment. Supplying unqualified SSAs at high levels, and qualified SSAs at lower levels simply tells DL/I where to begin the search.

MISSING LEVELS IN THE HIERARCHY. It's possible to make retrieval calls without supplying an SSA for each level in the hierarchy above the segment you're retrieving. For example, suppose you issued the Get-Unique call in figure 4.22. You'd retrieve segment 10, the *Wheeler* PATIENT segment. A normal fully qualified call requires an SSA for each level down to

```
GU      HOSPITAL(HOSPNAME =RIVEREDGE            )

        WARD    (WARDNO   =02)

        PATIENT
```

Figure 4.20 Unqualified and qualified SSAs

```
GU      HOSPITAL

        WARD
        PATIENT (PATNAME  =CAMPANA              )
```

Figure 4.21 Unqualified and qualified SSAs

```
GU      PATIENT (PATNAME  =WHEELER              )
```

Figure 4.22 Missing levels

```
GU      HOSPITAL

        WARD

        PATIENT (PATNAME  =WHEELER              )
```

Figure 4.23 Assumed unqualified SSAs

the segment you're retrieving. But if you skip any levels, DL/I will assume an unqualified SSA for each segment type that you skipped. So issuing the Get-Unique call in figure 4.22 has the same effect as issuing the call in figure 4.23.

CALLS WITH NO SSAs. You can even make a Get-Unique call with no SSAs at all. When you do that, DL/I will assume an unqualified SSA for the first level, the root segment. So a Get-Unique call with no SSAs will always get you the first occurrence of the root segment. You'll see later that this will come in handy at times.

Using Get-Unique Calls

We've just discussed the ways that you can use SSAs with Get-Unique calls. The most common type of Get-Unique call in random retrieval programs is a fully qualified call where the program supplies a fully qualified SSA for each level in the hierarchy down to the segment being retrieved. It's the most efficient way to retrieve a segment randomly. You'll use other combinations of SSAs only when you have to, and only when the situation warrants it.

Status Code Logic

Following each retrieval call, you must determine whether your retrieval was successful by examining one of the fields in the PCB. There's a two-position field in the PCB called the *status code field* that will tell you what happened as a result of your call. There are only two values that are normally of interest to you when making random retrievals using the GU function code. These values are *blanks* and *GE*. A status code of *blanks* tells you that your retrieval was successful. A status code of *GE* says that the segment that you asked for could not be found.

Let's suppose that you issued the Get-Unique call in figure 4.24. DL/I would place GE in the status code field, because there's no PATIENT segment with the name *Smith* in the data base.

The call in figure 4.25 would also give you a status code of GE. There is a PATIENT segment with the name *Moses* in the data base, but the fully qualified SSAs for the HOSPITAL and WARD segments caused DL/I to look for it under the wrong HOSPITAL and WARD segments.

Other Function Codes

In this chapter, we've been talking only about random retrievals. In the next one, we'll talk about sequential retrievals using the GN and GNP function codes. You'll see that the same combinations of qualified and unqualified SSAs give you slightly different results with these calls.

CHAPTER 4 EXERCISES

Following are four exercises dealing with the use of the Get-Unique call. The second exercise uses the data base diagram shown in figure 4.15.

1. Figure 4.26 shows a DL/I CALL statement and its parameter list. Below is a list of five statements describing the five indicated parts of the CALL statement. Match each part with the statement that best describes it.

   a. Address of an SSA
   b. Entry Point in DL/I Used by COBOL calls
   c. Address of I/O Area
   d. Name of PCB Mask in Your Program
   e. Address of Function Code

2. Figure 4.27 shows four sets of SSAs in Get-Unique calls. For each set of SSAs, indicate the segment in figure 4.15 that would be retrieved, if any, and the status code that DL/I would return.

3. Write internal representations of the SSAs that would be required to retrieve the following segments from the data base using Get-Unique calls.

   a. The PATIENT segment for the patient whose name is *Wheeler*. The patient is in an *Intensive* ward in the *Mac Neal* hospital.

```
GU      HOSPITAL(HOSPNAME =MAC NEAL                       )

        WARD

        PATIENT (PATNAME  =SMITH                          )
```
Figure 4.24 Retrieving a PATIENT segment

```
GU      HOSPITAL(HOSPNAME =RIVEREDGE                      )

        WARD     (WARDNO   =04)

        PATIENT (PATNAME  =MOSES                          )
```
Figure 4.25 Retrieving a PATIENT segment

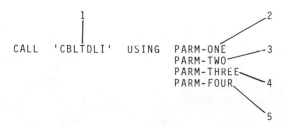

```
           1
           |
CALL    'CBLTDLI'   USING   PARM-ONE      -3
                            PARM-TWO
                            PARM-THREE
                            PARM-FOUR     4


                                    5
```
Figure 4.26 CALL statement for Exercise 1

```
a.  GU      PATIENT
    ^^^^     ^^^^^^^^^^


b.  GU      HOSPITAL
    ^^^^     ^^^^^^^^^^

            WARD
            ^^^^^^^^^^

            PATIENT (PATNAME  =WHEELER                 )
            ^^^^^^^^^^^^^^^^^^^^^^^^^^^^^^^^^^^^^^^^^^^^^^^^


c.  GU      HOSPITAL(HOSPNAME =RIVEREDGE              )
    ^^^^     ^^^^^^^^^^^^^^^^^^^^^^^^^^^^^^^^^^^^^^^^^^^^^^

            WARD
            ^^^^^^^^^^

            PATIENT (BEDIDENT =0017)
            ^^^^^^^^^^^^^^^^^^^^^^^^^^^^


d.  GU      PATIENT (PATNAME  =CAMPANA                )
    ^^^^     ^^^^^^^^^^^^^^^^^^^^^^^^^^^^^^^^^^^^^^^^^^^^^^^
```

Figure 4.27 Four sets of SSAs for Exercise 2

   b. A WARD segment for a ward that has more than 100 beds available. You don't
       care which hospital it's in.
   c. A DOCTOR segment for the doctor whose name is *Rogers*. He's the doctor
       for the patient whose name is *Bailey*. You don't know which hospital or ward
       the patient is in.
   d. The FACILITY segment under the *Mac Neal* HOSPITAL segment for the
       Cobalt facility type.

4. What are the meanings of the blank and GE status codes when received after
   Get-Unique calls?

5

Sequential Retrieval

Introduction

In this chapter we'll look at two DL/I calls, the *GN* or *Get-Next* call and the *GNP* or *Get-Next-Within-Parent* call. These calls are used to retrieve a series of segments in sequential order.

As with the Get-Unique call, you'll learn how to use Get-Next and Get-Next-Within-Parent calls with all combinations of SSAs, including no SSAs, unqualified SSAs, and qualified SSAs. You'll see how DL/I handles sequential retrieval within a DL/I data base, and you'll see the help that DL/I gives you in determining which segment types you're retrieving as you move up and down in level within the data base. We'll also cover the concept of parentage within a DL/I data base, which allows you to limit the range of retrieval in a series of sequential retrieval calls. And finally, after the topic of sequential retrievals has been covered, you'll learn an additional SSA feature that allows you to connect multiple search arguments with Boolean operators.

When you finish this chapter, you'll write a complete DL/I application program in either COBOL, PL/I, or Assembler Language using the following DL/I facilities:

The Get-Unique Call

The Get-Next Call

The Get-Next-Within-Parent Call

In using these calls you'll establish the necessary linkage between your program and DL/I, use precoded descriptions of segments, and write the necessary PCB and status code logic to implement those calls.

The Concepts of Sequential Retrieval

Before we get to the specific coding involved in using Get-Next and Get-Next-Within-Parent calls, let's take a look at how DL/I handles sequential retrievals and see the types of problems that can come up in writing sequential retrieval programs. For the examples in this chapter, let's assume that figure 5.1 shows all the segments in the HOSPITAL data base that your program can access.

DL/I Processing Sequence

You may remember from chapter 3 that hierarchical sequence within a DL/I data base is always top to bottom and left to right. Actually, if you look at figure 5.1, there's another dimension involved: front to back along twin chains. In figure 5.1, notice the segments are numbered in the upper right-hand corners of the boxes. The numbers correspond to hierarchical sequence within the data base: top to bottom, left to right, and front to back.

As you'll see later in the chapter, it's possible to issue Get-Next calls without SSAs to sequentially process all the segments in the data base. If you wrote a program to loop on a single Get-Next call with no SSAs, you'd get the segments in the sequence shown in figure 5.2. Figure 5.2 shows the segments in the indented form that you're familiar with from the previous chapter. It's easy to see the hierarchical sequence of the segments in a diagram like figure 5.2.

Reading Sequentially through the Data Base

Notice that as we read sequentially through the data base with an unqualified sequential retrieval call, we retrieve different segment types at different levels within the data base. The first call will retrieve a segment at the first, or root, level. It will retrieve the HOSPITAL segment for the *Mac Neal* hospital. The next call will move us down to the second level. The third call will retrieve a segment at the third level. And the fourth call will get us a segment at the fourth level. The fifth, sixth, seventh, and eighth calls will stay at the fourth level, but will retrieve different segment types. Finally, the ninth call will move us back from the fourth to the third level.

Notice also that it's possible to move up more than one level in one retrieval call. After we retrieve segment twelve, the last DOCTOR segment stored under the *0008* PATIENT segment, we'll jump up to segment thirteen, the *04* WARD segment. So we move from level four to level two in one call.

Problems with Sequential Retrieval

Many of the problems involved in processing segments sequentially involve figuring out which segment type you've retrieved after an unqualified call. Unless you have a chart like figure 5.2 to tell you the exact structure of the data base, it's very difficult to tell when you'll go up in level in the data base, down in level, or stay at the same level. One of the topics of this chapter will

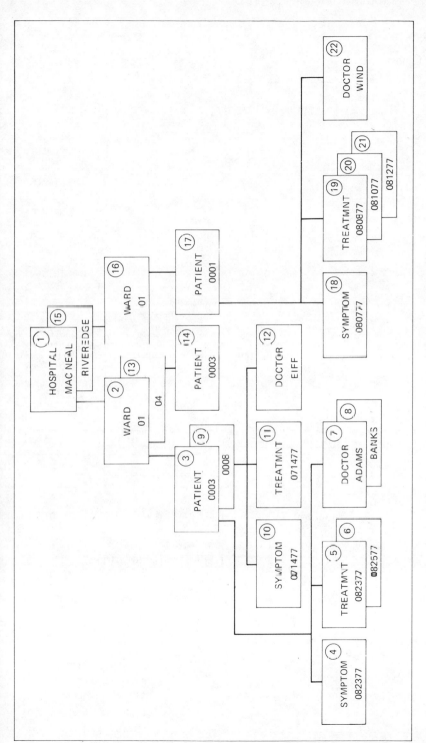

Figure 5.1 HOSPITAL data base hierarchy chart

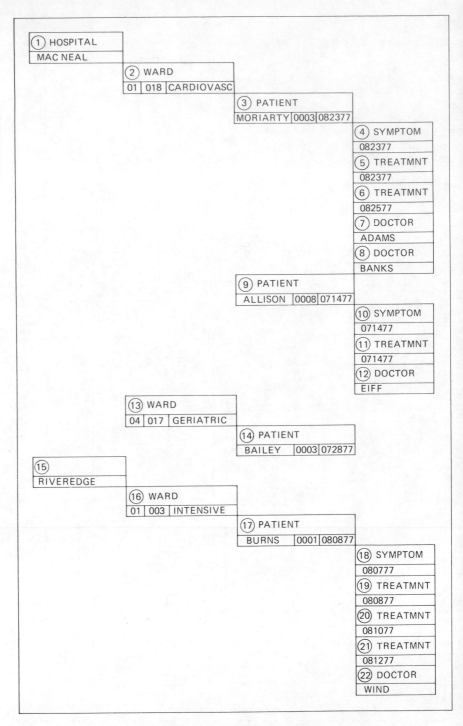

Figure 5.2 Indented structure chart

be to describe the fields in the PCB that help you determine what segment type you've retrieved when using unqualified sequential retrieval calls.

Get-Next Retrieval Calls

Before you issue a Get-Next call, you must consider one important concept that was not an issue with Get-Unique calls. That's the concept of *position within the data base.* A common way of establishing a position is to issue a Get-Unique call for a particular segment. After you issue a Get-Unique call, DL/I remembers the position of that segment, and a sequential retrieval that follows will be made relative to that location in the data base. In a retrieval program, a new position is established after each Get-Unique, Get-Next, or Get-Next-Within-Parent call. You'll see how current position is used when we look at how DL/I handles Get-Next calls without SSAs.

Get-Next Calls without SSAs

Using the Get-Next function code with no SSAs is the simplest sequential retrieval call that you can make. However, as you'll see later in this chapter, it can be the most complicated to handle as far as your program logic goes. Figure 5.3 shows the COBOL coding for a Get-Next call with no SSAs.

The Get-Next call without SSAs is a completely unqualified call, so you're giving DL/I no information as to which segment you would like. When you issue a Get-Next call with no SSAs, DL/I looks at the current position within the data base and retrieves the next segment in hierarchical sequence.

If the first call that you issue is a Get-Next without SSAs, you'll retrieve the first segment in the data base, the first occurrence of the root segment. Issuing a Get-Next call without SSAs as the first call in your program gives you the same result as issuing a Get-Unique call without SSAs, and is a handy way of establishing a position at the first segment in the data base. The status codes associated with this type of call are a bit different from the ones you saw in the last chapter, but we'll save the subject of status codes until after we look at the other two variations of Get-Next calls.

```
77  FUNCTION-CODE       PIC X(4)  VALUE 'GN '.
    .
    .
    .
    CALL  'CBLTDLI'  USING  FUNCTION-CODE
                           PCB-MASK
                           I-O-AREA.
```

Figure 5.3 Get-Next with no SSAs

Get-Next Calls With Unqualified SSAs

Get-Next calls without SSAs allow you to retrieve every segment in the data base in hierarchical sequence. Get-Next calls with unqualified SSAs let you restrict your sequential retrieval to only a particular segment type. For example, look at the call in figure 5.4. If you issued that call at the beginning of your program's execution, position would be established at the beginning of the data base; and the call would retrieve the first PATIENT segment, segment 3 in figure 5.2, the PATIENT segment whose bed identifier is *0003*. The next time you issued that same call, DL/I would scan through the data base until it found the next occurrence of the PATIENT segment. In this case, it would be segment 9, the PATIENT segment for patient *0008* in ward *01* under the *Mac Neal* HOSPITAL segment.

You would then scan ahead to segment 14, the PATIENT segment for patient *0003* in ward *04* under the *Mac Neal* HOSPITAL segment. Finally, the next execution of that call would cause DL/I to return a GE status code since there would be no more PATIENT segments in the data base.

Get-Next calls with unqualified SSAs are handy when you would like to retrieve segments in hierarchical sequence, but only segments of a particular type. Notice, however, that using Get-Next calls with unqualified SSAs does not restrict the retrieval of the PATIENT segments to those patients under a particular hospital. DL/I retrieves all the PATIENT segments, no matter what segments they're dependent on.

Get-Next Calls with Qualified SSAs

On first glance, the use of the Get-Next call with qualified SSAs does not seem to lend itself to sequential retrieval. For example, look at figure 5.5.

In the call in figure 5.5, we're asking DL/I to retrieve a particular occurrence of the PATIENT segment. If we look at this call out of context, there's no difference between it and a Get-Unique call. The main reason for using a Get-Next call instead of a Get-Unique call is to perform *skip-sequential processing*.

```
GN      PATIENT
~~~~    ~~~~~~~~~~
```

Figure 5.4 Get-Next with an unqualified SSA

```
GN      HOSPITAL(HOSPNAME =RIVEREDGE              )
~~~~    ~~~~~~~~~~~~~~~~~~~~~~~~~~~~~~~~~~~~~~~~~~~~~
        WARD    (WARDNO   =01)
        ~~~~~~~~~~~~~~~~~~~~~~~
        PATIENT (BEDIDENT =0001)
        ~~~~~~~~~~~~~~~~~~~~~~~~~
```

Figure 5.5 A fully qualified Get-Next call

Skip-Sequential Processing

When you perform skip-sequential processing, you process selected segments in hierarchical sequence. For example, you might want to retrieve selected PATIENT segments from a particular ward and hospital. If you know the key values for the PATIENT segments that you want, and can present them to the program in key sequence, you might use coding similar to that found in figure 5.6. The program reads a key value from an input file, stores the key value into an SSA, and then issues a Get-Next call using that SSA.

You might be wondering at this point about the difference between that program logic and the program logic for a Get-Unique call. The only difference is that when using the Get-Next call, you must be sure that the key values are presented to the program in key sequence. If you attempt to back up in the

```
        .
        .
        .
01   PATIENT-SSA.
     03   FILLER             PIC X(19)   VALUE 'PATIENT (BEDIDENT ='.
     03   BEDIDENT-SSA       PIC X(4).
     03   FILLER             PIC X       VALUE ')'.
        .
        .
        .
     MOVE INPUT-BEDIDENT TO BEDIDENT-SSA.
     CALL  'CBLTDLI'  USING  FUNCTION-CODE
                             PCB-MASK
                             I-O-AREA
                             HOSPITAL-SSA
                             WARD-SSA
                             PATIENT-SSA.
        .
        .
        .
```

Figure 5.6 Skip-Sequential processing with Get-Next

```
GN      HOSPITAL(HOSPNAME =MAC NEAL                )
        WARD     (WARDNO   =01)
        PATIENT (PATNAME  =ALLISON                  )
```

Figure 5.7 Retrieving the PATIENT segment for *Allison*

```
GN      HOSPITAL(HOSPNAME =MAC NEAL                )
        WARD     (WARDNO   =01)
        PATIENT (PATNAME  =MORIARTY                 )
```

Figure 5.8 Retrieving the PATIENT segment for *Moriarty*

data base with a Get-Next call, and present a key value that's lower than the one used in the previous call, DL/I will return a status code of GE, as if the segment did not exist. When you use Get-Unique calls, DL/I will back up in the data base and find the segment for you. The reason you would use Get-Next calls instead of Get-Unique calls is that a series of Get-Next calls is more efficient than the same series of calls using Get-Unique. With Get-Next calls, DL/I uses current position in performing the search for the next segment. When you use a Get-Unique call, DL/I normally goes back to the beginning of the data base before performing each search. In certain access methods, this can make a big difference in retrieval efficiency.

PROBLEMS WITH SKIP-SEQUENTIAL RETRIEVAL. A problem can occur when you would like to use skip-sequential processing and retrieve segments based on some search field rather than the key field. Suppose your program reads a series of patient names from an input file. If you sorted the input file by patient name, you would not be able to use Get-Next calls to perform skip-sequential processing to retrieve segments in patient name sequence.

Let's see what would happen if you tried to do it. Suppose your program first issued the Get-Next call in figure 5.7. That call would cause DL/I to retrieve segment 9 in the data base. Notice in figure 5.2, segment 9 has a bed identifier of *0008*. Suppose you now issued the Get-Next call in figure 5.8.

On first glance, this appears to be okay, since the search field values are being presented in alphabetical sequence. However, notice in figure 5.2, that the bed identifier for the *Moriarity* PATIENT segment is *0003*. This call would be asking DL/I to back up in the data base. Since this is not allowed with a Get-Next call, DL/I will return a status code of GE, and it will appear to you as if the *Moriarity* segment does not exist in the data base. So remember that skip-sequential processing requires you to process segments in *key* sequence.

Status Codes with Get-Next Calls

When you're using Get-Next calls with qualified SSAs, you can expect to see the same status codes as when you're using Get-Unique calls. The two most common status codes are blanks, for a successful retrieval call, and GE, for a segment-not-found condition.

When you're using Get-Next calls without SSAs, there are three more status codes that you must be concerned with. They're the GA, GK, and GB status codes shown in figure 5.9. When you're scanning through the data base sequentially, you test for the GB status code to find out when you've reached the end of the data base. If you issue another call after you have received a GB status code, DL/I will go back to the beginning of the data base.

When you're using unqualified Get-Next calls, you can use the GA and GK status codes to give you some idea of what segment type you've retrieved.

GA—Moved up in level

GK—New segment type at the same level

GB—End of data base

Figure 5.9 The GA, GK, and GB status codes

These status codes do not indicate error conditions. Figure 5.10 shows how you can use the GA and GK status codes with a series of Get-Next calls without SSAs. It shows the status codes that DL/I will issue after each execution of a Get-Next call, without SSAs, for the segment occurrences in figure 5.2.

Notice that each successive Get-Next call that retrieves a segment of the same type, or retrieves a segment lower in the hierarchy than the last one, will return a status code of blanks. Whenever a call retrieves a segment at a higher level, DL/I returns a status code of GA. If the call retrieves a segment of a different type, but at the same level, DL/I returns a status code of GK. You can use these status codes to help you find your way around in the data base when you're using a series of unqualified Get-Next calls.

Keep in mind, however, that the GA and GK status codes often don't give you all the information you need to determine what segment type you have. For example, the status code doesn't tell you when you move down in level. And when you get a GA status code, you don't know how many levels up you've moved since the last call. Later on in the chapter, we'll look at some of the other fields in the PCB. You'll see how you can use them for more positive identification of the segment you've retrieved.

Get-Next-Within-Parent Calls

The Get-Next-Within-Parent, or GNP function code, works in a very similar manner to the GN function code. It's used to perform sequential retrieval within the data base. However, Get-Next-Within-Parent calls limit your sequential retrieval to a particular range of segment occurrences within the data base. To understand how the GNP function code works, you have to understand the concept of *parentage.*

Setting Parentage

Whenever a Get-Next or Get-Unique call is issued, DL/I not only establishes a position on some segment occurrence, but it also establishes parentage on that occurrence. This means that the segment retrieved by the Get-Next or Get-Unique call is treated as the parent segment for any Get-Next-Within-Parent calls that follow. Get-Next-Within-Parent calls are only allowed to retrieve segments that are dependent on the segment at which parentage has been established. This allows you to limit the area of search within the data

Segment Number	Segment Level	Segment Type	Status Code
1	1	HOSPITAL	blanks
2	2	WARD	blanks
3	3	PATIENT	blanks
4	4	SYMPTOM	blanks
5	4	TREATMNT	GK
6	4	TREATMNT	blanks
7	4	DOCTOR	GK
8	4	DOCTOR	blanks
9	3	PATIENT	GA
10	4	SYMPTOM	blanks
11	4	TREATMNT	GK
12	4	DOCTOR	GK
13	2	WARD	GA
14	3	PATIENT	blanks
15	1	HOSPITAL	GA
16	2	WARD	blanks
17	3	PATIENT	blanks
18	4	SYMPTOM	blanks
19	4	TREATMNT	GK
20	4	TREATMNT	blanks
21	4	TREATMNT	blanks
22	4	DOCTOR	GK
--	-	------	GB

Figure 5.10 Reading sequentially through the data base

base. Let's look at a few Get-Next-Within-Parent calls to see how parentage works.

GNP Calls Without SSAs

A Get-Next-Within-Parent call with no SSAs is very similar to a Get-Next call with no SSAs, the difference being the range of segments that the two calls have access to. A series of Get-Next calls without SSAs will read segments from current position all the way to the end of the data base. A series of Get-Next-Within-Parent calls using no SSAs will read only those segments that are dependent on the segment at which parentage has been established. Let's use the segments in figure 5.2 to see how this works.

Let's suppose that you issue a Get-Unique call for the *Mac Neal* HOSPITAL segment. This establishes parentage at segment 1 in the data base. If you then issue a series of Get-Next-Within-Parent calls without SSAs, the first one will retrieve segment 2 in the data base, the first WARD segment. If you continue issuing Get-Next-Within-Parent calls without SSAs, the calls will scan through the data base and retrieve, in hierarchical sequence, all the segments that are dependent on the *Mac Neal* HOSPITAL segment. The last segment that the Get-Next-Within-Parent call would retrieve is segment 14. If you issued another Get-Next-Within-Parent call with no SSAs, DL/I would return a status code of GE. In this case the GE status code means that there are no more segments dependent on the segment at which parentage is currently established.

The lower in level that parentage is established, the fewer segments an unqualified Get-Next-Within-Parent call has access to. For example, let's suppose that you issued the Get-Unique call in figure 5.11. That would establish parentage at segment 3, the PATIENT segment for patient *0003*. If you followed that call with a series of Get-Next-Within-Parent calls without SSAs, those calls would only have access to segments 4, 5, 6, 7, and 8 in the data base. Once you retrieved segment 8, the next Get-Next-Within-Parent call would return a status code of GE, indicating that there are no more segments dependent on segment 3.

Get-Next-Within-Parent Using SSAs

You can use unqualified and qualified SSAs with the GNP function code just as you can with Get-Next calls. Unqualified SSAs will cause the Get-Next-Within-Parent call to sequentially retrieve only segments of a particular segment type. You can also use qualified SSAs with GNP to fully qualify your calls when performing skip-sequential processing.

Skip-sequential processing can often be simplified with GNP calls. Skip-sequential processing with Get-Next requires you to use SSAs at all levels in the hierarchy. With GNP, you can establish parentage on a particular segment occurrence. You then perform a series of Get-Next-Within-Parent calls using an SSA only for the segment type you're retrieving. An example will make this more clear. Suppose you'd like to retreive a set of PATIENT segments that

```
GU      HOSPITAL(HOSPNAME =MAC NEAL                     )
^^^^    ^^^^^^^^^^^^^^^^^^^^^^^^^^^^^^^^^^^^^^^^^^^^^^^^^
        WARD    (WARDNO    =01)
        ^^^^^^^^^^^^^^^^^^^^^^^^^
        PATIENT (BEDIDENT =0003)
        ^^^^^^^^^^^^^^^^^^^^^^^^^
```

Figure 5.11 Establishing parentage at the *0003* PATIENT segment

```
GN      HOSPITAL(HOSPNAME =MAC NEAL                     )
^^^^    ^^^^^^^^^^^^^^^^^^^^^^^^^^^^^^^^^^^^^^^^^^^^^^^^^
        WARD    (WARDNO    =01)
        ^^^^^^^^^^^^^^^^^^^^^^^^^
        PATIENT (BEDIDENT =   )
        ^^^^^^^^^^^^^^^^^^^^^^^^^
```

Figure 5.12 Retrieving certain PATIENT segments

```
GU      HOSPITAL(HOSPNAME =MAC NEAL                     )
^^^^    ^^^^^^^^^^^^^^^^^^^^^^^^^^^^^^^^^^^^^^^^^^^^^^^^^
        WARD    (WARDNO    =01)
        ^^^^^^^^^^^^^^^^^^^^^^^^^


GNP     PATIENT (BEDIDENT =   )
^^^^    ^^^^^^^^^^^^^^^^^^^^^^^^^
```

Figure 5.13 Using the Get-Next-Within-Parent call

are dependent on ward *01*. You can do this by issuing a series of Get-Next calls shown in figure 5.12. With those SSAs you must plug the appropriate BEDIDENT values into the last SSA before you issue each Get-Next call.

Notice that in this example you had to use qualified SSAs for all segments above the segment you were retrieving in order to limit DL/I's search. You would get the same result by first issuing a Get-Unique call for ward *01* as in the first call in figure 5.13. That would establish parentage at ward *01*. You could then issue GNP calls with a single qualified SSA for the PATIENT segment. By using GNP instead of the GN you automatically limit the area of search to only those segments dependent on ward *01*. A Get-Next call with that single SSA would cause DL/I to read through all the PATIENT segments in the data base, rather than stopping at the end of the ward *01* segments.

Using Fields in the PCB

Up to this point the only field in the PCB that we've examined is the status code field. In performing sequential retrievals within the data base, it's often necessary to examine other PCB fields to determine which segment type your program has retrieved. A number of fields in the PCB provide important information about the results of your calls.

PCB Linkage

Remember that the PCB is a DL/I control block that is loaded into memory by DL/I before your program is executed. The PCB mask coding in your program is set up in such a way that the data names in your program refer to fields in the PCB that DL/I loaded. This is done in COBOL by defining your PCB fields in the LINKAGE SECTION of your program. It's done in a similar manner in Assembler Language and PL/I programs.

Figure 5.14 shows the COBOL coding that establishes the linkage between DL/I and your program. (You saw this before in chapter 3.) The name of your PCB mask appears in the ENTRY statement of your program as well as in the LINKAGE SECTION. This establishes the linkage between your program and DL/I. All the data names in the PCB mask below the 01 level name now refer to the actual data areas of the PCB that was loaded before your application program got control. Let's take a look now at what each field can be used for in your program.

PCB Fields

The first field in the PCB is an eight-position character field which contains the name of the DBD referenced by this ACB.

The next field is a two-position, right-justified, decimal number, which indicates the level of the segment that you've just retrieved. With the HOSPITAL data base this field will contain 1 whenever a HOSPITAL segment has been retrieved, 2 whenever a WARD or FACILITY segment has been re-

```
         .
         .
         .
LINKAGE SECTION.
 01   PCB-MASK.
         03  DBDNAME                   PIC X(0).
         03  LEVEL-NUMBER              PIC XX.
         03  STATUS-CODE               PIC XX.
         03  PROC-OPTIONS              PIC XXXX.
         03  JCB ADDRESS               PIC XXXX.
         03  SEGMENT-NAME              PIC X(8).
         03  KEY-LENGTH                PIC S9(5)  COMP.
         03  NUMBER-SEGS               PIC S9(5)  COMP.
         03  KEY-FEEDBACK.
             05  HOSPNAME-KEY          PIC X(20).
             05  WARDNO-KEY            PIC XX.
             05  BEDIDENT-KEY          PIC XXXX.
         .
         .
         .
PROCEDURE DIVISION.
         ENTRY  'DLITCBL'  USING  PCB-MASK.
         .
         .
         .
```

Figure 5.14 COBOL entry linkage coding

trieved, 3 whenever a PATIENT segment has been retrieved, and 4 whenever a SYMPTOM, TREATMNT, or DOCTOR segment has been retrieved. The level number field can often give you a valuable clue as to the segment type you've retrieved.

The next field in the PCB is the status code field. You're already familiar with it.

The next field is a four-position field that shows the processing options that were coded in the PCB statement. The codes in this field tell you what types of calls you're allowed to use.

Next is a four-position field that is described in the IBM documentation as "reserved for DL/I." This field actually contains a four-type address, which is the address of an internal control block called the JCB. This field can often be useful in debugging situations, and its use will be described in appendix B.

The next field is eight positions long and can often be very valuable when you're performing sequential retrievals. After each retrieval call, this field contains the eight-position name of the segment just retrieved.

THE KEY FEEDBACK AREAS. The next three fields work together to describe the keys of all the segments along the retrieval path. The key length gives the length, in bytes, of the *concatenated key* of all the segments along the retrieval path. A concatenated key consists of the key values of all the segments along the retrieval path strung together one after the other. The number-of-segments field gives the number of key fields that are stored in the concatenated key area. The key feedback area contains the actual concatenated key of all the segments along the retrieval path. These are both full-word binary numbers. Some examples will show you how to use the key feedback fields.

Let's see what these last three PCB fields would look like after some segments have been retrieved. Figure 5.15 shows a Get-Next call to retrieve a PATIENT segment. Notice that we're searching for the PATIENT segment on one of the search fields, the PATNAME field. Figure 5.16 shows what the key-length, number-of-segments, and key-feedback fields will look like after this segment is retrieved. (As we said earlier, the key-length and number-of-segments fields are actually each full-word binary numbers, but we're showing them in decimal for clarity.)

The key-length field says that the key feedback area contains twenty-six bytes: the key field for the HOSPITAL segment is twenty bytes in length, the key field for the WARD segment is two bytes in length, and the key field for the PATIENT segment is four bytes in length. The number-of-segments field says that there are three concatenated keys in the key feedback area, and the key feedback area contains the key values for the three segments along the retrieval path.

Notice that the concatenated key area contains the key field of the PATIENT segment, even though it was retrieved using a search field. If a segment along the retrieval path has no key field, that level of the hierarchy

```
GN     HOSPITAL(HOSPNAME =RIVEREDGE                    )
^^^^   ^^^^^^^^^^^^^^^^^^^^^^^^^^^^^^^^^^^^^^^^^^^^^^^^^^
       WARD    (WARDNO   =01)
       ^^^^^^^^^^^^^^^^^^^^^^^
       PATIENT (PATNAME  =BURNS                        )
       ^^^^^^^^^^^^^^^^^^^^^^^^^^^^^^^^^^^^^^^^^^^^^^^^^^^
```

Figure 5.15 Retrieving a PATIENT segment

```
DBD  Name              Level     Status
|H|O|S|P|I|T|A|L|      | |3|     | | |

Proc.Options JCB Address  Segment  Name
| | | |G|    |X|X|X|X|     |P|A|T|I|I|E|N|T| |

Key  Length    No. of Segments
|0|0|2|6|      |0|0|0|3|

Key Feedback Area


HOSPNAME
|R|I|V|E|R|E|D|G|E| | | | | | | | | | | | |

WARDNO    BEDIDENT
|0|1|     |0|0|1|4|
```

Figure 5.16 PCB after successful PATIENT retrieval

will be skipped in the concatenated key. For example, the DOCTOR segment in the HOSPITAL data base contains no key field, only two search fields are defined. If you retrieve a DOCTOR segment using one of those search fields, the concatenated key area would contain the key fields for the HOSPITAL, WARD, and PATIENT segments, but would not contain the search field value for the DOCTOR segment. Only key field values can make up the concatenated key, not search fields.

DESCRIBING THE CONCATENATED KEY AREA. The concatenated key area is the only variable portion of the PCB. The rest of the fields are fixed in format for all data base PCBs. You set up your data names for the concatenated key area from the information in your PCB and DBD coding. If you look at figure 5.14 again and examine the concatenated key coding, you'll notice that the data areas defined there describe the hierarchical structure of the segments you have access to.

In setting up the coding for the concatenated key area, you use the SENSEG statements in your PCB and the FIELD statements for key fields in your DBD. With this information you set up the data fields that you'll need to describe the concatenated key for each retrieval path that you expect your program to handle.

PCB Fields for Unsuccessful Calls

The fields in the PCB come in handy even after unsuccessful retrieval calls. Suppose you issued a Get-Unique call with the SSA shown in figure 5.17 and suppose DL/I returned a status code of GE, indicating that the segment was not found. It might be useful for you to know whether it was only the PATIENT segment that was missing, or whether the WARD segment or even the HOSPITAL segment couldn't be found. To provide that information, DL/I stores information in the PCB to correspond to the highest level in the data base at which your search was satisfied.

For example, suppose that there was a *Mac Neal* HOSPITAL segment in the data base, and there was a WARD segment, but that the PATIENT segment that you wanted was not in that ward. Figure 5.18 shows you what the PCB fields would look like for that call. Notice that the status code field contains GE, indicating that the segment was not found, but other parts of the PCB look as if you tried to retrieve the ward *01* segment from the data base.

```
GU      HOSPITAL(HOSPNAME =MAC NEAL                    )
        WARD     (WARDNO   =04)
        PATIENT (PATNAME  =BAILEY                      )
```

Figure 5.17 Retrieving a PATIENT segment

```
DBD Name              Level    Status
|H|O|S|P|I|T|A|L|      | |2|    |G|E|

Proc.Options JCB Address  Segment Name
| | | |G|     |X|X|X|X|    |W|A|R|D| | | | |

Key Length    No. of Segments
|0|0|2|2|     |0|0|0|2|

Key Feedback Area


HOSPNAME
|M|A|C| |N|E|A|L| | | | | | | | | | | | |

WARDNO    BEDIDENT
|0|4|     | | | | | |
```

Figure 5.18 PCB for missing PATIENT segment

The PCB information indicates that the WARD segment level is the highest level at which the call was satisfied.

Let's suppose that you issued the same call, but that this time there was no ward *01* segment in the data base. The PCB fields would look like figure 5.19. Again, the status code is GE but the other fields in the PCB look as though you tried to retrieve a HOSPITAL segment. Notice especially the concatenated key and associated fields for the last two calls. Those fields can often be useful in determining what went wrong when you receive a GE status code.

Using the PCB Fields

The PCB will normally give you more than enough information to determine what happened as a result of any call. One thing to keep in mind, though, is that in your PCB logic, you should make use of as little of the information as you can. The reason for this is that the more use you make of the information stored in the PCB, the more dependent you are on the physical structure of the data base. So the more information in the PCB that you use, the more likely it is that your program will require changes if the physical structure of the data base changes.

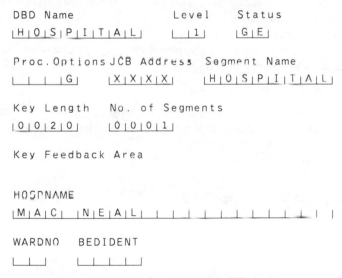

Figure 5.19 PCB for missing WARD segment

```
GU     TREATMNT(TRTYPE    =MORPHINE            &TRDATE   =080377)
```

Figure 5.20 Using the Boolean AND operator

Boolean SSA Statements

You'll find, at times, that you would like to perform a search for a segment based on more than one field in a segment. A good example of this would be retrieving a TREATMNT segment from the HOSPITAL data base. The key field is treatment date and another search field within the segment is treatment type. There may be many TREATMNT segments with the same treatment date and at the same time there might be many TREATMNT segments with the same treatment type given on different dates.

Suppose you wanted to search for a TREATMNT segment whose treatment type was *morphine* and whose treatment date was *080377.* You could issue the Get-Unique call in figure 5.20. Notice that the last SSA specifies two qualification statements connected by a *boolean operator.*

In this case the boolean operator is an ampersand, which specifies a logical AND operation. The last SSA means that we want to retrieve a TREATMNT segment whose treatment type is *morphine* and also whose treatment date is *080377.*

Boolean Operators

Figure 5.21 shows the other boolean operators that you can use in writing boolean qualification statements. You can use either the asterisk (*) or the ampersand (&) to indicate a logical AND. And you can use the plus (+) sign or the vertical bar (|) to indicate a logical OR operator. The special independent-AND operator indicated by the pound sign (#) will be described later in the section on secondary indexing.

Complex Boolean Statements

Figure 5.22 shows how a more complex group of qualification statements would be evaluated by DL/I. Any group of qualification statements connected

```
* —AND
& —AND
+ —OR
| —OR
# —Independent AND
```

Figure 5.21 Boolean operators

```
GU    FIELD  (A       =1*B        =2+C       =3*D       =4)
```

```
A = 1 AND B = 2 OR C = 3 AND D = 4
```

Figure 5.22 Complex Boolean statement

by AND operators is called a *set* of qualification statements. In order for the entire expression to be satisfied, any one set of qualification statements needs to be satisfied. In order for a set to be satisfied, all the qualification statements within that set must be satisfied. For example, in figure 5.22 the qualification statements would be considered satisfied if either field A equals *1* AND field B equals *2*, OR field C equals *3* AND field D equals *4*. As you can see, the normal logic rules of AND and OR apply in boolean SSA statements.

CHAPTER 5 EXERCISE (CODING PROBLEM)

There is only a single exercise associated with this chapter. However, in this exercise you'll get a chance to use all the skills you've learned up to this point. Following are the specifications for a complete DL/I batch application program. For this coding problem, you should code the complete program in COBOL, PL/I, or Assembler Language.

The Previous Hospital Stay Inquiry Program

The purpose of this program is to inquire into the HOSPITAL data base and print out lists of those patients in a particular hospital who are presently in wards whose WARD-TYPE search field equals *quarantine,* and who have had a previous hospital stay within one year of their present admittance date. The results should be provided in the form of Previous Stay reports.

INPUT TO THE PROGRAM. The program should read an 80-character card image file all of whose card images have the following format:

>   Columns 1–2   Constant—QR
>   Columns 3–22   Left-justified hospital name
>   Columns 23–80   Blanks

The cards can be presented in any sequence. Each card contains the name of a hospital for which the Previous Stay report should be prepared.

OUTPUT FROM THE PROGRAM. The program should print out a separate report for each input record. The report is called the Previous Stay report. The Previous Stay report should print out the hospital's name, address, and phone number at the top of the report. Following the hospital information, the report should print header information for each *quarantine* ward in the hospital, listing the information in each *quarantine* WARD segment.

Following each set of ward header information should be a single line for each patient in the ward that had a previous hospital stay in the last year. Each line should contain a patient's name, bed identifier, date admitted, name of the hospital at which the patient previously stayed, the date of the previous stay, and the reason for the previous stay.

Figure 5.23 shows a sample page from this report. Print a single page with the following line if a HOSPITAL segment is not found.

>   HOSPITAL nnnnnnnnnnnnnnnnnnnn NOT FOUND

Follow the hospital header information with the following line if the hospital does not have any quarantine wards:

PAGE 1

P R E V I O U S   S T A Y   R E P O R T

HOSPITAL NAME	HOSPITAL ADDRESS	HOSP PHONE
MAC NEAL	1234 MAIN STREET, CHICAGO IL	312554376

WARD NO	TOT ROOMS	TOT BEDS	BEDS AVAIL	WARD TYPE
01	34	112	018	QUARANTINE

PATIENT NAME	BED	ADMIT DATE	PREV DATE	PREVIOUS HOSPITAL	PREVIOUS REASON
O'HARA	0050	062377	1176	MAC NEAL	BUBONIC PLAGUE
OZIER	0051	052177	1176	ST JOSEPH	BUBONIC PLAGUE
PARELLA	0056	052777	1076	MAC NEAL	BUBONIC PLAGUE
WRIGHT	0057	052677	1176	MAC NEAL	BUBONIC PLAGUE
YANCEY	0058	052977	0976	RIVEREDGE	BUBONIC PLAGUE
ERIN	0059	051277	1176	MAC NEAL	BUBONIC PLAGUE
KAPP	0060	061777	1076	MAC NEAL	BUBONIC PLAGUE
CLAPPER	0070	071877	1176	MAC NEAL	BUBONIC PLAGUE
LEBEN	0071	080177	1076	ST JOSEPH	BUBONIC PLAGUE
CAROL	0072	080177	1176	MAC NEAL	BUBONIC PLAGUE
JOE	0074	071777	1076	RIVEREDGE	BUBONIC PLAGUE
KATIE	0077	080177	1176	MAC NEAL	BUBONIC PLAGUE
PAT	0078	072677	1076	ST JOSEPH	BUBONIC PLAGUE
LANOU	0079	072677	1076	MAC NEAL	BUBONIC PLAGUE
ELLGLASS	0080	072277	1176	MAC NEAL	BUBONIC PLAGUE
CARLSON	0082	072177	1176	MAC NEAL	BUBONIC PLAGUE
BUHL	0090	072477	1076	MAC NEAL	BUBONIC PLAGUE

Figure 5.23 Sample page of Previous Stay report

```
PRINT    NOGEN                                                        00000010
PCB      TYPE=DB,DBDNAME=HOSPDBD,PROCOPT=G,KEYLEN=26                   00000020
                                                                      00000025
SENSEG   NAME=HOSPITAL,PARENT=0                                       00000030
SENSEG   NAME=WARD,PARENT=HOSPITAL                                    00000040
SENSEG   NAME=PATIENT,PARENT=WARD                                     00000050
                                                                      00000055
PSBGEN   LANG=COBOL,PSBNAME=CHAP5C                                    00000060
END                                                                   00000070
```

Figure 5.24 Chapter 5 coding problem PSB

85

NO QUARANTINE WARDS

Follow the ward header information with the following line if there are no patients in that ward with a previous stay in the last year:

NO PATIENTS WITH PREVIOUS STAY

HOSPITAL Data Base Information

Figure 5.24 shows the coding for the PSB that your program should use. Notice that you are sensitive only to HOSPITAL, WARD, and PATIENT segments in this program.

Figure 5.24 shows the COBOL coding for the three segments your program is sensitive to. Assume that you have access to this coding, or to PL/I or Assembler Language versions, in a source statement library. Most of the information in the segments is self-explanatory. However, for this exercise, the field in the PATIENT segment named PREV-STAY-FLAG needs some explanation. This field contains a character zero if the patient has had no previous hospital stay, and a character one if the patient has had a previous hospital stay.

Appendix D summarizes all the information about the HOSPITAL data base that you need for this coding problem.

6

Loading and Inserting Segments

Introduction

In this chapter we'll look at a function code that can be used for two purposes. It's the *Insert* function code, spelled ISRT. You use Insert calls either to load a data base from scratch or insert segments into an existing data base. The way you use the Insert call is similar for both, but your program logic and your SSAs are sometimes quite different.

We'll look at both uses of the Insert call in this chapter, and you'll see a complete sample load program for the HOSPITAL data base. We'll also take a look at how DL/I processes your Insert calls and at the alternatives you have for Load and Insert status code logic.

The Insert Call

Let's begin by looking at a call statement and SSA which can be used to insert a segment. Figure 6.1 shows the COBOL coding that you might use to insert a PATIENT segment. Notice that only a single SSA is specified: an unqualified SSA for the PATIENT segment. The rest of the entries in the parameter list are the same as those for any other call. When your program executes this call, the I/O area should contain the actual PA-

```
77  FUNCTION   PIC X(4)  VALUE 'ISRT'.
77  SSA-AREA   PIC X(9)  VALUE 'PATIENT '.
    •
    •
    •
    CALL 'CBLTDLI' USING  FUNCTION
                          PCBMASK
                          IOAREA
                          SSA-AREA.
```

Figure 6.1 An Insert call

TIENT segment occurrence that you want to insert into the data base.

This type of call sequence can be used to load a data base or to insert a segment into an existing data base. Notice, however, that the single unqualified SSA does not give DL/I any information as to where in the data base to insert this particular PATIENT segment. As with other DL/I calls, unless you fully qualify the call, DL/I uses current position in determining where to insert or load the segment.

Using qualified SSAs with Insert Calls

When you load a data base or insert a segment into an existing data base, you are allowed to include qualified SSAs for all higher levels. Figure 6.2 shows an example of this. Notice that we've included qualified SSAs for both the HOSPITAL and WARD segments. The PATIENT segment is still referenced with an unqualified SSA. One important rule for using the ISRT function code is that the segment being loaded or inserted must be identified with an unqualified SSA. DL/I extracts further identification for that segment from the I/O area, and it's not valid to code a qualification statement in the last SSA.

For the most part, programs designed to load data bases from scratch normally use Insert calls with single unqualified SSAs. The reason for this will become more clear when we look at a load program in detail. Programs designed to insert segments into an existing data base generally use sets of qualified SSAs to completely describe the paths along which new segments are to be inserted. This ensures that segments are not inserted in the wrong place in the data base.

```
ISRT    HOSPITAL(HOSPNAME =MAC NEAL             )

        WARD    (WARDNO   =04)

        PATIENT
```

Figure 6.2 An Insert call with qualified SSAs

L —Load Mode

LS—Load Mode–Ascending Sequence

A —Get, Insert, Delete, Replace

AS—Get, Insert, Delete, Replace–Ascending Sequence

I —Insert Mode

IS —Insert Mode–Ascending Sequence

Figure 6.3 Insert call processing options

Insert Call Processing Options

DL/I knows whether your program is going to load a data base from scratch or insert segments into an existing data base by the processing options in your PCB. Figure 6.3 shows the processing options that apply for Insert calls.

PROCOPT=L says that you'll be using Insert calls in the load mode to load a data base from scratch. The PROCOPT=LS parameter says that you'll be using Insert calls in the load mode, and that you'll be loading segments in ascending sequence. Load programs normally load segments in ascending sequence. However, you'll see an exception to this rule later.

The PROCOPT=A parameter says that Get, Insert, Replace, and Delete calls are allowed for the data base. PROCOPT=AS means that Get, Insert, Replace and Delete calls may be specified, and segments must be processed in ascending sequence. With A and AS, Insert calls can only be used to insert segments into an existing data base. The PROCOPT=I parameter says that only Insert calls in the insert mode will be accepted for this data base. And the PROCOPT—IS parameter says that only Insert calls in the insert mode will be allowed, and segments must be inserted in ascending sequence.

If you're going to write a load program, make sure that your PCB has an L coded in the PROCOPT parameter. And similarly, if you expect to be able to use Insert calls in the insert mode, be sure that either A or I is coded.

Loading a Data Base

A load program is generally a lot more straightforward than a program written to process Insert calls in the insert mode, so we'll start with a load program. Figure 6.4 shows a complete program to load the HOSPITAL data base. We'll use this program to illustrate a few key concepts about using the Insert call in the load mode. Look this program over for a few minutes and see if you can follow the logic.

Notice that there is a single Insert call in this program. It's used to insert all segment types. Segment images are read from an input data set and the program determines what type of segment is being loaded. It then moves the proper unqualified SSA to the SSA area referred to by the CALL statement parameter list. The Insert call is executed, and some simple status code logic takes place. This process continues until the input data set is completely processed.

Two Approaches to Data Base Loading

One requirement of most data base load programs creates the need for two completely different approaches to data base loading. This requirement is that, for most applications, segments must be presented to the load program in *hierarchical sequence*. This means that root segments usually must be presented to the load program in root key sequence and all dependent segments

Figure 6.4 A complete load program

```
000010  ID DIVISION.
000020  PROGRAM-ID.  CHAP6C.
000030  AUTHOR.  JOSEPH F. LEBEN.
000040  DATE-COMPILED.
000041
000050  REMARKS.  LOADING THE HOSPITAL DATA BASE - CAUTION: THIS PROGRAM
000060          DOES VERY LITTLE ERROR CHECKING AND ASSUMES THAT THE
000070          INPUT DATA SET CONTAINS SEGMENT IMAGES IN PROPER
000080          HIERARCHICAL SEQUENCE.  EACH SEGMENT IMAGE IS CONTAINED
000090          IN TWO CARDS.  CARD FORMAT IS:
000100
000110              COLUMNS  1 -  8   SEGMENT NAME
000120                       9        BLANK
000130                      10 - 72   FIRST OR SECOND HALF OF SEGMENT
000140                      73 - 80   SEQUENCE NUMBER.
000150
000160  ENVIRONMENT DIVISION.
000170  CONFIGURATION SECTION.
000180  SOURCE-COMPUTER. IBM-370-168.
000190  OBJECT-COMPUTER. IBM-370-168.
000200  INPUT-OUTPUT SECTION.
000210  FILE-CONTROL.
000220      SELECT  CARDFILE    ASSIGN TO   UT-S-INPUT.
000230      SELECT  OUTFILE     ASSIGN TO   UT-S-OUTPUT.
000240
000250  DATA DIVISION.
000260  FILE SECTION.
000270
000280  FD  CARDFILE
000290      LABEL RECORDS ARE STANDARD
000300      RECORDING MODE IS F
000310      BLOCK CONTAINS 0 RECORDS
000320      DATA RECORD IS  VARIED-INFO.
000330
000340  01  VARIED-INFO.
000350      03  SEG-NAME        PIC X(8).
```

```
000360           03  FILLER          PIC X.
000370           03  CARD-DATA       PIC X(63).
000380           03  FILLER          PIC X(8).
000390
000400     FD  OUTFILE
000410         LABEL RECORDS ARE STANDARD
000420         RECORDING MODE IS F
000430         BLOCK CONTAINS 0 RECORDS
000440         DATA RECORD IS PRINT-LINE.
000450
000460     01  PRINT-LINE.
000470           03  CARR-CNTL       PIC X.
000480           03  CARD-INFO       PIC X(80).
000490           03  FILLER          PIC X(52).
000500         EJECT
000510     WORKING-STORAGE SECTION.
000520
000530     77  INSERTION       PIC X(4)        VALUE 'ISRT'.
000540     77  LINE-COUNT      PIC S99  COMP-3 VALUE 50.
000550
000560     01  UNQUAL-SSA.
000570           03  SEGNAME                   PIC X(8).
000580           03  FILLER          PIC X     VALUE ' '.
000590
000600     01  I-O-AREA.
000610           03  FIRST-HALF                PIC X(63).
000620           03  SECOND-HALF               PIC X(62).
000630
000640     LINKAGE SECTION.
000650     01  PCB-MASK COPY MASKC.
000670     PROCEDURE DIVISION.
000680     START-OF-PROGRAM.
000690
000700         ENTRY 'DLITCBL' USING PCB-MASK.
000710
000720     BEGIN-HERE.
000730         OPEN INPUT CARDFILE.
000740         OPEN OUTPUT OUTFILE.
000750
```

```
000760  READ-CARD.
000770      READ CARDFILE  AT END GO TO FINIS.
000780      MOVE CARD-DATA  TO FIRST-HALF.
000790      PERFORM PRINT-ROUTINE.
000800      READ CARDFILE  AT END GO TO FINIS.
000810      MOVE CARD-DATA  TO SECOND-HALF.
000820      PERFORM PRINT-ROUTINE.
000830      MOVE SEG-NAME OF VARIED-INFO TO SEGNAME OF UNQUAL-SSA.
000840
000850  LOAD-1.
000860      CALL 'CBLTDLI' USING  INSERTION
000870                            PCB-MASK
000880                            I-O-AREA
000890                            UNQUAL-SSA.
000900
000910      IF  STATUS-CODE IS  NOT EQUAL TO '   '  GO TO BAD-END.
000920          GO TO READ-CARD.
000930
000940  PRINT-ROUTINE.
000950      IF LINE-COUNT = 50
000960          MOVE ZERO TO LINE-COUNT
000970          MOVE SPACE TO PRINT-LINE
000980          WRITE PRINT-LINE AFTER ADVANCING 1 LINES.
000990      MOVE VARIED-INFO TO CARD-INFO.
001000      WRITE PRINT-LINE AFTER ADVANCING 1 LINES.
001010
001020  FINIS.
001030      CLOSE CARDFILE.
001040      CLOSE OUTFILE.
001050      GOBACK.
001060
001070  BAD-END.
001080      DISPLAY 'BAD STATUS', STATUS-CODE.
001090      CLOSE OUTFILE.
001100      GOBACK.
```

must be presented to the load program in hierarchical sequence following each root.

When you use the Insert call in the insert mode, segments may normally be inserted into an existing data base in any sequence. Since it is sometimes quite difficult to sort segments into hierarchical sequence, a two-step load process is sometimes performed. An initial load program, using Insert calls in the load mode, processes all of the root segments and some of the dependent segments under each root. This program loads a skeleton data base consisting of only a portion of the total segments. In the second step, a program using Insert calls in the insert mode is used to insert the remaining segments into the data base.

In deciding which approach to use, keep in mind that a program designed to load all of the segments in one pass is bound to run faster than the two programs required with the two-step approach. So if it's possible to sort the segments into hierarchical sequence, the one-pass approach is usually best. In many cases, however, it's next to impossible to sort all the segments into hierarchical sequence, so the two-step approach may be necessary. The thing to keep in mind is to try to load as many of the segments in the first pass as you can.

When you're forced to use the two-step approach to data base loading, you might consider reorganizing the data base immediately after the initial load. As you'll see later in chapter 12, the chapter on access methods, inserting a large volume of segments into an existing data base can alter the physical structure of the data base to the point where access to segments becomes very inefficient. Reorganizing the data base immediately after the load eliminates these inefficiencies.

SSAs for Load Mode Insert Calls

Figure 6.5 shows the CALL statement and SSA area used in the sample load program. Notice that the SSA area for this program consists of one nine-byte data item. The appropriate unqualified SSA is moved into this area before each segment is inserted. This illustrates the only SSA requirement for the Insert call in load mode. Only a single unqualified SSA for the segment type being loaded is required. As we stated earlier, it's not valid to qualify this SSA since DL/I gets qualification information from the I/O area which contains the segment being inserted. Since you normally load segments in hierarchical sequence, DL/I never has to stray from current position in loading each subsequent segment. So for most load programs, additional qualification of the Insert calls is not necessary.

It's perfectly valid, however, to include qualified SSAs to completely describe the path along which each segment is to be loaded. The only restriction here is that you can't include a qualification statement for the final SSA, the one for the segment being loaded. And of course, you can't include SSAs at levels lower than the level at which you're loading the segment.

When you use high-level qualified SSAs in an Insert call, those SSAs

```
                .
                .
                .
01   UNQUAL-SSA.
     03  SEGNAME              PIC X(8).
     03  FILLER               PIC X      VALUE SPACE.
                .
                .
                .
     CALL 'CBLTDLI' USING  INSERTION
                           PCB-MASK
                           I-O-AREA
                           UNQUAL-SSA.
                .
                .
                .
```

Figure 6.5 Call and SSA for data base load

function exactly as they do in a Get-Unique call. They cause DL/I to locate the path along which you would like to load the segment. Keep in mind, however, in a program designed to load segments in hierarchical sequence, high-level SSAs that describe a path other than the one pointed to by current position will normally cause the call to be unsuccessful.

Load Mode Status Codes

Four status codes are of particular interest to you when you're using ISRT calls in the load mode. (See figure 6.6.) There are many more status codes that you can get as a result of an Insert call in the load mode. If you get one of them you can look it up in your *Application Programming Reference Manual.*

You'll get the LB when you try to load the same segment twice. The LC status code tells you that your segments are not in hierarchical sequence. The LD status code also tells you that something is wrong with the sequence of your segments in the input data set. You can't load a dependent segment until its parent has been loaded. LE indicates another type of sequencing problem. This might occur if you tried to load a FACILITY segment before a PA-TIENT segment.

Inserting Segments into an Existing Data Base

An Insert call to insert a segment into an existing data base looks exactly the same as the Insert call used to load a data base. Figure 6.7 shows the Insert call and SSA that could be used to insert a PATIENT segment into the data base. We saw this same coding earlier in this chapter. Yes, this is the same call that was used to load a PATIENT segment when we built the data base from scratch. The only difference in coding between inserting segments into an existing data base and loading a data base is the processing options in the PCB.

LB—Segment already exists

LC—Key values out of sequence

LD—No parent for segment being loaded

LE—Segment types out of sequence

Figure 6.6 Load mode status codes

```
77  FUNCTION    PIC X(4)   VALUE 'ISRT'.
77  SSA-AREA    PIC X(9)   VALUE 'PATIENT
     •
     •
     •
    CALL 'CBLTDLI' USING   FUNCTION
                           PCBMASK
                           IOAREA
                           SSA-AREA.
```

Figure 6.7 Insert mode Insert call

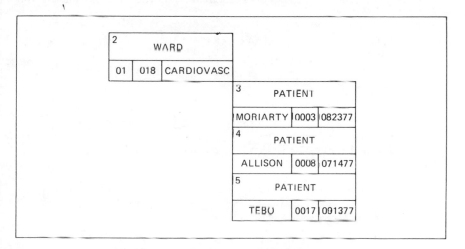

Figure 6.8 PATIENT segments before Insert

We said earlier that if you intend to insert segments into an existing data base, the A or I must be coded in the PROCOPT operand.

Using Qualified SSAs for Segment Insertion

In general, you must be very careful about describing to DL/I where each segment should be inserted when you're inserting segments into an existing data base. When you're loading segments in hierarchical sequence, current position always indicates the place where you would like the next segment to be inserted. This is not normally the case when you're inserting segments into an existing data base. Unless you have just issued a retrieval call that points to exactly where you would like the next segment inserted, you must supply DL/I with additional qualified SSAs to completely describe the path along which the insertion is to be made.

Let's suppose that figure 6.8 shows the segments in a portion of the HOSPITAL data base. Let's say that you would like to add a PATIENT segment to ward *01* under the *Mac Neal* HOSPITAL segment. Figure 6.9 shows the function code, SSAs, and part of the contents of the I/O area for this Insert call.

After this Insert call is executed, the PATIENT segments dependent on the ward *01* segment would look like those shown in figure 6.10.

Since the PATIENT segment has a unique key field, DL/I uses the key of the new PATIENT segment to determine where in the twin chain to insert the new segment. In other words, DL/I maintains twin chains in key sequence wherever a key field has been specified for a segment type.

Notice that the SSAs in figure 6.9 completely describe the path along which to insert the new PATIENT segment. Another way to handle the

```
ISRT    HOSPITAL(HOSPNAME =MAC NEAL              )
        ^^^^    ^^^^^^^^^^^^^^^^^^^^^^^^^^^^^^^^^^^^^^^^
        WARD    (WARDNO   =01)
        ^^^^^^^^^^^^^^^^^^^^^^^^
        PATIENT
        ^^^^^^^^^

FREDERICKS              ~ 0011 ~ 101177
^^^^^^^^^^^^^^^^^^^^^^^^^^^  ^^^^   ^^^^^^
```

Figure 6.9 Function code, SSAs, and I/O area for Insert call

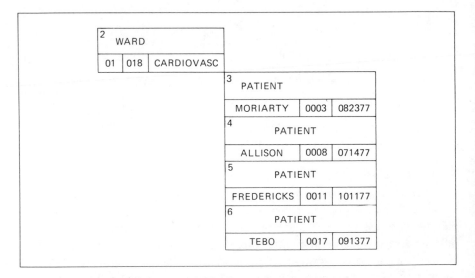

Figure 6.10 PATIENT segments after Insert

insertion is to perform some retrieval call to establish a position within the data base. For example, a Get-Unique call with the SSAs shown in figure 6.11 will retrieve the ward *01* segment and establish a position within the data base at that point. You could follow that Get-Unique call with an Insert call referring to a single unqualified SSA for the PATIENT segment. That would accomplish the same insertion. The important thing is either to establish the proper position within the data base before you issue the Insert call, or fully qualify the Insert call and completely describe the path along which you would like to make the insertion.

The DBD Insert Rules

When the DBA defines a segment type that does not have a key field, or has a non-unique key field, it's necessary to tell DL/I where to insert new occurrences of that segment type. The RULES parameter of the SEGM statement tells DL/I how to handle segment insertions in that kind of situation. Figure 6.12 shows a possible SEGM statement for the DOCTOR segment. It also shows the three options that the DBA has when coding the second subparameter of the RULES operand. The second subparameter tells DL/I where in the twin chain to insert a new segment when a segment does not have a unique key field. This second subparameter is called the *insert rule*. The insert rule FIRST says that a new segment will always be inserted at the beginning of the twin chain. The insert rule LAST says the segment will always be inserted at the end of the twin chain. This is the default if no RULES operand is coded. The insert rule HERE says that you will normally establish a position within the twin chain before issuing an Insert call. This segment will then be inserted after the segment on which current position is established.

INSERTING A SEGMENT WITH NO KEY FIELD. Figure 6.13 shows a portion of the data base containing DOCTOR segments. Since the DOCTOR segment has two search fields, but no key field, the insert rule helps to determine where new DOCTOR segments will be inserted. Suppose we issued

```
GU      HOSPITAL(HOSPNAME =MAC NEAL                        )
        ^^^^    ^^^^^^^^^^^^^^^^^^^^^^^^^^^^^^^^^^^^^^^ ..........
        WARD    (WARDNO    =01)
        ^^^^^^^^^^^^^^^^^^^^^^^
```

Figure 6.11 Get-Unique call for the ward *01* segment

```
SEGM    NAME=DOCTOR,PARENT=PATIENT,
        BYTES=20,RULES=(,HERE)


        RULES=(,FIRST)
               LAST
               HERE
```

Figure 6.12 Specifying the insert rule

the Insert call in figure 6.14. The SSAs will establish a position within the data base at the appropriate PATIENT segment occurrence. The insert rule then tells DL/I where in the DOCTOR segment twin chain to place the new segment. The insert rules of FIRST or LAST clearly tell DL/I where to place the new segment. If the insert rule were HERE and you issued the call in figure 6.14, the new segment would be placed at the beginning of the twin chain. This is because we haven't established a position within the DOCTOR segments yet. With the insert rule HERE, a new segment is always placed at the beginning of the twin chain if no position has been established within that twin chain.

INSERTING SEGMENTS WITH NON-UNIQUE KEY FIELDS. An insert rule may also be specified for a segment that has a non-unique key field. In this case DL/I can use the key field to find the approximate position within the twin chain to insert the segment. The insert rule is then used to determine where to put the new segment relative to all the segments having the same key field value. For example, figure 6.15 shows a TREATMNT segment twin chain. If we try to insert a new TREATMNT segment with the key value *060776* into the data base, DL/I would have to use the insert rule to determine where to

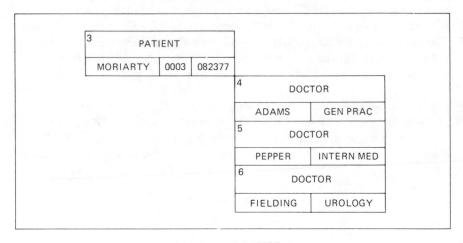

Figure 6.13 Some DOCTOR segments

```
ISRT    HOSPITAL(HOSPNAME =MAC NEAL              )
^^^^    ^^^^^^^^^^^^^^^^^^^^^^^^^^^^^^^^^^^^^^^^^^^^^
        WARD    (WARDNO   =01)
        ^^^^^^^^^^^^^^^^^^^^^
        PATIENT (BEDIDENT =0003)
        ^^^^^^^^^^^^^^^^^^^^^^^^^
        DOCTOR
        ^^^^^^^^
```

Figure 6.14 Inserting a DOCTOR segment

insert the new segment relative to the other TREATMNT segments having the same key value.

The insert rule FIRST tells DL/I to insert the segments at the beginning of all of those segments having the same key value. An insert rule LAST tells DL/I to put the new segment after all of those segments having the same key value. And the insert rule HERE says that you will establish a position within the twin chain before you issue the Insert call. If you have not established position on a segment having the appropriate key field value, DL/I will insert the new segment at the beginning of the set of segments having the same key value.

Insert Mode Status Codes

Figure 6.16 shows two status codes that are common to Insert calls in the insert mode. The status codes indicate two error conditions. The II status code is self-explanatory. It's never valid to insert a segment that already exists in the data base.

You'd get the IX status code if you tried to insert a segment into the wrong place in the data base. Suppose you issued the Insert call in figure 6.17. You'd get an IX status code with that call because the PATIENT segment is dependent on the WARD segment, not the FACILITY segment. This is an example of trying to insert a PATIENT segment into the wrong place in the data base.

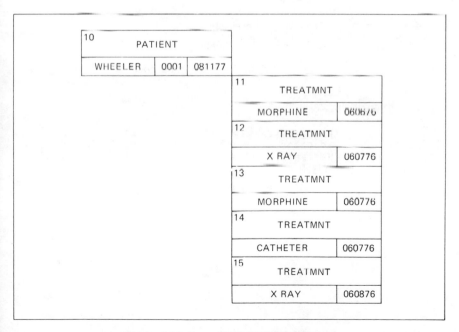

Figure 6.15 Some TREATMNT segments

CHAPTER 6 EXERCISES

1. Figure 6.18 is a list of all the PCB processing options that can be specified for Insert calls. Below is a list of statements describing those processing options. Match each processing option with the statement that best describes it.

   a. Insert segments in the load mode.
   b. Get, replace, delete, and insert segments in the insert mode, in hierarchical sequence only.
   c. Insert segments in the insert mode in hierarchical sequence only.
   d. Insert segments in the load mode in hierarchical sequence only.
   e. Get, replace, delete, and insert segments in the insert mode.
   f. Insert segments in the insert mode.

2. Write the function code and SSAs to load a PATIENT segment in a new data base. Assume that you are positioned correctly in the data base, and the PATIENT segment is already in the I/O area.

3. Write the function code and SSAs to insert a DOCTOR segment into an existing data base. The new DOCTOR segment should be inserted under the *Valentine* PATIENT segment, under ward *04*, under the *Mac Neal* HOSPITAL segment. Assume that you do not know current position, and that the DOCTOR segment is already in the I/O area.

4. Figure 6.19 shows the segments that are stored in a portion of the hospital data base. Current position within the data base is described by referencing the numbers

II —Segment already in data base

IX—Insert rule violation

Figure 6.16 Insert mode status codes

```
ISRT    HOSPITAL(HOSPNAME =MAC NEAL                  )
~~~~    ~~~~~~~~~~~~~~~~~~~~~~~~~~~~~~~~~~~~~~~~~~~~~~^
        FACILITY(FACTYPE  =PUMP-OXYGENATOR    )
        ~~~~~~~~~~~~~~~~~~~~~~~~~~~~~~~~~~~~~~~~~~~~~~^
        PATIENT
        ~~~~~~~~~~
```

Figure 6.17 An invalid Insert call

1. L

2. LS

3. A

4. AS

5. I

6. IS

Figure 6.18 PCB processing options for Insert calls

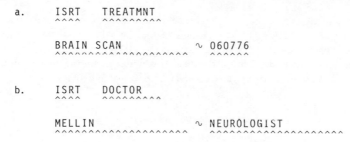

Figure 6.19 Segments for Exercise 4

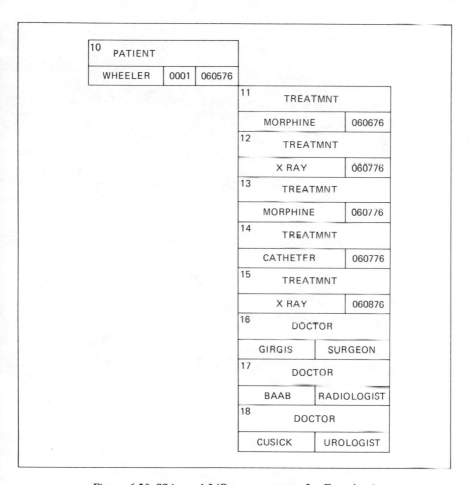

Figure 6.20 SSAs and I/O area contents for Exercise 4

in the upper left hand corner of each segment. Remember that the numbers are shown here for reference only; they are not stored in the data base. Figure 6.20

shows an SSA and the key and search field values of new segments for Insert calls. Indicate after which segment each new segment would be inserted. Assume that before each call current position is on segment 10. If a segment insertion depends on the insert rule in the DBD, indicate after which segment the new segment would be inserted for each insert rule: FIRST, LAST, and HERE.

7

Deleting and Updating Segments

Introduction

Deleting or replacing segments always requires you to perform a sequence of two calls. In the first call you use a special Get-Hold function code to retrieve the segment that you would like to delete or replace. You follow that with a call that will either delete or replace the segment.

In this chapter you'll learn the rules for using Get-Hold function codes, and you'll also learn the rules for using the Delete and Replace calls.

When you finish this chapter, you'll write a complete program using the following DL/I calls:

Get-Hold Calls

Replace Calls

Insert Calls

Delete Calls

In addition to using the above calls, you'll write the appropriate PCB and status code logic to support them.

Get-Hold Calls

Figure 7.1 shows the function codes for the three special retrieval calls, one of which must precede each Replace or Delete call. These function codes perform similar functions to those of the three retrieval calls you've already learned. The Get-Hold-Unique call corresponds to the Get-Unique call, the Get-Hold-Next call corresponds to the Get-Next call, and the Get-Hold-Next-Within-Parent call corresponds to the Get-Next-Within-Parent call. Everything that you've learned about the Get-Unique, Get-Next, and Get-Next-Within-Parent function codes also applies to these three. The Get-Hold calls cause DL/I to perform additional functions as well. When you issue a Get-

Hold call, DL/I saves information about the segment's location so that you can later delete or replace the segment. Get-Hold calls also cause DL/I to write information on data sets called the *system log data sets* that can be used to restore a data base should recovery ever be necessary. The main purpose of the Get-Hold calls is to retrieve a segment that you may want to delete or update and replace in the data base.

You use the same kinds of SSAs with Get-Hold calls as with normal Get calls. The status codes that DL/I returns to your program are also identical, given the same set of circumstances. Again, the only difference between Get-Hold calls and Get calls is that with Get-Hold calls you are allowed to follow that call with a Delete or Replace call. Following a normal Get call with a Delete or Replace is not allowed.

Delete and Replace Rules

Figure 7.2 shows the function codes for Delete and Replace calls. There are four important rules that you must keep in mind in using these function codes. Let's go through the rules before looking at Delete and Replace calls in detail.

Delete and Replace Rule 1

The first rule to keep in mind in using the DLET or REPL function code is that before you issue the Delete or Replace call you must issue a Get-Hold call. The Get-Hold call brings a particular segment into the I/O area and causes DL/I to save information about that segment. You can then examine the segment in the I/O area and decide whether you would like to delete or replace it. If you decide to delete the segment, you issue a call with the DLET function code. If you decide to replace the segment in the data base, you make any desired modifications to the segment and then issue a call with the REPL function code. That will cause the segment in the I/O area to be written back into the data base.

GHU —Get-Hold-Unique

GHN —Get-Hold-Next

GHNP—Get-Hold-Next-Within-Parent

Figure 7.1 The three Get-Hold calls

DLET—Delete function code

REPL—Replace function code

Figure 7.2 The DLET and REPL function codes

Delete and Replace Rule 2

Between the time that you issue the Get-Hold call and the time that you issue the Delete or Replace call, you are not allowed to issue any other call using the same PCB. If you issue a call other than a Delete or Replace, you'll nullify the effect of the Get-Hold call. Unless that call were another Get-Hold call, you would not be allowed to issue the Delete or Replace.

Delete and Replace Rule 3

You do not normally include SSAs when you issue a call with the DLET or REPL function code. The only exception to this rule is a Delete or Replace call following a Get-Hold that specified one or more SSAs using the D command code. The D command code causes more than one segment to be brought into the I/O area with a single call. We'll talk about this in more detail later in this chapter, but we'll go into it more in chapter 8, the chapter on command codes.

Delete and Replace Rule 4

As we stated earlier, your program can perform almost any kind of processing between the time that you perform the Get-Hold, and the time that you issue the Delete or Replace call. However, your program is not allowed to modify the key field of the segment. The Delete or Replace call will not work if you modify the key field.

Deleting Segments from the Data Base

As we mentioned earlier, deleting segments is a two-step process. Your first requirement is to retrieve the segment that you would like to delete. This may be done with any sequence of retrieval calls. The only requirement is that your last retrieval call, the one that's used to actually retrieve the segment to be deleted, must be of the Get-Hold variety. Figure 7.3 shows the function codes and SSAs for a call sequence to delete a PATIENT segment from the data base.

Notice that in this case we knew exactly which PATIENT segment we wanted to delete, so all we had to issue was a single Get-Hold-Unique call to

```
  ·     GHU     HOSPITAL(HOSPNAME =MAC NEAL                  )
              ^^^^ ^^^^^^^^^^^^^^^^^^^^^^^^^^^^^^^^^^^^^^^^^^^^^^
                   WARD    (WARDNO   =01)
                   ^^^^^^^^^^^^^^^^^^^^^^^
                   PATIENT (BEDIDENT =0008)
                   ^^^^^^^^^^^^^^^^^^^^^^^^^^

        DLET
        ^^^^
```

Figure 7.3 Deleting a PATIENT segment

bring that segment into the I/O area. As soon as you determine that you would like to delete the segment, issue a call using the DLET function code. Notice that this call does not include an SSA.

If, after you issue the Get-Hold-Unique call, you determine that you don't want to delete the segment, you can perform any processing that you like, including issuing other calls. Using the Get-Hold variety of retrieval call does not require you to follow that call with a Delete or Replace call.

Delete Calls Using an SSA

You'll see later in the chapter on command codes that you can include a D command code in your SSAs for a retrieval call. This type of Call is called a *path call* and will cause more than one segment to be brought into the I/O area. When you follow a path call with a Delete call, you are allowed to specify a single SSA using the N command code. You use this SSA to tell DL/I which segment to delete. If you don't include an SSA in a Delete following a path call, the last segment in the I/O area will be the one deleted. You'll learn more about using the N command code in chapter 8, the chapter on command codes.

Automatic Deletion of Dependent Segments

A very important point to remember is that when you issue a Delete call for a segment that has other segments dependent on it, all of its dependent segments will be deleted along with it.

Figure 7.4 shows the segments stored in the HOSPITAL data base. If we retrieve the ward number *08* segment from the data base with a Get-Hold call and follow that with a Delete call, we would delete not only that WARD segment, but also segments 10 through 15 in the chart. Those are all the PATIENT segments dependent on the ward number *08* segment. This should illustrate that a single Delete call can cause a lot of segments to be deleted from the data base.

Deleting root segments from the data base can be even more dangerous. Suppose you retrieved the *Mac Neal* HOSPITAL segment with a Get-Hold call, and followed that call with a Delete. You would then delete all the segments dependent on the *Mac Neal* HOSPITAL segment. That would be segments 1 through 15 in figure 7.4. In this particular example you'd wipe out three quarters of the data base with a single Delete call.

Replacing Segments in the Data Base

As with Delete calls, the first requirement when replacing a segment is to issue a Get-Hold call for it. Again, you can use any call sequence to retrieve the segment that you'd like to replace, the only requirement is that the call that actually brings the segment into the I/O area must be of the Get-Hold variety. Once you have in the I/O area the segment that you're going to replace, you're allowed to make any changes desired except to the key field. Figure 7.5 shows

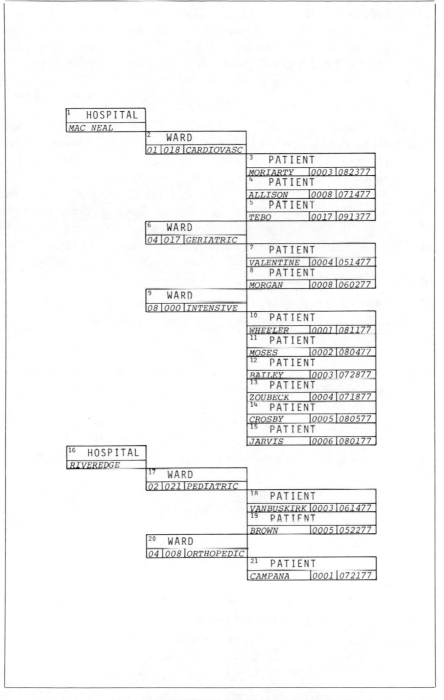

Figure 7.4 **HOSPITAL** data base segments

a call sequence to replace a WARD segment in the data base. Notice that, like the Delete call, the REPL call uses no SSAs.

After you've made all the changes to the segment in the I/O area you then issue a call using the REPL function code. You normally use no SSAs in this call. The REPL call will cause that segment to be rewritten in the data base, so the new version will replace the old version.

Replace Calls Following a Get-Hold Path Call

As we mentioned earlier with Delete calls, we'll talk in more detail about path calls in chapter 8, the chapter on command codes. However, when you use a Get-Hold path call to bring more than one segment into the I/O area, you are allowed to follow that call with a Replace call with one or more SSAs. If you bring multiple segments into the I/O area with a Get-Hold path call and issue a REPL call with no SSAs, all the segments in the I/O area will be written back into the data base. You are allowed to use SSAs with the N command code to tell DL/I not to replace certain segments. You'll learn more about using the N command code in the chapter on command codes.

Delete and Replace Status Codes

The status codes that can be returned as a result of the three Get-Hold calls are the same ones that you can receive with Get-Unique, Get-Next, and Get-Next-Within-Parent calls. As far as status code logic is concerned, Get-Hold calls are identical to Get calls.

There are four status codes that are quite common when you're using Delete or Replace calls. Figure 7.6 shows these status codes. DJ means that

```
GHU    HOSPITAL(HOSPNAME =MAC NEAL                    )
^^^^   ^^^^^^^^^^^^^^^^^^^^^^^^^^^^^^^^^^^^^^^^^^^^^^^
       WARD    (WARDNO   =04)
       ^^^^^^^^^^^^^^^^^^^^^^^^


REPL
^^^^
```

Figure 7.5 Deleting a WARD segment

DJ—No previous Get-Hold call

DA—Key field changed

DX—Delete rule violation

RX—Replace rule violation

Figure 7.6 Delete and Replace call status codes

you issued either a Delete call or a Replace call, but you neglected to precede it with a Get-Hold call. The DA status code is returned if you change the key field in the I/O area before you issue the DLET or REPL call. The DX status code indicates that you've violated some delete rule. And finally the RX status code is returned if you violate some replace rule. You normally get these last two status only codes if your data base uses logical relationships.

CHAPTER 7 EXERCISE (CODING PROBLEM)

There is only a single coding problem for this chapter. In this coding problem, you'll write a complete program that will use all of the function codes you've learned so far. In this program you'll code the following types of DL/I calls:

Get-Hold Calls
Replace Calls
Insert Calls
Delete Calls

The purpose of the program is to prepare a Recovery Room Schedule report having two parts. The first part lists all patients who are scheduled for surgery on a particular day. Assume that all of the patients will require the use of the recovery room. The second part of the report lists all patients who are released from the recovery room that day. Assume that all patients stay in the recovery room for a fixed period of time. The following instructions show you what your program should do:

1. Read a parameter card containing a date. This date will tell your program which patients are to be released from the recovery room.

2. Look for all the patients in the *Columbus* hospital who are scheduled for surgery on today's date. The SURGERY-FLAG field in the last TREATMNT segment for a patient must contain a character one if the patient is scheduled for surgery. It contains a character zero if the patient is not scheduled for surgery. The SURG-ERY-DATE field tells you what day the patient is scheduled for surgery.

3. For each patient who's scheduled for surgery today, insert a copy of that patient's PATIENT segment, and the last TREATMNT and DOCTOR segments for that patient, under the *Columbus* hospital WARD segment whose WARDTYPE is equal to *Recovery Room*. At the same time, write a line on the part of the recovery room report that lists patients that are scheduled for surgery on the date in the parameter card.

4. After you've found all the patients who are scheduled for surgery that day, check all the patients who are currently in the *Recovery Room* ward to see which ones should be released. For each patient whose first TREATMNT segment has a treatment date equal to or less than the date read in on the parameter card, delete that patient's PATIENT, TREATMNT, and DOCTOR segments. Delete the segments dependent on the recovery room WARD segment, not the original segments.

5. For each patient's segments that you delete, write a line on the second part of the recovery room report, the list of patients released from the recovery room.

```
PRINT       NOGEN                                                           00000010
FCB         TYPE=DB,DBDNAME=HOSPDBD,KEYLEN=32                               00000020
                                                                            00000030
SENSEG      NAME=HOSPITAL,PARENT=0,PROCOPT=G                                00000040
SENSEG      NAME=WARD,PARENT=HOSPITAL,PROCOPT=G                             00000050
SENSEG      NAME=PATIENT,PARENT=WARD,PROCOPT=A                              00000060
SENSEG      NAME=SYMPTOM,PARENT=PATIENT,PROCOPT=G                           00000070
SENSEG      NAME=TREATMNT,PARENT=PATIENT,PROCOPT=A                          00000080
SENSEG      NAME=DOCTOR,PARENT=PATIENT,PROCOPT=A                            00000090
                                                                            00000110
PSBGEN      LANG=COBOL,PSBNAME=CHAP7C                                       00000120
END                                                                         00000130
```

Figure 7.7 PSB coding

110

```
R E C O V E R Y   R O O M   S C H E D U L E

DATE 06/30/77                                                    PAGE    1

        PATIENTS SCHEDULED FCR SURGERY

PATIENT NAME        PATIENT ADDRESS                 PATIENT PHONE    BED ID

CARLSON             1234 WAVERLY, CHICAGO, IL       312-555-1234     0002
BIDWELL             3344 STREET, CHICAGC, IL        312-555-4455     0004
EO SANG Y           3312 ROSE PLACE, CHICAGO, IL    312-555-1187     0006
OLSON               3256 BURLINGTON, CHICAGO, IL    312-555-5562     0010
WOLF                5562 ROSE PLACE, CHICAGO, IL    312-555-9935     0012

        PATIENTS TO BE RELEASED FRCM RECOVERY ROOM

PATIENT NAME        PATIENT ADDRESS                 PATIENT PHONE    BED ID

PONIC               1276 COLFAX, CHICAGC, IL        312-555-5519     0005
O'HARA              1298 BURLINGTON, CHICAGO, IL    312-555-6620     0007
TEKCOM              9834 COLFAX, CHICAGC, IL        312-555-8892     0009
KASPER              7345 WAVERLY, CHICAGO, IL       312-555-9034     0013
POPEYE              8834 1ST STREET, CHICAGO, IL    312-555-8832     0015
```

Figure 7.8 The Recovery Room Schedule report

Figure 7.7 is a listing of the PSB coding that you should assume already exists. Figure 7.8 is a sample listing of the Recovery Room Schedule Report. Assume that the segment description coding is stored in a sample library. You can use the listings in Appendix D for the data names to use.

8

Using Command Codes

Introduction

In this chapter we'll cover one of the most powerful features of the SSA. You'll see how you can use command codes to cause DL/I to treat your SSAs differently from the way it treats SSAs without command codes. You'll find that command codes offer you a lot of opportunities to save programming and processing time.

In this chapter, we'll show you a few situations that might come up in working with the HOSPITAL data base. We'll show you how each situation might be handled without a command code, and then we'll show you how a command code can simplify each task.

The Format of SSAs with Command Codes

Using a *command code* in an SSA causes DL/I to modify the way the call is handled for the segment the SSA refers to. There are ten command codes, and you can use them in combination to perform various functions that would be difficult, or impossible, with SSAs that do not use command codes.

Figure 8.1 is a summary of how DL/I treats SSAs with command codes, and gives you a preview of the things you can do with them. We'll cover each of the command codes in detail, but before we do, let's look at the format of an SSA that uses command codes.

Command Codes in Qualified SSAs

Figure 8.2 is an example of a qualified SSA containing the D command code.

Notice that position nine does not contain a left parenthesis; it contains an asterisk instead. When DL/I finds an asterisk in position nine, it assumes that one or more command codes follow the asterisk. In a qualified SSA, DL/I

Command

Code	Meaning
D	Put this segment into the I/O Area (Path call)
N	Don't replace this segment
C	Concatenated key in this SSA
F	Locate first occurrence
L	Locate last occurrence
P	Establish parentage at this level
Q	Enqueue this segment
U	Maintain current position at this level
V	Maintain current position at this and higher levels
–	Null command code

Figure 8.1 Command code summary

```
WARD    *D(WARDNO   =04)
```

Figure 8.2 A qualified SSA with the D command code

```
PATIENT *DNP(PATNAME  =SMITH              )
```

Figure 8.3 A qualified SSA with three command codes

```
WARD    *PD
```

Figure 8.4 An unqualified SSA with two command codes

treats all characters following the asterisk as command codes until it reaches a left parenthesis or blank, so you can use as many command codes in combination as you like. Figure 8.3 is an example of a qualified SSA using three command codes.

Command Codes in Unqualified SSAs

In an unqualified SSA, a blank tells DL/I where the command codes end. Figure 8.4 shows an unqualified SSA with two command codes. Now let's look at each of the ten command codes and see what you can do with them.

The D and N Command Codes

The D and N command codes work together to let you process multiple segments in a single call. The D command code lets you perform a *path call.* When you retrieve segments with a path call, DL/I places multiple segments along the retrieval path into your I/O area. In retrievals that don't use the D command code only the segment identified in the last SSA is placed into the I/O area. By coding D command codes in one or more higher-level SSAs, you ask DL/I to place additional segments into the I/O area.

Let's look at an example where this might be useful. Suppose you want to print hospital and ward information for a patient, and you also want to update the PATIENT segment. To do that, you have to retrieve the PATIENT segment and the WARD and HOSPITAL segment above it. Let's retrieve segment 19 in the data base. Figure 8.5 shows the segments in the data base that we're sensitive to. Figure 8.6 shows the processing logic that you would probably follow to perform the retrieval without using command codes.

Now let's see how you might perform the retrieval part of the same procedure using the D command code. A single Get-Hold-Unique call will retrieve all three segments for you and store them, one after another, into the I/O area. (See figure 8.7.) In a call that does not use command codes, only the PATIENT segment would be placed into the I/O area. The D command codes in the higher-level SSAs cause those segments to be placed into the I/O area as well. The segments are stored in the I/O area in hierarchical sequence.

It's not necessary, in a path call, to retrieve all the segments in the hierarchical path. You can code the D command code in the SSAs for only the segments you'd like DL/I to place in the I/O area.

A processing option of P must be coded in your PSB for a segment in order to use the D command code in an SSA for that segment.

Replacing Segments after a Path Call

Whenever you make a Get-Hold Path call, DL/I remembers how many segments it stored in the I/O area. When you make a subsequent Replace call without SSAs, DL/I replaces all of the segments in the I/O area. In the example, we want to replace only the PATIENT segment. To do that you have to issue a Replace call using SSAs that include N command codes for those segments that you don't want to replace.

In a normal Replace Call, SSAs are not used. SSAs with the N command code are an exception to this rule. Figure 8.8 shows the SSAs that you'd use in your Replace call to cause DL/I to replace only the PATIENT segment. If you wanted to use the same set of SSAs for both the retrieval path call and the Replace call, you could use both D and N command codes in combination in the first two SSAs. (See figure 8.9.)

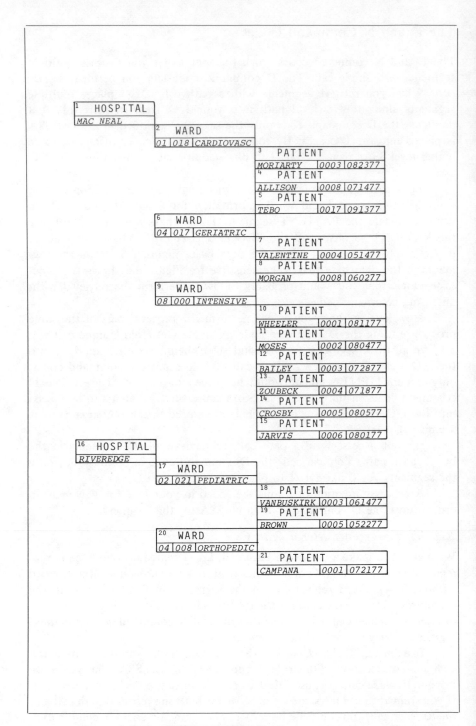

Figure 8.5 The HOSPITAL data base segment occurrence chart

```
1.  Store HOSPITAL, WARD and PATIENT identification into

    the appropriate SSAs.

2.  GU      HOSPITAL(HOSPNAME =RIVEREDGE              )
    ^^^^    ^^^^^^^^^^^^^^^^^^^^^^^^^^^^^^^^^^^^^^^^^^^^
3.  Save appropriate hospital information.

4.  GN      WARD    (WARDNO   =02)
    ^^^^    ^^^^^^^^^^^^^^^^^^^^^^^
5.  Save appropriate ward information.

6.  GHN     PATIENT (BEDIDENT =0005)
    ^^^^    ^^^^^^^^^^^^^^^^^^^^^^^^^
7.  Print patient, ward and hospital information.

8.  Update information in the PATIENT segment.

9.  REPL
    ^^^^
```

Figure 8.6 Retrieving and replacing without command codes

```
GHU     HOSPITAL*D(HOSPNAME =RIVEREDGE              )
^^^^    ^^^^^^^^^^^^^^^^^^^^^^^^^^^^^^^^^^^^^^^^^^^^^^
        WARD    *D(WARDNO   -02)
        ^^^^^^^^^^^^^^^^^^^^^^^^^
        PATIENT (BEDIDENT =0005)
        ^^^^^^^^^^^^^^^^^^^^^^^^^
```

Figure 8.7 A Retrieval Path call with the D command code

```
HOSPITAL*N(HOSPNAME =RIVEREDGE              )
^^^^^^^^^^^^^^^^^^^^^^^^^^^^^^^^^^^^^^^^^^^^^^
WARD    *N(WARDNO   =02)
^^^^^^^^^^^^^^^^^^^^^^^^^
PATIENT (BEDIDENT =0005)
^^^^^^^^^^^^^^^^^^^^^^^^^
```

Figure 8.8 SSAs with the N command code

```
HOSPITAL*DN(HOSPNAME =RIVEREDGE              )
^^^^^^^^^^^^^^^^^^^^^^^^^^^^^^^^^^^^^^^^^^^^^^^
WARD    *DN(WARDNO   =02)
^^^^^^^^^^^^^^^^^^^^^^^^^^
PATIENT (BEDIDENT =0005)
^^^^^^^^^^^^^^^^^^^^^^^^^
```

Figure 8.9 D and N command code combination

DL/I would ignore the N command codes when you make the Get-Hold call, and would ignore the D command codes when you make the Replace call.

The C Command Code

The C command code can save you some programming and processing time in situations where you would normally use fully qualified calls. It allows you to use a *concatenated key* in a single SSA rather than using a set of fully qualified SSAs. Let's suppose that you wanted to retrieve DOCTOR segments from the HOSPITAL data base. We'll assume that your program reads input records like the one in figure 8.10. To retrieve a DOCTOR segment, the program would have to follow logic similar to that in figure 8.11 if you used no command codes.

If you take a close look at the input record in figure 8.10 you'll notice that the information in the record consists of the entire concatenated key of

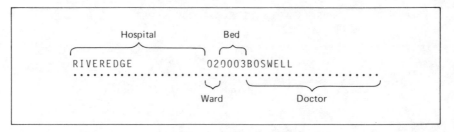

Figure 8.10 Retrieval program transaction

```
      1.   Move hospital name to HOSPITAL SSA.

      2.   Move ward number to WARD SSA.

      3.   Move patient key to PATIENT SSA.

      4.   Move doctor name to DOCTOR SSA.

      5.   GU      HOSPITAL(HOSPNAME =RIVEREDGE            )

                   WARD    (WARDNO   =02)

                   PATIENT (BEDIDENT =0003)

                   DOCTOR  (DOCTNAME =BOSWELL             )
```

Figure 8.11 Retrieving without the C command code

```
GU    DOCTOR  *C(RIVEREDGE            020003BOSWELL                    )
^^^^  ^^^^^^^^^^^^^^^^^^^^^^^^^^^^^^^^^^^^^^^^^^^^^^^^^^^^^^^^^^^^^^^^^^^^^^
```

Figure 8.12 Using the C command code

a DOCTOR segment. To retrieve a DOCTOR segment, you could move the entire 46 positions of the input record to a single SSA that has the C command code and use it in a Get-Unique call. Such a call is shown in figure 8.12.

In using the C command code, you must use only a single SSA naming the segment you're retrieving. The entire concatenated key for the segment you're retrieving must be enclosed in parentheses, and you can't skip any levels as you can when you use a separate SSA for each segment type.

The L and F Command Codes

The L and F command codes are used in unqualified SSAs when you would like to locate the *first* or *last* twin occurrence of a segment type. Let's see first how the L command code works.

The L Command Code

We'll retrieve the last twin occurrence of the TREATMNT segment type in the structure shown in figure 8.13. Without using command codes, your program would look something like figure 8.14.

By coding the L command code in an unqualified SSA for the TREATMNT segment, you ask DL/I to search for the last twin occurrence. So you can accomplish the same retrieval with a single call, shown in figure 8.15.

The F Command Code

The F command code is similar to the L command code, but instead of the last, it gets you the first occurrence in a twin chain. The main use for the F command code is to back up in the data base when doing sequential retrievals.

Here's an example that will illustrate when this might be useful. Suppose you'd like to search through all the TREATMNT segments under a particular PATIENT segment occurrence for a treatment type of *morphine*. If you find one, you'd like to print out all the TREATMNT segments for that patient.

Figure 8.16 shows logic that would accomplish this without using command codes. If you used the F command code, you could simplify the search somewhat and use the logic shown in figure 8.17.

The second example may not seem much simpler to write than the first. However, in many cases, the unqualified SSA with the F command code works a lot faster than the fully qualified SSA in the Get-Unique call. That's because the GNP call with the F command code takes advantage of current position,

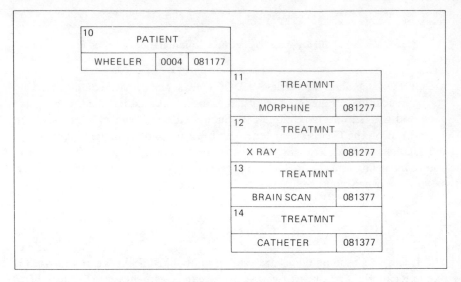

Figure 8.13 A TREATMNT segment twin chain

1. Move keys to the SSAs.

2. GU   HOSPITAL(HOSPNAME =MAC NEAL   )

           WARD   (WARDNO   =08)

           PATIENT (BEDIDENT =0004)

3. GNP   TREATMNT

4. Loop back to step 3 until you receive a GE status code. The I/O area will

    contain the last twin occurrence of TREATMNT.

Figure 8.14 Retrieving the last occurrence without command codes

GU   HOSPITAL(HOSPNAME =MAC NEAL   )

       WARD   (WARDNO   =08)

       PATIENT (BEDIDENT =0004)

       TREATMNT*L

Figure 8.15 Using the L command code

```
1.  GU      HOSPITAL(HOSPNAME =RIVEREDGE              )

            WARD    (WARDNO   =04)

            PATIENT (BEDIDENT =0008)

2.  GNP     TREATMNT(TRTYPE   =MORPHINE             )

3.  If the status code is GE, exit from the procedure.

    If the status code is blanks, go to step 4.

4.  GU      HOSPITAL(HOSPNAME =RIVERFDGE             )

            WARD    (WARDNO   =04)

            PATIENT (BEDIDENT =0008)

5.  GNP     TREATMNT

6.  Print a TREATMNT segment.

7.  Loop back to step 5 until a GE status code.
```

Figure 8.16 Backing up without command codes

```
1.  GU      HOSPITAL(HOSPNAME =RIVEREDGE              )

            WARD    (WARDNO   =04)

            PATIENT (BEDIDENT =0008)

2.  GNP     TREATMNT(TRTYPE   =MORPHINE             )

3.  If the status code is GE, exit from the procedure.

    If the status code is blanks, go on to step 4.

4.  GNP     TREATMNT*F

5.  Print a TREATMNT segment.

6.  GNP     TREATMNT

7.  Loop back to 5 until a GE status code.
```

Figure 8.17 Using the F command code

while Get-Unique calls usually begin the search at the beginning of the data base.

The P Command Code

The P command code allows you to set parentage on a segment occurrence other than the one identified by your last SSA. You code the P command code in the SSA for the segment at which you would like parentage established. DL/I still retrieves the segment identified by the last SSA, but sets parentage where you set the P command code.

Let's say you wanted to retrieve all the PATIENT segments under a particular WARD segment. Without the P command code, your logic would have to look something like figure 8.18.

By using the P command code, you can save one call by retrieving the first PATIENT segment in the Get-Unique call and setting parentage at the WARD level. (See figure 8.19.)

```
1.  GU      HOSPITAL(HOSPNAME =MAC NEAL                    )

            WARD     (WARDNO   =08)
2.  GNP     PATIENT
3.  Print a PATIENT segment.
4.  Loop back to step 2 until a GE status code.
```

Figure 8.18 Retrieving PATIENT segments

```
1.  GU      HOSPITAL(HOSPNAME =MAC NEAL                    )

            WARD     *P(WARDNO   =08)

            PATIENT
2.  Print a PATIENT segment.
3.  GNP     PATIENT
4.  Loop back to step 2 until a GE status code.
```

Figure 8.19 Using the P command code

The programming logic isn't any simpler, but you do save one call every time you execute this procedure.

The Q Command Code (IMS/VS Only)

The Q command code is a special-purpose command code that's only used when multiple applications will be accessing the same data base at the same time. It allows you to enqueue a segment occurrence so that no other user is able to make a Get-Hold type of Call for it. When you use the Q command code, you follow the Q with a one-character class identifier, one of the letters from A through J. You can then issue a system service DEQ call referencing that class identifier in order to dequeue the segment.

When you set the Q command code at the root segment level, no other user will be allowed to gain access to any segment in that data base record. When you set it at a segment lower in the hierarchy, no user is able to issue a Get-Hold call for that segment occurrence, but they can gain access to it with non-Hold calls.

The Q command code is generally only used in message processing programs. These usually run in an environment where many programs execute concurrently and may access the same data bases. We'll talk about message processing programs in chapters 10 and 11, the chapters on IMS Data Communications.

The U and V Command Codes

The U and V command codes provide you with some control over movement forward in the data base when you're making unqualified Get-Next or Get-Next-Within-Parent calls. They let you exercise some control over calls that can't be satisfied for a particular parent, but can be satisfied further in the data base under a different parent. The U and V command codes can be used to prevent a GN or GNP call from leaving the current position.

Let's suppose you'd like to read sequentially through the HOSPITAL data base and prepare a report for one hospital, listing all the patients in each ward. A likely way to do that would be to use GNP calls with unqualified SSAs. To limit your search to a single hospital, you might establish parentage on a HOSPITAL segment occurrence. Look at the sequence of calls in figure 8.20. Since parentage is established at the root level by the first Get-Unique call, the GNP call with the unqualified call for the PATIENT segment in step 3 will not stop at segment 5 in the data base. That call would read through all the PATIENT segments under the *Mac Neal* HOSPITAL segment. You would be given no indication when ward changes occurred.

A way to solve this problem would be to use a qualified SSA for the

```
   1.  GU      HOSPITAL(HOSPNAME =MAC NEAL              )
       ^^^^    ^^^^^^^^^^^^^^^^^^^^^^^^^^^^^^^^^^^^^^^^^^^
   2.  GNP     WARD
       ^^^^    ^^^^^^^^^^
   3.  GNP     PATIENT
       ^^^^    ^^^^^^^^^^

   4.  Loop back to step 3.
```

Figure 8.20 Sequentially processing PATIENT segments

WARD segment in the call for PATIENT segments, and fill in the key value each time you retrieve a WARD segment. In figure 8.21, you have to get the key out of the PCB every time you execute step 2 of the procedure. You then store it into the qualified SSA in step 4 before starting the loop that retrieves PATIENT segments. This keeps the GNP calls within the same domain in the data base. You would then receive a GE status code after you run out of PATIENT segments for each WARD, just as though you had established parentage at the WARD level. This would give you the control breaks that you need for the report.

Another way to handle this situation is to use the U command code. Coding the U command code in an unqualified SSA has the same effect as using a qualified SSA at that level. Look at the procedure in figure 8.22. Using the U command code at the WARD level tells DL/I not to leave the current position established on the WARD segment. So it has the same effect as a qualified SSA for that particular segment occurrence.

The V command code is similar to the U command code. The difference is that the V command code causes DL/I to act as though a U command code were set at that level, and at all levels above it. Suppose you were retrieving SYMPTOM segments sequentially. The two sets of SSAs in figure 8.23 are functionally equivalent. The V command code saves you the trouble of coding an SSA at each level when you want the function of the U command code at each level.

The Null Command Code

In some cases, you may find it necessary to store a command code into an SSA while your program is in execution. Take a look at the SSA in figure 8.24. The SSA will be treated as though no command codes were coded. The null command code ($-$) gives you the opportunity to reserve one or more positions in an SSA into which you can store command codes, should you need them when your program is in execution. In this way, it's possible to use the same set of SSAs for more than one purpose. Keep in mind, however, that dynami-

```
1.  GU        HOSPITAL(HOSPNAME =MAC NEAL                    )
    ^^^^      ^^^^^^^^^^^^^^^^^^^^^^^^^^^^^^^^^^^^^^^^^^^^^^^^^^
2.  GNP       WARD
    ^^^^      ^^^^^^^^^^
3.  Get a WARD key from PCB and store in WARD SSA.

4.  GNP       WARD      (WARDNO    = )
    ^^^^      ^^^^^^^^^^^^^^^^^^^^^^^^^
              PATIENT
              ^^^^^^^^^
5.  Loop back to step 4 until a GE status code.
```

Figure 8.21 Solving the problem with a qualified SSA

```
1.  GU        HOSPITAL(HOSPNAME =MAC NEAL                    )
    ^^^^      ^^^^^^^^^^^^^^^^^^^^^^^^/^^^^^^^^^^^^^^^^^^^^^^^^
2.  GNP       WARD
    ^^^^      ^^^^^^^^^^
3.  GNP       WARD      *U
    ^^^^      ^^^^/^^^^^^
              PATIENT
              ^^^^^^^^^
4.  Loop back to step 3 until a GE status code.
```

Figure 8.22 Using the U command code

```
GNP       WARD      *U
^^^^      ^^^^^^^^^^
          PATIENT *U
          ^^^^^^^^^^
          SYMPTOM
          ^^^^^^^^^


GNP       PATIENT *V
^^^^      ^^^^^^^^^^
          SYMPTOM
          ^^^^^^^^^
```

Figure 8.23 Using the V command code

cally modifying your SSAs in any way may increase the time it takes for you to debug your program. This is because it's sometimes difficult to tell what your SSAs actually look like during any particular point in your program's execution.

CHAPTER 8 EXERCISES

1. In figure 8.25 is a list of ten command codes that may be specified in an SSA. Below is a list of ten statements. Match each command code with the statement that best describes it.

   a. Establishes parentage at other than the segment identified by the last SSA.
   b. Used to bring more than one segment into the I/O area in a single call.
   c. Locates the last occurrence in a twin chain.
   d. The null command code
   e. Causes a segment to be enqueued.
   f. The SSA contains a concatenated key rather than a qualification statement.
   g. Can be used to back up in the data base even during sequential retrieval.
   h. Can be used in place of a qualified SSA to maintain position in the data base.
   i. Used to specify which segments not to replace following a path call.
   j. Performs the function of the U command code in higher level SSAs.

```
HOSPITAL*---(HOSPNAME =MAC NEAL              )
^^^^^^^^^^^^^^^^^^^^^^^^^^^^^^^^^^^^^^^^^^^^^^
```

Figure 8.24 Using the null command code

1. D
2. N
3. C
4. F
5. L
6. P
7. Q
8. U
9. V
10. –

Figure 8.25 The command codes for Exercise 1

2. Write a set of SSAs to do the following:

   a. Bring the HOSPITAL segment for the *Mac Neal* hospital, the WARD segment for ward number *01*, and the PATIENT segment whose bed identifier is *0002*, into the I/O area with a single Get-Hold-Unique call.

   b. Cause only the WARD segment to be replaced if the same set of SSAs is referenced in a Replace call.

   c. Reserve one extra position in the SSA for the WARD segment to allow the program to set a command code during program execution.

3. Write a single SSA to retrieve the WARD segment for ward number *08* in the *Riveredge* hospital. Use a concatenated key instead of qualification statements.

4. Write a set of SSAs to do the following:

   a. Retrieve the last PATIENT segment in a ward whose ward type is *Recovery* in the *Mac Neal* hospital.

   b. The SSAs should also cause subsequent Get-Next-Within-Parent calls to treat the *Mac Neal* HOSPITAL segment as the parent segment.

9

Advanced Data Base Features

Introduction

In this chapter, we'll look at four more facilities of IMS. The first two, multiple positioning and multiple PCBs, can be used with both IMS/360 and IMS/VS. These features allow you to maintain positions on more than one segment at a time in the same data base. Multiple PCBs also allow you to access segments from more than one physical or logical data base in the same program.

The other two facilities, variable-length segments and secondary indexing, are available only with IMS/VS. Variable length segments allow you to save space within the data base for segments types whose occurrences have varying space requirements. Secondary indexing allows you to retrieve segments more efficiently when a sequence other than standard hierarchical sequence is desirable from an efficiency point of view.

We'll present the programming considerations of these four important facilities, and examples of how you can use each. When you finish the chapter, you'll write a complete application program that uses multiple positioning and many of the other facilities, such as command codes, that you've learned up to this point.

Multiple Positioning

Before discussing the multiple positioning facility, we have to expand on the concept of position within the data base. Remember first that DL/I maintains a position within the data base for the purpose of sequential retrieval. The result of any Get-Next call with either unqualified SSAs or no SSAs is partially determined by where position has been established within the data base at the time of the call.

When single positioning is in effect, DL/I maintains a single position within the data base. When multiple positioning is in effect, DL/I maintains a separate position for each dependent segment type at each level in the data base. First we'll look at some examples of the effects of single and multiple positioning on sequential retrieval in the HOSPITAL data base. Then we'll see how the DBA specifies either single or multiple positioning for your PCB.

SYMPTOM, TREATMNT, and DOCTOR Segments

The relationships between the SYMPTOM, TREATMNT, and DOCTOR segments in the data base illustrates the need for multiple positioning for some types of sequential retrievals. Let's suppose that the design of the data base requires that there be a one-to-one relationship between SYMPTOM, TREATMNT, and DOCTOR segments. For each SYMPTOM segment there must be corresponding TREATMNT and DOCTOR segments. This may be

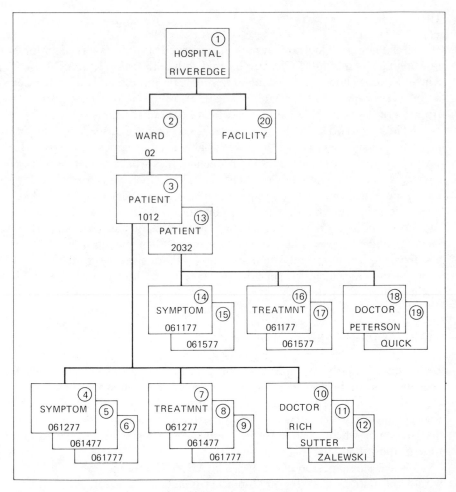

Figure 9.1 Hierarchy chart

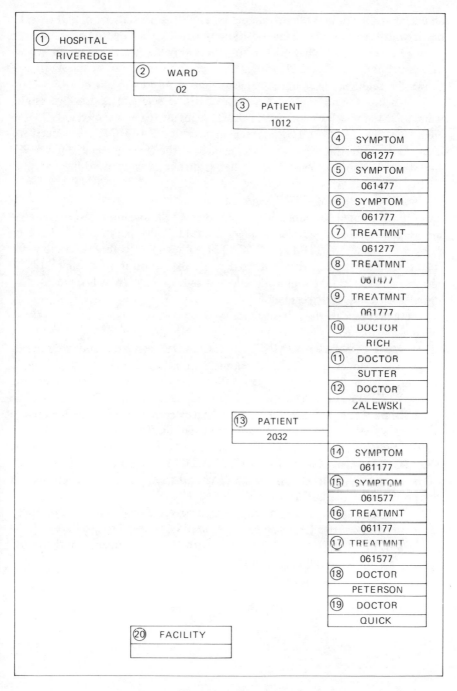

Figure 9.2 Indented structure chart

an oversimplification of the way an actual HOSPITAL data base might work, but it will illustrate why single positioning can be very restrictive.

The segments we'll work with in the following examples are shown in figures 9.1 and 9.2. Figure 9.1 shows the hierarchical structure, and figure 9.2 shows the segments in hierarchical sequence in an idented form.

If a one-to-one relationship between those segments exists, we might want to list, for a particular PATIENT segment, each set of SYMPTOM, TREATMNT, and DOCTOR segments under that PATIENT segment. If we didn't care about the sequence of the segments, the call sequence in figure 9.3 would do the job very easily. With that sequence of calls, we'd first retrieve all the SYMPTOM segments, followed by all the TREATMNT segments, followed by all the DOCTOR segments.

If we wanted to maintain the one-to-one relationship between the segments in the report, that call sequence wouldn't do, because we'd have to retrieve all the SYMPTOM and TREATMNT segments before we could write the first line of the report. What we'd really like to do in this situation is to retrieve a SYMPTOM segment, followed by a TREATMNT segment, followed by a DOCTOR segment.

On first glance, the call sequence in figure 9.4 would seem to do the trick. What we'd like to do is loop through the GNP calls, each time retrieving a set of SYMPTOM, TREATMNT, and DOCTOR segments, until we run out of segments under a PATIENT segment. If DL/I is maintaining a single position within the data base, the call sequence works fine the first time through. We'll retrieve segments 4, 7, and 10, exactly what we want. But the second time through, we'd receive a GE status code indicating that there are no more SYMPTOM segments under that parent. The second time we issue the call sequence, current position is on segment 10, the first occurrence of the DOCTOR segment. To get the next SYMPTOM segment, DL/I would have to remember the position of the last SYMPTOM segment retrieved, as well as the positions of the last TREATMNT and DOCTOR segments.

To illustrate this problem even more clearly, let's see how single positioning would work with a Get-Next call instead of Get-Next-Within-Parent. Let's see how DL/I would retrieve segments with the call sequence in figure 9.5 looping on the GN calls, with single positioning. This time the sequence of

```
GU      HOSPITAL(HOSPNAME =RIVEREDGE                      )

        WARD    (WARDNO   =02)

        PATIENT (BEDIDENT =1012)


GNP
```

Figure 9.3 Retrieving all SYMPTOM, TREATMNT, and DOCTOR segments

```
GU       HOSPITAL(HOSPNAME =RIVEREDGE              )
         ^^^^    ^^^^^^^^^^^^^^^^^^^^^^^^^^^^^^^^^^^^^^^^^
         WARD    (WARDNO   =02)
         ^^^^^^^^^^^^^^^^^^^^^^^
         PATIENT (BEDIDENT =1012)
         ^^^^^^^^^^^^^^^^^^^^^^^^^^

GNP      SYMPTOM
^^^^     ^^^^^^^^^

GNP      TREATMNT
^^^^     ^^^^^^^^^

GNP      DOCTOR
^^^^     ^^^^^^^^^
```

Figure 9.4 Using unqualified SSAs

```
GU       HOSPITAL(HOSPNAME =RIVEREDGE              )
^^^^     ^^^^    ^^^^^^^^^^^^^^^^^^^^^^^^^^^^^^^^^^^^^^^^^
         WARD    (WARDNO   =02)
         ^^^^^^^^^^^^^^^^^^^^^^^
         PATIENT (BEDIDENT =1012)
         ^^^^^^^^^^^^^^^^^^^^^^^^^^

GN       SYMPTOM
^^^^     ^^^^^^^^^

GN       TREATMNT
^^^^     ^^^^^^^^^

GN       DOCTOR
^^^^     ^^^^^^^^^
```

Figure 9.5 Using Get-Next calls with unqualified SSAs

segments would be 4, 7, 10, 14, 16, 18, followed by a GE status code. That call sequence would go through the entire data base getting you only the first occurrence of the SYMPTOM, TREATMNT, and DOCTOR segments under each PATIENT segment. There would be no way to get past the first occurrence of any of the segments.

Can you see how difficult it is to retrieve segments in the order that you really want them with single positioning? Your program would have to be quite complex to maintain the one-to-one relationship between the three segment types. Now let's see how multiple positioning simplifies the situation.

Retrieving with Multiple Positioning

In the previous example, the problem was caused by the fact that DL/I maintained only a single position within the data base. With multiple positioning, DL/I maintains a separate position within a data base record for each dependent segment type, at each level. Figure 9.6 shows the different points at which DL/I would maintain a position within the data base. The positions that we're interested in for our example are the positions indicated by D, E, and F in the hierarchy chart.

Let's see how the call sequence in figure 9.4 would work with multiple positioning. The first time through, we'd retrieve segments 4, 7, and 10, as in the single positioning example. This time, the next execution of the call sequence would get us segments 5, 8, and 11. This is because current position for SYMPTOM segments would have been at segment 4 and current position for TREATMNT segments would have been at segment 7. DL/I maintains a different position for each segment.

Specifying Single or Multiple Positioning

It's up to your data base administrator to specify either single or multiple positioning when the PCB statement in the PSB is coded. Figure 9.7 shows the PCB statements for single and multiple positioning. The POS= operand is used to specify either single or multiple positioning. If the POS= operand is not coded, the default is single positioning. The DBA must code POS= for multiple positioning. It's very important for you to know whether single or

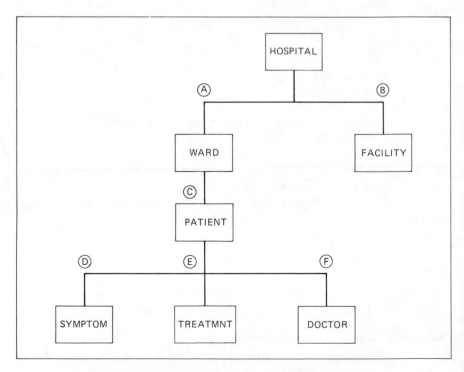

Figure 9.6 Positions maintained with multiple positioning

multiple positioning is in effect for your PCB before you code your program. As you can see from the last few examples, your program can operate quite differently depending on whether single or multiple positioning is in effect.

It's dangerous to change a PCB from multiple positioning to single positioning. A program that operates properly when multiple positioning is in effect may produce strange results if you try to run that same program with single positioning.

Multiple PCBs

You read earlier in the book that it's possible to have more than one PCB statement in a PSB. Each PCB statement defines a separate PCB that your program has access to during execution. In this section we'll look at how your program gains access to the PCBs and how multiple PCBs can help you simplify some otherwise complex programming.

Reasons for Multiple PCBs

There are several reasons for using multiple PCBs. The most obvious one is the case where your program requires access to more than one physical or

```
PCB     TYPE=DB,NAME=HOSPITAL,POS=M


PCB     TYPE=DB,NAME=HOSPITAL,POS=S
```

Figure 9.7 PCB statements for single and multiple positioning

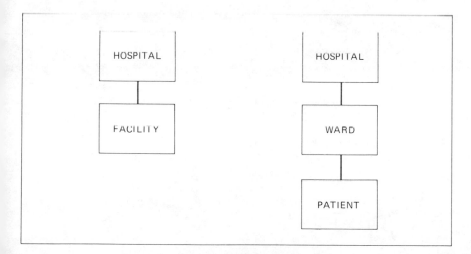

Figure 9.8 Two logical data structures

logical data base. A single PCB can refer to only one DBD. So if your program requires access to two or more data bases, you'll need a PCB for each one.

There are times that you'll need more than one data base PCB, even if you're working with a single data base. You may require access to two completely different logical data structures, each describing different segments in the same data base. For example, figure 9.8 shows two different HOSPITAL data base logical data structures that could possibly be useful in the same program. Each logical data structure is described by a PCB statement and a set of SENSEG statements in a single PSB. Figure 9.9 shows a PSB that describes those two logical data structures.

```
PRINT     NOGEN
PCB       TYPE=DB,NAME=HOSPITAL,PROCOPT=G
SENSEG    NAME=HOSPITAL,PARENT=0
SENSEG    NAME=FACILITY,PARENT=HOSPITAL
PCB       TYPE=DB,NAME=HOSPITAL,PROCOPT=A
SENSEG    NAME=HOSPITAL,PARENT=0
SENSEG    NAME=WARD,PARENT=HOSPITAL
SENSEG    NAME=PATIENT,PARENT=WARD
PSBGEN    LANG=COBOL,PSBNAME=HOSP2PCB
```

Figure 9.9 A PSB with two PCBs

```
          .
          .
          .
LINKAGE SECTION.
01  PCB-MASK-ONE.
          .
          .
          .
01  PCB-MASK-TWO.
          .
          .
          .
PROCEDURE DIVISION.
     ENTRY 'DLITCBL' USING  PCB-MASK-ONE  PCB-MASK-TWO.
          .
          .
          .
     CALL  'CBLTDLI' USING  FUNCTION
                            PCB-MASK-ONE
                            IOAREA
                            SSA-AREA.
          .
          .
          .
     CALL  'CBLTDLI' USING  FUNCTION
                            PCB-MASK-TWO
                            IOAREA
                            SSA-AREA.
          .
          .
          .
```

Figure 9.10 COBOL coding for multiple PCBs

Gaining Access to the Two PCBs

In COBOL, your ENTRY statement must include a parameter for each PCB statement that you require access to. Other programming languages follow similar conventions. The parameters must be coded in the order in which the PCBs appear in the PSB. Figure 9.10 shows COBOL coding that you'd use to access the two PCBs in your PSB. You must be aware of the structure of your PSB when you code your program, because DL/I passes the addresses of the PCBs to your program in the order in which the PCB statements are coded in the PSB.

Notice that your CALL statements must reference the appropriate PCB mask coding to indicate which PCB each CALL statement refers to.

Other Uses for Multiple PCBs

In the above example, it isn't clear why the FACILITY segment wasn't included in the first PCB, rather than set up in a separate logical data structure. In some cases, that approach will work, and in others it won't. Multiple PCBs can be used in the same physical or logical data base where you have to access segments from more than one place in the data base at the same time.

In the last section, on multiple positioning, you saw an example of parallel processing within one portion of a data base record. Multiple positioning allows you to process different segment types in parallel, as long as those segment types are dependent upon the same parent. Multiple PCBs allow you to process segments in parallel, no matter where in the data base the segments are.

A Parallel Processing Example

A good example of where parallel processing would be handy is in transferring a patient from one hospital to another. To do that you'd have to retrieve a PATIENT segment from one part of the data base, and insert it in a different part. You would then sequentially process that patient's SYMPTOM, TREATMNT, and DOCTOR segments, and insert them under the new copy of the PATIENT segment.

With a single PCB, as soon as you insert the PATIENT segment under a new WARD segment occurrence, you lose position on the old PATIENT segment. You won't be able to find the dependent segments without retrieving the old PATIENT segment again.

And each time you insert one of the dependents under the new parent, you lose position again. The only practical way to handle the move, with a single PCB, is to retrieve the PATIENT segment, and all of its dependents, and store them away somewhere before you start inserting them under the new WARD segment.

Figure 9.11 shows the coding that you could use to accomplish the move if you had two PCBs. In this case, the PCBs describe the same logical data structure. You need two of them so that you can maintain two positions in

```
CALL   'CBLTDLI'   USING   GET-UNIQUE  PCB1  IOAREA  HOSPSSA
                                                     WARDSSA
                                                     PATSSA.
  .
  .
CALL   'CBLTDLI'   USING   INSERT      PCB2  IOAREA  NEWHOSPSSA
                                                     NEWWARDSSA
                                                     PATSSA-UNQUAL.
  .
  .
CALL   'CBLTDLI'   USING   GNP         PCB1  IOAREA.
  .
  .
MOVE   PCB1-SEGTYPE TO UNQUAL-SSA
  .
  .
CALL   'CBLTDLI'   USING   INSERT      PCB2  IOAREA  UNQUAL-SSA
```

Figure 9.11 Moving a PATIENT segment and its dependents

different parts of the data base at the same time. Multiple positioning lets you do somewhat the same thing. However, with multiple positioning, you can never maintain two different positions on the same segment type. And within a group of dependent segments, separate positions can be maintained only on segments that are dependent on a particular parent.

Other Types of PCBs

Another case where multiple PCBs are required is when you need to use PCBs that are other than the standard data base PCBs. In message processing programs, PCBs are used to describe terminals that the program will communicate with. This is how IMS allows you to write application programs that are independent of any actual physical terminal devices. You'll learn more about these kinds of PCBs in chapters 10 and 11, which deal with message processing programs.

A third kind of PCB describes a GSAM data base. You'll learn more about GSAM PCBs in appendix C, the appendix on GSAM programming.

Variable-Length Segments (IMS/VS Only)

The variable-length segments feature is a very powerful feature of IMS/VS, yet is very easily implemented. Variable-length segments can be used to save space when occurrences of a segment type normally contain variable amounts of information. In the HOSPITAL data base, some segments have description fields, such as PREV-REASON, DIET-COMMENT, and SURGERY-COMMENT. We've arbitrarily limited description fields to thirty positions. In many segment occurrences, these fields will be blank; in others, the thirty characters might not be enough to hold the required information. Segment types containing these fields would be likely candidates for variable-length segments in an actual implementation of this data base.

Variable-Length Segment Format

Figure 9.12 shows what a variable-length segment occurrence looks like in the I/O area. Each segment starts with a two-byte length field. This field gives the length, in bytes, of the segment, including the two-byte length field. The length is expressed as a binary number. Since the length field appears in the I/O area, the programmer has the responsibility for maintaining it. For example, if you're inserting a segment, either into an existing data base or into a new data base, your program must calculate the length of the new segment and insert the proper value into the first two bytes of the I/O area before you issue the Insert call.

In retrieving a variable-length segment, your program uses the first two bytes of the segment in determining how much of the I/O area contains useable information.

The same considerations apply in replacing an existing segment. If the length of the segment changes during the update, the program must change the length field before issuing the Replace call.

Variable-Length Segment Restrictions

Variable-length segments are supported only in IMS/VS. In addition, they're supported only for HISAM, HDAM, and HIDAM data bases, and only when VSAM is the access method. Variable-length segments are not supported for ISAM/OSAM data bases. You'll learn more about these access methods in chapter 12.

In working with the length field in the segments, you must be aware of the maximum and minimum values that the DBA has specified for the segment type you're working with. The DBA specifies variable-length segments in the SEGM statement in the DBD. Figure 9.13 shows how the DBA could specify

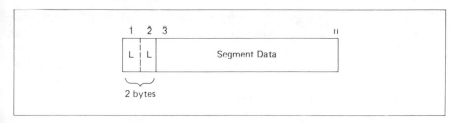

Figure 9.12 Variable-length segment format

```
SEGM    NAME=TREATMNT,PARENT=PATIENT,BYTES=(90,160)
```

Figure 9.13 Specifying a variable-length TREATMNT segment

that the TREATMNT segment type is a variable-length segment. The first subparameter of BYTES tells you the maximum size of the TREATMNT segment, including the two-byte length field. The second subparameter of BYTES tells you the minimum size. The length field that you place in a segment occurrence must be between these two ranges for your program to operate properly.

Secondary Indexing (IMS/VS Only)

Sequential retrievals are normally made using key sequence. The secondary indexing feature allows you to sequentially retrieve segments, or search for segments, in a sequence other than normal hierarchical sequence. In most cases, the use of a secondary index is transparent to the application program, but there are some cases where you have to know about them. In this section, we can't go into the design or implementation of secondary indexes to any great extent; this is best left to the data base administrator. What we'll try to do here is define some of the terms used in describing a secondary index, show how they can be used, and, through the use of a few examples, show you how they effect the application program.

What is a Secondary Index?

Basically, a secondary index is a small, self-contained data base that stores a series of index segments that point to segments in the data base being indexed. The secondary index allows you to process segments in a sequence other than in key sequence. Each secondary index is a separate data base having its own DBD. Secondary index data bases are connected to the main data base with special DBDGEN parameters. We won't go into DBDGEN coding here. The definitions of some terms, along with some examples, will illustrate how a secondary index can be used.

Definition of Terms

We'll use figure 9.14 to help illustrate how a secondary index can be used, and to help define four terms that are used to describe a secondary index. These four terms are *index target segment, index source segment, index pointer segment,* and *indexed field.* What we're trying to accomplish with the secondary index in figure 9.14, is to allow programs to process PATIENT segments in patient name sequence as well as in bed identifier sequence. Let's see how our four terms relate to this example.

INDEX TARGET SEGMENT. The index target segment is the segment in the data base being indexed that the secondary index indexes. In the example, the PATIENT segment is the target segment. In essence, the target segment represents the segment type that the secondary index resequences for us. When we retrieve segments via this secondary index, we'll retrieve PATIENT seg-

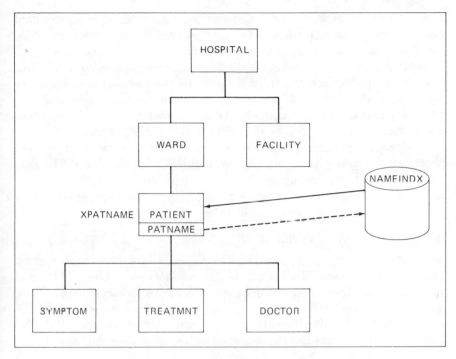

Figure 9.14 The NAMEINDX secondary index

ments, so the index target segment tells us what kind of segments we'll retrieve when using the secondary index.

INDEX SOURCE SEGMENT. This is the segment in the data base being indexed from which the *indexed field* comes. In the example, the index source segment and the index target segment are the same segment, the PATIENT segment. The *indexed field* is the field, or combination of fields, from the index source segment, that we would like to sequence the secondary index on. In the example, the indexed field is the PATNAME field in the PATIENT segment. The secondary index will be sequenced on that field. The indexed field can be made up of from one to five fields in the index source segment.

The indexed field is of special significance to the application program. The indexed field is actually a new field that's defined in the DBD for the data base when a secondary index is set up. You can reference this field in an SSA when you want DL/I to use the secondary index to search for a segment. We'll have a lot more to say about the indexed field later. In our patient name example, the indexed field consists of only the PATNAME field. The name of the indexed field is XPATNAME. Many installations use the convention of preceding the names of indexed fields with the letter X, to distinguish them from other fields in the target segment.

INDEX POINTER SEGMENT. This segment resides in the secondary index data base. It's not a part of the data base being indexed. It's a new segment type that's created when the secondary index is built. Each index pointer segment points to an index target segment in the data base being indexed. The key field of the index pointer segment is made up of the indexed field from the index source segment. The key field can contain other information as well, and we'll talk about that later. In our example, the index pointer segments all reside in a secondary index described by the DBD named NAMEINDX.

The index pointer segment is created and maintained by DL/I, and the application programmer is normally not required to work with it. The only time an application programmer would work with the index pointer segment is in the special case where an application program processes the secondary index as data. We won't go into that here.

Using the Secondary Index

There are two ways that a program can use a secondary index. Each method requires that you use a PSB that names the secondary index DBD. In the first method, you use the secondary index to sequence the segments in the data base using the secondary index. In this method, each PCB statement in your PSB may use the PROCSEQ parameter to name a single secondary index. With this method, your program can also use the indexed field name in SSAs. In the second method, your program uses the normal processing sequence of the data base, but your program is allowed to use the indexed field name in SSAs. In this method, each SENSEG statement for an index target segment may contain the INDICES parameter to name one or more secondary index DBDs. Let's see how each of these methods work.

USING THE SECONDARY PROCESSING SEQUENCE. The secondary index can be used to give the data base a secondary processing sequence. To give your program access to the secondary processing sequence, a PCB statement must identify the secondary index DBD used to create the secondary processing sequence. Figure 9.15 shows the PSB for the NAMEINDX secondary index. (This PSB assumes that the DBDGENs have already been performed to define the secondary index and the indexed field.) The PROCSEQ= operand defines the name of the DBD for the secondary index.

```
PRINT    NOGEN
PCB      TYPE=DB,NAME=HOSPITAL,PROCOPT=A,PROCSEQ=NAMEINDX
SENSEG   NAME=PATIENT,PARENT=0
SENSEG   NAME=WARD,PARENT=PATIENT
SENSEG   NAME=HOSPITAL,PARENT=WARD
SENSEG   NAME=SYMPTOM,PARENT=PATIENT
SENSEG   NAME=TREATMNT,PARENT=PATIENT
SENSEG   NAME=DOCTOR,PARENT=PATIENT
PSBGEN   LANG=COBOL,PSBNAME=HOSPSCNX
```

Figure 9.15 PSB using the secondary index

RESTRUCTURING THE HIERARCHY. When you process the data base using a secondary processing sequence, it may appear to the program that the data base has a completely different hierarchical structure. This happens whenever the index target segment is not the root. In our example, since we're going to process segments using the patient name secondary index, it will appear to the program that the PATIENT segment is the root. Notice that the first SENSEG statement in the PSB names the PATIENT segment.

This is one of the most powerful features of secondary indexing. You can define any segment in the data base to be the root segment of a new hierarchical structure, simply by creating a secondary index with that segment as the target segment. The rules for restructuring the hierarchy are simple. In determining the new hierarchy, the target segment always becomes the root. Under the target segment will be the segments directly above it in reverse hierarchical sequence.

The target segment's children remain in normal hierarchical sequence, except that they are displaced one segment to the right in the hierarchy to make room for the target segment's parents. Figure 9.16 shows the hierarchical structure of the new segments defined in the secondary processing sequence PSB. Notice that the FACILITY segment does not appear in the new structure. Only the segments directly above the target segment in the hierarchy, and the target segment's children are in the new structure.

When you're using a secondary processing sequence to retrieve PATIENT segments with Get-Next calls, your program is actually written in the same way that it would be written if the physical data base were structured as in Figure 9.16. In this sense, the use of a secondary index is actually transparent to your program. All you have to know is the order of the SEN-

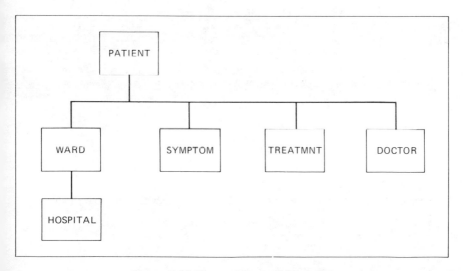

Figure 9.16 The restructured hierarchy

SEG statements in the PSB in order to write your program. However, the use of a secondary index in certain retrieval situations can adversely effect the performance of your program.

CALLS USING THE SECONDARY PROCESSING SEQUENCE. Let's see some examples of DL/I calls using the secondary processing sequence. The most obvious application would be to list all the patients in patient name sequence. You could do that with a loop on a call like the one in figure 9.17. Since your PCB defines a secondary index, that index will be used to satisfy each Get-Next call.

Although your program logic is very simple, the work that DL/I does to get those segments is another matter. Remember, PATIENT segments are not *stored* in patient name sequence in the data base, so each Get-Next call will result in a random retrieval. Alternatives to the secondary index should be considered for this type of application. For example, in a large data base, it might be quicker to retrieve PATIENT segments using the normal processing sequence on BEDIDENT, and then sort them into patient name sequence.

Remember that the WARD and HOSPITAL segments appear below the PATIENT segment in the hierarchy created by the secondary index, so SSAs must be coded in the new sequence when accessing WARD and HOSPITAL segments through the secondary index. Figure 9.18 shows a call you might use

```
GN      PATIENT
```

Figure 9.17 Retrieving PATIENT segments in name sequence

```
GU      PATIENT(PATNAME  =WHEELER                        )
        WARD    *D
        HOSPITAL
```

Figure 9.18 Retrieving the WARD and HOSPITAL segments

```
GU      HOSPITAL
        WARD
        PATIENT (PATNAME  =WHEELER                       )
```

Figure 9.19 Retrieving a PATIENT segment without the secondary index

```
GU      PATIENT (XPATNAME=WHEELER                        )
```

Figure 9.20 Retrieving a PATIENT segment via the secondary index

to retrieve WARD and HOSPITAL segments using the secondary index. This allows you to find out which WARD and HOSPITAL a particular patient is in without having to search through the entire data base.

USING THE SECONDARY INDEX WITH NORMAL PROCESSING SEQUENCE. You can also use the secondary index by referencing the *indexed field* in an SSA.

Here's an example. Let's suppose that your PCB specifies the normal processing sequence by excluding the PROCSEQ parameter, and you'd like to retrieve a particular PATIENT segment by name. Figure 9.19 shows how you'd do that without using the secondary index. This will cause DL/I to start at the beginning of the data base and scan through it until it finds a PATIENT segment having the name *Wheeler*. This could be very inefficient. Figure 9.20 shows an SSA that causes DL/I to use the secondary index. The XPATNAME field is defined in the DBD, and it can be used to gain access to a target segment via the secondary index. In this example, DL/I goes directly to the *Wheeler* PATIENT segment occurrence through the secondary index. It doesn't have to search through the data base to find it. Using the field name PATNAME causes DL/I to make a normal search. Using the name XPATNAME tells it to use the secondary index. This illustrates the power of secondary indexing.

Remember, if your PCB statement includes the PROCSEQ parameter, identifying your secondary index, you can always code the indexed field name in an SSA. If your PCB statement does not include the PROCSEQ parameter, the SENSEG statement for the index target segment must contain an IN-DICES parameter naming the secondary index PCB. If your PSB contains neither of these parameters, your program has no knowledge of the secondary index, and you may not reference the indexed field in an SSA, nor may you take advantage of the secondary processing sequence. So your PSB controls the way that you can use a secondary index.

Defining the Indexed Field

The source segment fields that the DBA picks for the indexed field are used to make up the key field in the index pointer segments in the secondary index data base. It's the field that DL/I uses to sequence the index pointer segments in the secondary index. The DDA chooses from one to five segments from the source segment to make up the indexed field. In addition to the one to five fields that make up the indexed field, the DBA may include additional information in the index pointer segments. Figure 9.21 shows the format of an index pointer segment in a secondary index data base. Much of this additional information is of little consequence to application programs.

CONSTANT INFORMATION. The DBA may choose to put a one-byte constant at the beginning of each indexed field in the index pointer segment. A constant is only specified when two or more secondary indices share the same physical data base.

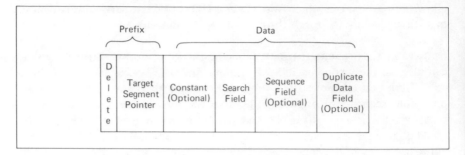

Figure 9.21 Index pointer segment format

SUBSEQUENCE FIELDS. It's often desirable to ensure that each index pointer segment in the secondary index data base has a unique key field value. The DBA can specify subsequence fields to make the key values unique. For example, the HOSPITAL data base may contain more than one PATIENT segment with the same PATNAME value. If we only placed the PATNAME value in the index pointer segment, more than one index pointer segment might contain the same key value. This can cause inefficiencies in the secondary index data base.

If one of the fields in the PATIENT segment happened to be social security number, the DBA might choose to use this field as a subsequence field. This would make the index pointer segment key field unique. A good choice for a subsequence field is often the key field of the source segment. For example, it's unlikely that two patients would have the same name and the same bed identifier in two different hospitals.

DUPLICATE DATA FIELDS. In addition to subsequence data, the DBA may also choose to include other fields from the source segment in the index pointer segment. This is useful if a program processes the secondary index as data. For example, suppose you want to find out a patient's bed identifier when you know the patient's name. You might choose to store the value for BEDIDENT in the secondary index as duplicate data. This would allow you to access only the secondary index in a program. This is much faster than accessing the HOSPI-TAL data base just to find out a patient's bed identifier. However, it would require duplicating the BEDIDENT field in both the HOSPITAL data base and the secondary index. This would be a storage-space versus processing-time tradeoff.

When Source and Target Segments Are Not the Same

In the previous example, the index source segment and the index target segment were the same segment. This is not a requirement. DL/I allows the source segment to be any segment dependent on the target segment as well as the target segment itself. Figure 9.22 shows an example where the source segment is the DOCTOR segment. This time we're using the DOCTNAME field to create the indexed field. Since the PATIENT segment is still the target segment, each secondary index pointer segment will point to a PATIENT segment. Since the key field value of each secondary index pointer segment will consist of a doctor's name, this secondary index can be used to find out which patients are using a particular doctor.

Since the PATIENT segment is still the target segment, the restructured hierarchy for this secondary processing sequence still looks like that shown in figure 9.16. It's the target segment that determines the new root segment, not the source segment. This time, Get-Next calls with unqualified PATIENT SSAs will not retrieve PATIENT segments in patient name sequence. They'll retrieve PATIENT segments in sequence on the names of the doctors in the DOCTOR segments dependent on them. In this particular example, Get-Next calls using the secondary processing sequence might not be very useful.

But by using the indexed field, named XDOCNAME in this example, we could use a very simple call sequence to retrieve all PATIENT segments in a particular ward using some doctor. Figure 9.23 shows the call that you'd loop on to retrieve those PATIENT segments. This time the PATIENT segments would be retrieved in BEDIDENT sequence for a particular doctor.

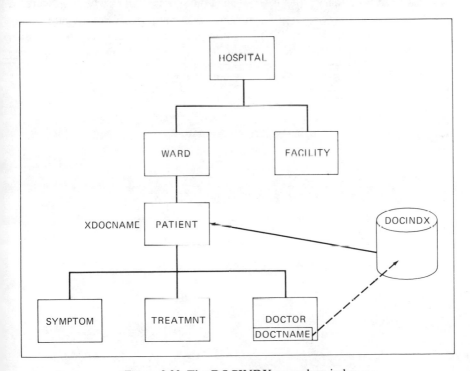

Figure 9.22 The DOCINDX secondary index

Using the Independent-AND Boolean Operator

When your target segment and source segment are not the same, the Independent-AND Boolean operator can often be quite useful. For example, suppose you'd like to find a PATIENT segment that has DOCTOR segments for two doctors dependent on it. For example, let's find a patient in a particular ward who is using both Doctor *Payne* and Doctor *Neiman*. Figure 9.24 shows an SSA using the independent-AND operator. It says to find a PATIENT segment that has DOCTOR segments with the names *Payne* and *Nieman* dependent on it. Suppose you coded the SSA, as in figure 9.25, using the normal AND operator. This says to find the PATIENT segment that has a single DOCTOR segment whose DOCTNAME field is equal to PAYNE and is also equal to NIEMAN. That's an impossibility, and that call could never find a segment that satisfies the search argument.

Using Multiple Secondary Indices

Figure 9.26 shows the HOSPITAL data base with two secondary indices indexing it. For this example, assume that an additional field in the TREATMNT segment is defined as a search field. This field is SURGDATE. It was not defined as a search field in our original data base example. The SURGINDX secondary index is sequenced on SURGDATE, which indicates when each patient is scheduled for surgery. A secondary index sequenced on surgery date, and having the PATIENT segment as the target segment, will

```
GN       HOSPITAL(HOSPNAME =RIVEREDGE              )

         WARD     (WARDNO   =01)

         PATIENT (XDOCNAME =PAYNE                   )
```

Figure 9.23 Using the indexed field

```
GU       HOSPITAL(HOSPNAME =RIVEREDGE              )

         WARD     (WARDNO   =01)

         PATIENT (XDOCNAME =PAYNE      #XDOCNAME =NIEMAN    )
```

Figure 9.24 Using the independent-AND operator

```
GU       HOSPITAL(HOSPNAME =RIVEREDGE              )

         WARD     (WARDNO   =01)

         PATIENT (XDOCNAME =PAYNE      *XDOCNAME =NIEMAN    )
```

Figure 9.25 Using the normal AND operator

allow us to find all patients that are scheduled for surgery on a given day.

By using this secondary index in combination with the DOCINDX secondary index, we can find all patients having a particular doctor who are scheduled for surgery on a particular day. Figure 9.27 shows the call that you'd loop on to retrieve all the PATIENT segments for patients using Doctor *Payne* and scheduled for surgery on *July 4, 1977*. This time the call is not limited to a particular hospital or ward.

Sparse Indices

The SURGINDX secondary index can be used to illustrate another secondary indexing facility called sparse indexing. The secondary index need not contain an index pointer segment for each occurrence of the index source segment. For example, the SURGINDX secondary index need not contain an index pointer

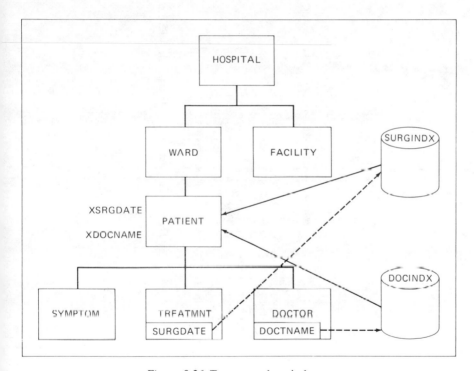

Figure 9.26 Two secondary indexes

```
GN      HOSPITAL
^^^^    ^^^^^^^^^
        WARD
        ^^^^^^^^^
        PATIENT (XDOCNAME =PAYNE      *XSRGDATE =070477      )
        ^^^^^^^^^^^^^^^^^^^^^^^^^^^^^^ ∿ ^^^^^^^^^^^^^^^^^^^^^ ∿ ^^
```

Figure 9.27 Using two secondary indexes

```
PRINT    NOGEN                                                            00000010
FCB      TYPE=DB,DBNAME=HOSPDBD,PROCOPT=G,POS=MULTIPLE,                    *00000020
         KEYLEN=32                                                         00000025
                                                                          00000030
SENSEG   NAME=HOSPITAL,PARENT=0                                           00000040
SENSEG   NAME=WARD,PARENT=HOSPITAL                                        00000050
SENSEG   NAME=PATIENT,PARENT=WARD                                        00000060
SENSEG   NAME=SYMPTOM,PARENT=PATIENT                                     00000070
SENSEG   NAME=TREATMNT,PARENT=PATIENT                                    00000080
SENSEG   NAME=DOCTOR,PARENT=PATIENT                                      00000090
                                                                          00000110
PSBGEN   LANG=COBOL,PSBNAME=CHAP9C                                       00000120
END                                                                       00000130
```

Figure 9.28 Chapter 9 coding problem PSB

```
                            P A T I E N T   H I S T O R Y                    PAGE    1

DATE  06/30/77

HOSPITAL NAME   MAC NEAL

WARD TYPE       INTENSIVE

PATIENT NAME      PATIENT ADDRESS                       PHONE          BED ID  ADMIT DATE

BINKIS            1234 ROSE PLACE, CHICAGO, IL          312-555-1234   0003    06/29/77

PREVIOUS HOSPITAL   PREVIOUS DATE   PREVIOUS REASON

RIVEREDGE           05/23/77        GALL BLADDER

PREVIOUS DOCTOR   PHONE             DIAGNOSIS           TREATMENT DESCRIPTION  DATE

GRILL             312-555-1144      UNKNOWN             NONE                   06/24/77

MEDICATION TYPE   DIET COMMENT                          SURGERY DATE  SURGERY COMMENT

NONE              NONE                                                NONE

DOCTOR NAME       DOCTOR ADDRESS                        DOCTOR PHONE  SPECIALTY

AHAB              1134 BURLINGTON, CHICAGO, IL          312-555-6667  GENERAL PRACTICE
```

Figure 9.29 Patient history report

segment for each occurrence of the TREATMNT segment. This would be wasteful if the TREATMNT segment did not specify surgery as a treatment.

When building the SURGINDX secondary index, the DBA could write a routine to test the SURGERY-FLAG field in the TREATMNT segment. If the SURGERY-FLAG field indicates that the patient is not scheduled for surgery, the index pointer segment for that segment could be left out of the secondary index. This way, secondary index pointer segments would only point to relevant segments in the HOSPITAL data base. This can be a big performance improvement.

CHAPTER 9 EXERCISE (CODING PROBLEM)

There is only a single exercise associated with this chapter. However, in this exercise, you'll get a chance to use most of the skills you've learned. Following are the specifications for a complete DL/I batch program. You can write this program in either COBOL, PL/I, or Assembler Language.

The PATIENT History Program

The purpose of this program is to print the history of each patient, by ward, for all the hospitals in the data base. Since the entire data base is to be processed, there is no input to the program other than the HOSPITAL data base. Figure 9.28 shows the PSB to use for this coding problem.

OUTPUT FROM THE PROGRAM. Figure 9.29 shows a sample page of the report that your program is to prepare. The information relating to the doctors to be printed for each patient is obtained from two places. Information about the first doctor is obtained from the patient's first SYMPTOM segment (SYMP-DOCTOR and SYMP-DOCT-PHONE). Information about the second doctor is obtained from the patient's last DOCTOR segment (DOCTNAME, DOCT-PHONE, and SPECIALT). Print the information from the SYMPTOM and TREATMNT segments in ascending sequence by date.

Assume that you can use path calls and multiple positioning when you code your solution to this problem. Appendix D summarizes all the information about the HOSPITAL data base that you need to code your solution.

10

IMS Data Communications Concepts

Introduction

Up to this point, we've been talking primarily about accessing *data base segments* using DL/I calls. In this chapter and the next, we'll be talking about the other major part of the IMS software, the *data communications portion*. Since there is no data communications support provided in DL/I DOS/VS systems, these chapters only apply to IMS/VS and IMS/360 installations. We'll begin with a brief overview of the differences between the DL/I batch environment and the data base/data communications environment. Then we'll look at the various resources that are under the control of IMS.

After that we'll see what types of information flow through an IMS data communications system, and how the information is processed by IMS and application programs. Then we'll concentrate on application programs in the data communications environment and how they are written. We'll end up with discussions of three commonly used features of IMS, conversational programming, Message Format Service, and the Batch Terminal Simulator.

The IMS DB/DC Environment

An IMS application program that uses only DL/I, the interface to IMS data bases, uses only a portion of the IMS software. A full implementation of IMS uses both DL/I and the data communications interface. This type of system is called an IMS *data base/data communications* (DB/DC) system. It is possible to use only DL/I in the batch mode, or only the data communications portion of IMS. But most installations that use either IMS/360 or IMS/VS operate in the DB/DC environment. As an alternative, however, some installations use DL/I for access to data bases, and CICS instead of the IMS data communications software. CICS is another IBM program product that handles communication with remote terminals. CICS has interfaces that allow it to be used with DL/I. This chapter and the next one deal only with the IMS

153

data communications interface. Let's begin by reviewing the DL/I batch environment. We'll then look at the main differences between the batch environment and the DB/DC environment.

The Batch Environment

In the batch environment, you supply the JCL for the execution of a single DL/I batch program. Figure 10.1 shows what your program looks like when it's operating in the batch mode. In MFT and VS1 systems, your program occupies one of the operating system's *partitions*. In MVT and VS2 release 1 (SVS) systems, it occupies a *region*. In VS2 systems at release 2 and later (MVS systems) your program occupies an *address space*. Throughout this chapter and the next, we'll use the term *region* to mean either partition, region, or address space.

Notice that the region that's assigned to your program contains a copy of DL/I. Everything that your program needs is contained within its own region, and your program is independent of any other job in the system. Your application program, in combination with DL/I modules, operates like any other operating system job.

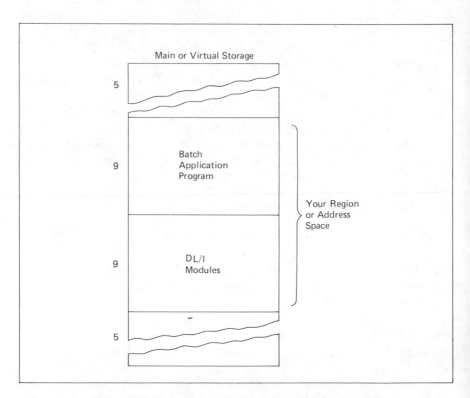

Figure 10.1 Executing a DL/I batch application program

In the batch environment, application programmers and designers need not be concerned with the IMS system definition process. The IMS system definition is performed once for all users, and data bases and application programs may be added at any time without requiring another IMS system definition.

DB/DC Differences

In the DB/DC environment, application programs can be automatically scheduled by IMS as a result of information coming into the system from remote terminals. The data communication portion of the DB/DC system handles information in the form of *messages* that flow between remote terminals and application programs.

An IMS DB/DC system is usually set up to handle a great number of application programs, and the resources under the control of IMS have a more system-wide orientation. For this reason, the IMS system definition for a DB/DC system must include information about the various application programs that will be under the control of IMS. Let's begin by looking at the types of resources that are under the control of IMS in the DB/DC environment, and how those resources are defined to IMS.

The Resources that IMS Controls

In the DB/DC system, you cannot add programs and data bases to the system at will as you can when you operate in the batch mode. All programs and data bases that will run under the control of IMS must be defined in the IMS system definition. There are two main categories of system resources that are defined to IMS during IMS system definition: *application resources* and *data communications resources*. Let's look at each one individually.

Application Resources

These are the system resources that are related to application programs that will operate in the IMS DB/DC system. Specifically, these resources consist of application programs, transaction codes, and data bases.

APPLICATION PROGRAMS. There are two types of application programs in the IMS DB/DC environment. These are *message processing programs,* or MP programs for short, and *batch message processing programs,* or BMP programs for short. The scheduling of message processing programs is entirely under the control of IMS. A message processing program is scheduled after a message to be processed by that program is received by IMS. A batch message processing program is manually scheduled by the system operator. It's more or less a cross between a normal DL/I batch application and a message processing program. A typical BMP program is used to process information that has been received from remote terminals, but stacked up and held by IMS in a *message queue*. More about message queues in a minute.

MP programs and BMP programs are identified to IMS during IMS system definition in APPLCTN system definition macros. The first APPLCTN macro in figure 10.2 is an example of one for an MP program. The second is for a BMP program. Basically, there's an APPLCTN macro for each MP and BMP program that will be allowed to execute in the system. An APPLCTN macro names the PSB that will be used by a program. The convention that MP and BMP programs follow in the DB/DC environment is that the program's load module name and the PSB name must be the same.

TRANSACTION CODES. Messages may be sent to MP and BMP programs either from remote terminals, or from other programs. When information is sent from one program to another it's called a *program-to-program message switch*. A message that has an MP or BMP program as a destination, whether it originates at a terminal or in a program, is called a *transaction*. Each type of transaction that can be processed by an MP or BMP program is identified with a unique one- to eight-character transaction code. These transaction codes are defined to IMS during IMS system definition with TRANSACT macros. Figure 10.3 shows an example of a TRANSACT macro. A TRANSACT macro names a transaction code, and follows the APPLCTN macro for the program that processes it. In this way the DBA tells IMS which program processes each type of transaction. One, and only one, program may be assigned to process a given transaction, but a given program may process more than one type of transaction.

THE MESSAGE QUEUES. As transactions arrive from remote terminals or are generated within programs, they are processed by IMS and stored in *message queues*. There is a separate message queue maintained for each valid transaction code defined during IMS system definition. For transactions that are processed by MP programs, IMS automatically schedules the appropriate MP program after IMS receives those transactions. Because there are normally more transactions in the queues than can be processed at one time, a priority scheme is used in determining which transaction to

```
APPLCTN   PSB=PROGRAM1

APPLCTN   PSB=BMPPGM1,PGMTYPE=BATCH
```
Figure 10.2 APPLCTN macros

```
TRANSACT   CODE=TRANS1
```
Figure 10.3 A TRANSACT macro

select from the queue first. We'll see how this priority scheme works a little later.

Transactions that are processed by BMP programs remain in message queues until the appropriate BMP program is manually scheduled by the operator. The BMP program then reads the transactions from the appropriate message queue as if it were any other sequential data source.

DATA BASES. Programs that run in the DB/DC environment cannot indiscriminately access any DL/I data base. DBD names for the data bases that MP and BMP programs will access must be defined to IMS in DATABASE system definition macros. Figure 10.4 shows an example of a DATABASE macro. You don't have to identify which data bases will be processed by which programs. You simply include a DATABASE macro for each data base that programs in the system will access.

DEFINING APPLICATION RESOURCES TO IMS. Let's say our system supports four transaction codes: TRANS1, TRANS2, TRANS3, and TRANS4. Transactions with transaction codes TRANS1 and TRANS2 will both be processed by an MP program named PROGRAM1. Transactions having transaction codes TRANS3 will be processed by an MP program named PROGRAM2. Transactions with transaction code TRANS4 will be processed by a BMP program named BMPPGM1. The MP and BMP programs in the system will require access to three data bases. Their DBD names are DBD1, DBD2, and DBD3. Figure 10.5 shows the IMS system definition macros that might be used to define these application resources to IMS.

Data Communications Resources

A second category of resources that must be defined during IMS system definition includes all the data communications hardware in the communications network. The most important of these physical resources are the com-

```
DATABASE   DBD1
```

Figure 10.4 A DATABASE macro

```
DATABASE   DBD1
DATABASE   DBD2
DATABASE   DBD3
APPLCTN    PSB=PROGRAM1
  TRANSACT   CODE=TRANS1
  TRANSACT   CODE=TRANS2
APPLCTN    PSB=PROGRAM2
  TRANSACT   CODE=TRANS3
APPLCTN    PSB=BMPPGM1
  TRANSACT   CODE=TRANS4
```

Figure 10.5 IMS system definition macros

munications lines that handle data communications, usually phone lines, and the remote terminals themselves.

COMMUNICATIONS LINES. In an **IMS DB/DC** network, a single communications line can handle one or more remote terminals of a particular type. A line can be switched or nonswitched. Users gain access to a switched line by dialing a phone number. A nonswitched line is dedicated to the use of a set of terminals, and the terminals remain connected at all times. Lines that connect terminals of a similar type may be grouped together into *line groups.* Each line group is identified in the IMS DB/DC JCL by a DD statement.

The LINEGRP and LINE system definition macros are used to define the network of communication lines to IMS. We'll look at examples of these macros after we define the rest of the communication resources.

PHYSICAL TERMINALS. One or more physical terminals can be connected to each communication line through one or more levels of controllers. In a switched line network, each terminal may be connected to any one of several lines. In a nonswitched network, a terminal is always connected to the same line. Defining a switched network is beyond the scope of this book, so we'll show an example of a nonswitched network in this chapter.

Different types of physical terminals require different combinations of IMS system definition macros. A common type of network uses remote 3277 display terminals. In this type of network, use the DBAs a CTLUNIT macro to define each 3271 control unit, followed by a set of TERMINAL macros to define the 3277 display terminals connected to each control unit.

LOGICAL TERMINALS. MP and BMP programs do not communicate directly with physical terminals. That would cause programs to be tied to a particular hardware environment. Messages that are destined for remote terminals include a one to eight character logical terminal name instead of a transaction code. As with transactions, logical terminal messages are held in the message queues. There is one message queue for each valid logical terminal name defined in the system. NAME system definition macros are used to define logical terminal names to IMS. During IMS system definition, each TERMINAL macro that defines a particular physical terminal can be followed by one or more NAME macros which assign one or more logical terminal names to each physical terminal.

When a logical terminal name message is sent, the physical terminal that happens to be assigned to that logical terminal name will receive the message. The system operator has commands that allow the logical and physical terminal assignments to change at any time. This way, the operator can cope with equipment malfunctions by reassigning logical terminal names.

Logical terminal messages may be sent by MP and BMP programs, or by other terminals. When a terminal sends a logical terminal name message to another terminal, it performs a *terminal-to-terminal message switch.* It does this by beginning a message with a logical terminal name instead of a transaction code.

DEFINING DATA COMMUNICATIONS RESOURCES TO IMS. Figure 10.6 shows a sample set of IMS system definition macros that could be used to define a very simple data communications network to IMS. There is a single line group consisting of two lines. Each has a single 3271 control unit attached to it. Each control unit supports three 3277 display terminals. The NAME macros define the logical terminal names that will be initially assigned to each physical terminal.

Data Communications Messages

The messages that flow through the IMS DB/DC system are categorized according to their destinations within the system. There are basically three different types of messages. You've already briefly seen two of them, transaction code messages and logical terminal name messages. The third type is an IMS terminal command. Let's look at each of them in more detail.

Transaction Code Messages

A *transaction code message,* or *transaction* for short, has an MP or BMP program as a destination. It can originate at a remote terminal, or in another application program. Figure 10.7 shows what a transaction code message might look like as it's entered at a terminal. It begins with a one- to eight-character transaction code. This must be one of the valid transaction codes defined to IMS in a TRANSACT macro. The transaction code is followed by

```
LINEGRP        DDNAME=LINEDD,UNITYPE=3270
  LINE         ADDR=0C9
    CTLUNIT    ADDR=C1,MODEL=2
      TERMINAL ADDR=40
        NAME     LTERM1
        NAME     LTERM2
      TERMINAL ADDR=C1
        NAME     LTERM3
      TERMINAL ADDR=C2
        NAME     LTERM4
  LINE         ADDR=0CA
    CTLUNIT    ADDR=C2,MODEL=2
      TERMINAL ADDR=40
        NAME     LTERM5
      TERMINAL ADDR=C1
        NAME     LTERM6
        NAME     LTERM7
        NAME     LTERM8
      TERMINAL ADDR=C2
        NAME     LTERM9
```

Figure 10.6 IMS data communications macros

an optional one- to eight-character password in parentheses. A program called the *Security Maintenance Program,* or SMP, can be used to assign passwords to protect certain transaction codes. If this is done, a particular password must accompany the transaction code for the transaction to be accepted by IMS. The password (or transaction code if there is no password) is followed by the text of the message.

MESSAGE SEGMENTS. Messages may be broken into one or more *message segments.* Each group of message segments making up a message is transmitted at one time by IMS. In an MP or BMP program, you retrieve messages one segment at a time with calls to IMS, much as you retrieve data base segments. We'll look in more detail at how this works later. When IMS passes a message segment to your program, it strips off the transaction code and password and adds some control information to each segment.

MESSAGE SEGMENTS IN THE APPLICATION PROGRAM. As far as an MP or BMP program is concerned, the transaction code and the password are not a part of the message. Figure 10.8 shows a message segment as an MP or BMP program sees it. Each message segment consists of four bytes of control information, followed by the message text.

   The first two bytes of control information in the message consist of the *message length.* It's a two-byte binary field that indicates the total length of the message text, plus the four bytes of control information. The second two bytes of control information, called the *ZZ field,* are normally manipulated by IMS. On an input message, you ignore this two-byte field, and on an output message, you normally store binary zeros in it. An exception to this is when you're working with display terminals. With display terminals, the ZZ field is used to indicate where on the screen you would like your message to be written.

TRANS1(PASSWORD)MESSAGE TEXT

Figure 10.7 A transaction

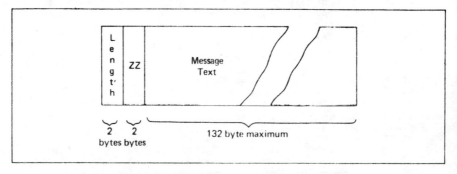

Figure 10.8 Message format in application program

The ZZ field is device dependent, and you can learn more about how it's used in your *Application Programming Reference Manual.* We'll talk about output messages next.

Logical Terminal Name Messages

Logical terminal name messages have logical terminals as their destinations. As with transactions, they may originate either in programs or at other logical terminals. A logical terminal name message that originates at a terminal is called a *terminal-to-terminal message switch.* Figure 10.9 shows what a logical terminal message segment might look like if you entered one at a terminal. Instead of a transaction code the message segment begins with one of the valid logical terminal names. This must be one of the names defined during IMS system definition in a NAME macro. No password is allowed in a logical terminal name message.

Figure 10.10 shows a logical terminal name message segment in an MP or BMP program's message I/O area. Notice that the logical terminal name does not appear in the message itself. It's supplied in another way, which you'll learn about when we get to programming techniques.

IMS Terminal Commands

The third kind of message is represented by one of the IMS terminal commands. These begin with a slash followed by one of the valid terminal command verbs. These terminal commands are described in detail in the *Operator's Reference Manual.* They're used to control the operation of the IMS DB/DC

LTERM1 MESSAGE TEXT

Figure 10.9 A logical terminal name message

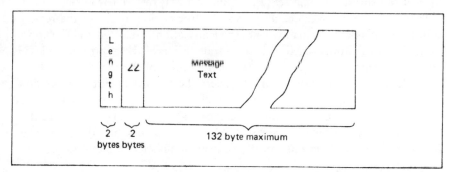

Figure 10.10 A logical terminal name message in the program

/DIS STATUS

Figure 10.11 An IMS terminal command

system. Figure 10.11 shows an example of an IMS terminal command. This is a command that's used to get a status display. IMS terminal commands are used most often by the IMS master terminal operator. The IMS master terminal is the main control center of the IMS DB/DC system, and is normally able to enter all of the IMS terminal commands. Normally, all other remote terminals are able to enter only certain IMS terminal commands.

The IMS DB/DC Operating Environment

In the DB/DC environment, multiple operating system regions are used for MP and BMP programs. All of these regions are under the control of IMS. There are three types of regions, the IMS control region, MP regions, and BMP regions. Figure 10.12 shows a typical IMS DB/DC region configuration. Let's look at each region type individually to see how the DB/DC system operates.

The IMS Control Region

There is only one control region allowed in an IMS DB/DC system, and it's required. It handles all communication between IMS and remote terminals. The IMS control region also controls the use of the various MP regions in the system.

Message Processing Regions

Programs are not scheduled into MP regions in the same way that normal operating system jobs are scheduled. The scheduling of MP programs into the MP regions is handled by the IMS control region. Each of the transaction codes defined to IMS is assigned to a transaction class identified with a number from 1 to 255. Each MP region is set up to process transactions from one to four of the transaction classes. Each time an MP region becomes available, IMS checks the message queues to see if a transaction in one of the region's transaction classes is available. If so, the transaction is selected and the appropriate MP program is scheduled. If no transaction of the appropriate class is available, the region remains idle. If there are multiple transactions to choose from, IMS uses a priority scheme to select the highest priority transaction.

Different transaction codes may have different priority values within the system, so messages are not always selected on a first-in/first-out basis. Rather, more important messages may be scheduled ahead of less important messages. You'll learn more about this priority scheme in a later section in this chapter.

Batch Message Processing Regions

BMP programs are not scheduled into MP regions. If your system supports BMP programs, one or more BMP regions must be available. It's up to the system operator to schedule BMP programs into the BMP regions at the appropriate times.

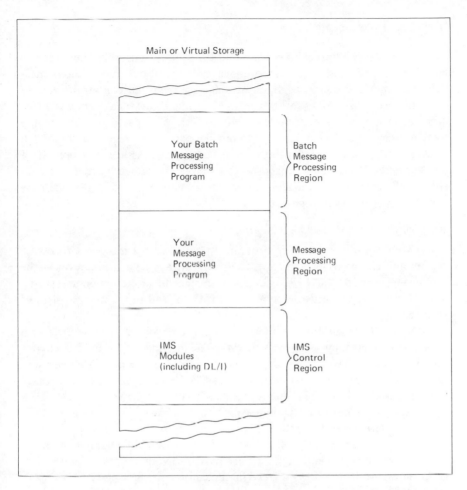

Figure 10.12 Executing in a data communications environment

BMPs are used when it's necessary to receive information from remote
terminals, but when each individual message might require substantial processing. It's not desirable to tie up a message processing region for more than
a few seconds to process each transaction, so if more time than that would be
required, and a response is not immediately required, a BMP program might
be more efficient than a message processing program. Batch message processing programs are often used when it's desirable to submit input from a terminal, but when a response back to the terminal is not required. With BMPs, the
output is often supplied in the form of a listing, rather than a direct response
to the terminal.

Message Processing

In this section we'll see how MP and BMP programs send and receive messages to and from logical terminals. First, let's talk more about messages and message segments. Each message segment can contain up to 130 bytes of text. This 130-byte limit is used to make message segments manageable. In general, a message segment consists of a particular line of the total message. For example, if a terminal operator is required to send a message that consists of five individual lines, that message will consist of five segments. By the same token, if you would like to send a message consisting of seven lines of information to a remote printer, the message would consist of seven segments.

Receiving the First Message Segment

When your message processing program is loaded into a message processing region, and control is passed to it, there will always be a transaction in the message queue with one of your program's assigned transaction codes waiting for it. Your program must issue a call to IMS to read in the first segment of your message.

You retrieve message segments in much the same way as you retrieve data base segments: by using calls to IMS. The interface is set up so that your message queue behaves like a sequential data set. You read the first segment of your message by issuing a Get-Unique call. A Get-Unique call for a message segment uses no SSAs. The only difference between a Get-Unique call for a message segment and a Get-Unique call for a data base segment is in the PCB that you reference in the call. Calls for message segments use special *data communications PCBs* rather than data base PCBs. We'll be talking about the format of these PCBs, and how they are passed to your program, later in this chapter. Figure 10.13 shows a Get-Unique call for the first message segment.

Reading the Remaining Message Segments

The manner in which a message is broken into segments must be communicated to the application program. If a message consists of more than one message segment, the programmer that writes the application program must

```
CALL   'CBLTDLI' USING GET-UNIQUE
                         I-O-PCB
                         MESSAGE-AREA.
```

Figure 10.13 Getting the first message segment

```
CALL   'CBLTDLI' USING  GET-NEXT
                         I-O-PCB
                         MESSAGE-AREA.
```

Figure 10.14 Getting all other message segments

know about it. The first segment is always read with a Get-Unique call (except in conversational programs which we'll talk about later). Succeeding segments of the same message are always read with Get-Next calls. Figure 10.14 shows a call to read any message segment after the first.

You can see that getting the segments of a message is exactly like reading any other sequential input source. Just remember that a Get-Unique call always gets the first segment, and Get-Next calls are used to get the rest. If you should make a mistake and issue another Get-Unique call in your message processing program, IMS will search the message queues for another message having the same transaction code. This causes all remaining segments of the first message to be lost.

Sending Information Back to the Terminal

Just as you use Get-Unique and Get-Next calls to read segments, you use Insert calls to send messages back to the terminal. Again, the Insert call that you use to send a message is exactly the same as a data base Insert call, except that it references a data communications PCB. Figure 10.15 shows an example of an Insert call used to send a message segment.

In most common situations, your program will send a message back to the same terminal that sent the input message. Your program can also send messages to other terminals, and it can also put a message back into a message queue so that it can be read later by some other program.

Flow of Information Through the System

Now that you've gotten a brief overview of each of the individual parts of the IMS data communication system, let's take an overall look at how information flows through the system. This will put these individual parts into better perspective.

Message Input

The first thing that normally happens in the IMS data communications environment is that an operator enters a transaction at a remote terminal. The IMS control region handles the actual transmission of this transaction from the remote terminal to the central system. Routines within the control region check the transaction code against a list, to see if the transaction code is valid, and check the password if required. If the transaction code and the password are valid, the message is stored in the appropriate message queue. Remember

```
CALL  'CBLTDLI'  USING  INSERT
                        I-O-PCB
                        MESSAGE-AREA.
```

Figure 10.15 Sending a message

that messages are maintained in individual message queues by transaction code or logical terminal name.

Message Selection

Only a part of the IMS control region handles the transmission of messages from the remote terminals to the message queues. Another program in the control region decides which message to select next from the message queue. When IMS determines which message to select, the operating system loads the appropriate MP program into an MP region. Remember that each transaction code known to IMS is handled by a particular message processing program. IMS looks up which application program is needed to handle a particular transaction.

Message Processing

Once the message processing program is loaded into the appropriate region, IMS passes control to it. The first thing that the program normally does is to issue a Get-Unique call for the first message segment. The program can then process the information in that message segment, which may require making any number of DL/I calls to data bases. If the message consists of more than one segment, the program issues Get-Next calls for the remaining message segments. At any time, the program is able to make more calls to DL/I data bases.

Message Output

If the application determines that a reply is necessary, the program issues Insert calls to send messages back to the originating terminal. Optionally, the program can send messages to other terminals, and can also put messages back into a message queue to be read later by other MP or BMP programs.

Sending Information to Terminals and Other Programs

Sending and receiving messages requires that you use a special data communications PCB when you issue the Get and Insert calls. In this section we'll look at the various types of PCBs that the IMS data communication system provides to you, and how the data base administrator sets them up.

Sending Messages to the Originating Terminal

One of the simplest forms of message processing programs receives a message from a terminal, processes one or more segments in DL/I data bases, and sends a message back to the same terminal. Two PCBs are required, one for the terminal and one for the data base.

DATA BASE PCBS. Data base PCBs are those PCBs that you're familiar with from earlier chapters. They describe the hierarchical structure of the sensitive segments, and tell you the types of DL/I Calls that you can issue. Data base PCBs are always defined in a PSB. Your program's PSB contains all the data base PCBs that your program can use.

DATA COMMUNICATIONS PCBS. Data Communications PCBs allow your program to communicate with remote terminals. There is always at least one data communications PCB required for an MP or BMP program; this is the PCB that describes the logical terminal from which the input message was received. It's called the *I/O PCB*. Your PSB does not contain any reference to the I/O PCB. Before control is passed to your message processing program IMS sets up an I/O PCB for you. The I/O PCB is always the first PCB identified in the parameter list passed to your MP or BMP program.

In our example, the MP program that we're working with requires an I/O PCB to send and receive messages to and from the originating terminal, and one data base PCB to access a DL/I data base. Figure 10.16 shows what the PSB might look like for this message processing program. Notice that there's only one PCB, the one for the data base. IMS supplies the I/O PCB automatically.

Figure 10.17 shows what the entry coding would look like for this MP

```
PRINT    NOGEN
PCB      TYPE=DB,DBDNAME=HOSPITAL,PROCOPT=A
SENSEG   ...
  .
  .
  .
PSBGEN   LANG=COBOL,PSBNAME=MYPSB
END
```

Figure 10.16 PSB with no alternate PCB

```
       .
       .
       .
LINKAGE SECTION.
01   DB-PCB.
       .
       .
       .
01   I-O-PCB.
       .
       .
       .
PROCEDURE DIVISION.
     ENTRY   'DLITCBL'   USING I-O-PCB DB-PCB
       .
       .
       .
```

Figure 10.17 Entry linkage

program. Notice that the data base PCB parameter is the second one in the parameter list. The first parameter identifies the I/O PCB. We'll look at the format of the I/O PCB in the next chapter.

USING THE I/O PCB. The I/O PCB can be used to retrieve transaction messages segments sequentially from a message queue, and can also be used to transmit logical terminal name messages back to the originating terminal. The I/O PCB contains information that describes the input message segments and also contains a status code that can be checked to see if your calls are successful. The I/O PCB can be used with Get-Unique and Get-Next calls to retrieve messages from the message queue, and it can also be used with Insert calls to transmit segments back to the originating terminal.

The key point to remember is that when you are simply sending responses back to the originating terminal, no special PSB statements are required for a message processing program. IMS automatically supplies the address of the I/O PCB to your program. The only difference between a batch program and a data communications program, in this respect, is that the data base PCB is the second PCB in the list rather than the first.

Sending Messages to Other Terminals

In addition to sending responses back to the originating terminal, a message processing program can route messages to other terminals in the system. To do this, the message processing program must have access to another type of data communications PCB called an *alternate PCB*.

ALTERNATE PCBS. To use an alternate PCB, another PCB statement must be included in your PSB. Figure 10.18 shows the PSB for a program that can send messages to a terminal other than the one that sent the original transaction. This program will be provided with an I/O PCB automatically by IMS, so the program will have access to three PCBs, the I/O PCB, and the two PCBs identified in the PSB. This program will be able to receive a message from the originating terminal, send messages back to that same terminal, and send messages to the terminal identified in the alternate PCB. Notice that a parameter in the alternate PCB gives the name of the logical terminal that the message will be sent to.

Figure 10.19 shows the entry coding for a program that would use the PSB in figure 10.18. Notice that the I/O PCB is still identified by the first parameter in the parameter list. The alternate PCB is next, followed by the data base PCB.

MODIFIABLE ALTERNATE PCBS. If the DBA requires that a message processing program send a response to a terminal other than the originating terminal, and it is always known which logical terminal the response should be sent to, the PCB will contain the name of the logical terminal. Figure 10.18 is an example of that case. If, on the other hand, the MP program itself is going to

```
PRINT    NOGEN
PCB      TYPE=TP,LTERM=T11234
PCB      TYPE=DB,DBDNAME=HOSPITAL,PROCOPT=A
SENSEG   ...
         .
         .
         .
PSBGEN   LANG=COBOL,PSBNAME=MYPSB
END
```

Figure 10.18 PSB with alternate PCB

```
         .
         .
         .
LINKAGE SECTION.
01    DB-PCB.
         .
         .
         .
01    ALT-PCB.
         .
         .
         .
01    I-0-PCB.
         .
         .
         .
PROCEDURE DIVISION.
      ENTRY   'DLITCBL'   USING   I-0-PCB ALT-PCB DB-PCB.
         .
         .
         .
```

Figure 10.19 Entry coding

```
PCB      TYPE=TP,LTERM=T11234,MODIFY=YES
```

Figure 10.20 Modifiable alternate PCB

determine the destination of the message, the DBA can make the alternate PCB *modifiable*. A PCB statement for this is shown in figure 10.20. With this type of PCB, the message processing program can issue a call with the CHNG function code to store the appropriate logical terminal name in the modifiable alternate PCB. In this way, a message processing program can send the response to any logical terminal in the system.

Program-to-Program Message Switching

You learned earlier that an MP program may send messages to other message processing programs as well as to logical terminals. To do this, an alternate PCB must be available to the program, and that alternate PCB must either be modifiable or must reference a *transaction code* rather than a logical terminal.

When an MP program issues an Insert call to an alternate PCB specifying a transaction code rather than a logical terminal name, that message will be sent to the message queue, rather than to a terminal.

Messages that are placed in the message queue by MP programs are treated no differently than messages that come from remote terminals. Eventually the particular message processing program associated with the message's transaction code will be scheduled by IMS, and that program will treat the message as if it had come from a terminal.

IMS Message Scheduling Techniques

As we mentioned earlier, messages from terminals are stored into queues before they're passed to message processing programs. IMS uses a priority scheme in deciding which message to select next from the message queues. In this section we'll talk in more detail about the priority scheme that IMS uses.

Allocating the Message Processing Regions

One of the things that the DBA must decide when planning the data communications environment is how many MP regions to use. The DBA then decides which transaction codes each region should handle. Transactions are normally separated into classes based on the response time that they require. For example, a particular environment may have a particular transaction that occurs very frequently and must be given very high response time. One or more MP regions might be set aside for that transaction type only. The MP regions are set up based on the requirements of the individual MP programs that will be running in them.

Message Selection

IMS attempts to select a transaction for each of the message processing regions currently in operation. It does this based on a priority scheme. Each transaction that IMS can handle has two priorities associated with it. These priorities are called the transaction's *normal priority* and its *limit priority.* In addition to these two priorities, each transaction has another number associated with it called that transaction's *limit count.* These three numbers may be defined by the DBA in the TRANSACT macro for each transaction.

Remember, we said that a separate message queue is maintained for each transaction code. Messages are queued serially by transaction code. When an MP region becomes available, IMS looks at the first message in each message queue for the transaction codes that particular MP region can handle. It then schedules the transaction having the highest priority. Remember that each transaction has both a normal priority and a limit priority associated with it. In order to determine whether to use the normal priority or the limit priority, IMS looks at how many transactions with each transaction code are stored in each message queue. If the number of transactions in a particular queue is greater than or equal to that transaction code's limit count, the limit priority is used. If the number of messages queued is less than the processing limit, the normal priority is used. A few examples will make this more clear.

A MESSAGE SELECTION EXAMPLE. Let's assume, for example, that a particular message processing region has become available, and that region is able to handle transactions T11234 and transaction T11432. Figure 10.21 shows what the message queues look like for those transaction codes. Figure 10.21 also shows the normal priority, the limit priority and the limit count for those two transaction codes, and it shows the number of transactions for each of those transaction codes stored in the message queues.

Notice that the number of transactions of each of those transaction codes has not equaled or exceeded the limit count yet. So, in determining which message to select, transaction T11234 has a normal priority of seven and T11432 has a normal priority of four, so the first transaction with transaction code T11234 will be selected.

Now let's see what might happen after a period of time. Figure 10.22 shows the new condition of the message queues. Notice that the number of transactions with transaction code T11432 now equals the limit count. When priorities are now compared, IMS will compare the normal priority of transac-

Transaction Code	T11234	T11432
Normal Priority	7	4
Limit Priority	9	8
Limit Count	20	50
Entries in Queue	15	40

Figure 10.21 Message queues for T11234 and T11432

Transaction Code	T11234	T11432
Normal Priority	7	4
Limit Priority	9	8
Limit Count	20	50
Entries in Queue	13	50

Figure 10.22 Message queues after a time interval

tion type T11234 with the limit priority of transaction type T11432. In this case, a transaction with transaction code T11432 will be selected.

The normal priority, limit priority and limit count must be chosen very carefully by the DBA for each transaction code. This is the only way that the DBA has of making sure that important transaction types are processed ahead of less important transaction types.

Other Data Communications Facilities

The facilities that we've talked about thus far are more or less standard data communications facilities that most IMS DB/DC shops use. There are a number of other facilities that are optional, and are used less frequently than the ones we've covered. We'll cover three of them in this chapter. These optional facilities are *conversational programming, Message Format Service,* and the *Batch Terminal Simulator.*

Conversational Programming

The MP programs that we've looked at so far all process nonconversational transaction types. MP programs can also process conversational transaction types. Whether a transaction is conversational or nonconversational is determined by parameters that are coded in the TRANSACT macro for a particular transaction code. When a nonconversational transaction is processed by an MP program, the operator at a remote terminal enters a transaction at a remote terminal. This message is placed in the message queue, and eventually an MP program is scheduled to handle it. That program then processes the transaction and might send a response back to the terminal. When the operator at the remote terminal sees the response the choice might be made to enter another transaction. When this new transaction is processed by another MP program, or perhaps, the same MP program, that MP program has no knowledge of any previous interaction with the operator. This can be a severe disadvantage in certain applications. In many cases, the MP program must engage in a dialogue with the operator.

One way that IMS could have been designed to handle a situation like this, is to have the MP program reside permanently in the message processing region during the time that the conversation is in progress. This would be very wasteful, however, because the response time of a terminal operator is far slower than the response time of the data communication system. (Or so we would hope.) The way that IMS actually implements conversational processing is through the use of a *scratch pad area* or *SPA.*

THE SCRATCH PAD AREA. The scratch pad area is a small area of main or virtual storage, or a small area of direct access storage, that's used to store the intermediate results of a series of executions of a message processing program. In the first execution of an MP program that handles a conversational transaction, the program might read in a transaction, and, based on the information in it, store certain information in the SPA and send a response back to the terminal. The terminal operator can communicate with the MP program in a conversational manner even though the message processing program does not reside permanently in the MP region. When the MP program is brought in the second time, as a result of a conversational response by the terminal operator, the program can read in the scratch pad area to determine what happened during the last execution of that program.

WRITING CONVERSATIONAL PROGRAMS. The only major difference between an MP program that processes a nonconversational transaction, and one that processes a conversational transaction is in the use of the scratch pad area. The SPA is a predefined area of either main or virtual storage, or direct access storage. Its size and format are predefined by the DBA and given to you as part of your program specifications. The first Get-Unique call that you issue to the I/O PCB, in a conversational program, gets you the SPA, rather than your first message segment. This standard departs from the standard for nonconversational programs, where the Get-Unique call to the I/O PCB will get you the first message segment.

In conversational programs all message segments, including the first one, are gotten with Get-Next calls to the I/O PCB. Also, the first Insert call to the I/O PCB will return the scratch pad area to IMS. This is so your program can store information to be used the next time your program is scheduled.

We'll have a look at the format of the scratch pad area, and go into more detail on conversational programming considerations, in chapter 11.

Message Format Service (MFS)

A very powerful facility provided by IMS is called *Message Format Service,* or MFS for short. This facility is most useful in helping you format messages that will be transmitted to and from display screens. When you use MFS, your program only works with certain fields of data in the screen. IMS inserts and removes filler characters and control characters that will actually be used to format the screens at the terminal.

INPUT MESSAGE FORMATTING. When display terminals are used, messages to be sent to your message processing program from the terminal often consist of full screens of information. These screens often contain a lot of descriptive information that helps make the screen readable. MFS provides two control blocks, set up by macros, to separate out information of direct interest to the MP or BMP program.

One control block, called the *Message Input Descriptor* or *MID,* is used to describe an input message as your program would like to see it. The MID describes just those fields on the screen that your program is interested in. Another control block, called the *Device Input Format* or *DIF,* describes the screen format as the terminal operator formats it.

OUTPUT MESSAGE FORMATTING. Two other MFS control blocks are used to help you format screens that will be transmitted from your program to a display terminal. The *Message Output Descriptor,* or *MOD,* describes the message as your program formats it. Another control block, called the *Device Output Format* or *DOF,* describes the screen format as it will appear on the screen. MFS uses the MOD and the DOF to translate the data fields that your program places in the output message into a complete screen format as it will appear on the display screen.

MFS ADVANTAGES. MFS allows your program to work with information on the data field level rather than worrying about where on the screen the information is stored or should appear. It allows quite complex screen formats to be used without tying the application program to where on the screen the pertinent information is stored.

The subject of screen formatting, and the writing of the four control blocks that MFS uses to help you format display terminal screens, is almost the subject of a book in itself, and we won't go into MFS in any more detail here. If your installation uses MFS you can consult with your data base administration group to learn more about how it's used in your installation.

The Batch Terminal Simulator

Almost all new MP programs must be tested in the batch environment before they are run in actual production. This is normally done by using standard SYSIN and SYSOUT data sets to simulate the transmission of information to and from terminals.

There is a special facility, called the *Batch Terminal Simulator,* or BTS for short, which allows you to write very simple control statements that allow you to use sequential data sets to simulate your terminals. These control statements can be written to simulate almost any terminal that the IMS data communications system has access to. As with MFS we won't be going into the details on the BTS control statements in this book.

If your installation does not have access to the batch terminal simulator, you can still test message processing programs in the batch environment. Your *IMS System/Application Design Guide* has an appendix that includes instructions for writing program modules that allow an MP program to be tested as a batch DL/I program. You can consult that appendix if you'd like to know more about it.

CHAPTER 10 EXERCISES

1. List the three types of regions that can be used in an IMS DB/DC system.

2. List the three types of PCBs that can be used in an MP program, and describe the purpose of each.

3. Following is a list of ten terms. After that are definitions of those terms. Match each term with the statement that best defines it.

Terms

a. Physical Terminal
b. Logical Terminal
c. Message Queues
d. Message Processing Program
e. Batch Message Processing Program
f. Master Terminal
g. Message Segment
h. Password
i. ZZ Field
j. Scratch Pad Area

Definitions

1. Used to store information between two executions of a conversational message processing program.
2. Control information in a message segment used to indicate where on a display screen the information should be written.
3. Name by which message processing programs refer to terminals.
4. Name used to describe a hardware terminal.
5. The terminal used to control the IMS DB/DC system.
6. Used to store messages from terminals before they are processed by message processing programs.
7. An application program used to handle a particular type of transaction from a remote terminal
8. A portion of a message.
9. An application program that runs in the batch mode but has access to the message queues.
10. Used to protect the system from unauthorized access.

11

Data Communications Programming Techniques

Introduction

In the last chapter, you saw how IMS data communications facilities are implemented and, in general, how you use them. In this chapter, we'll be looking specifically at MP programs. You'll see a complete MP program that reads a one segment transaction and sends messages back to the originating terminal. In addition to the sample program, you'll see programming techniques for using alternate PCBs to send messages back to an alternate terminal and also for program-to-program message switching.

We'll look at the format of the SPA that's used in writing conversational programs to see the differences between nonconversational MP programs and conversational MP programs. And you'll find a series of hints on how to make MP programs efficient.

At the end of the chapter, you'll find another coding problem. In this problem you'll modify the PATIENT segment retrieval program that you saw in chapter 4 to make it operate as an MP program.

A Message Processing Program

Coming up is a listing of a complete COBOL MP program. The program reads a transaction that consists of a single message segment. Figure 11.1 shows the

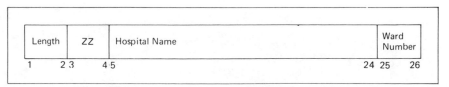

Length	ZZ	Hospital Name		Ward Number
1	2 3	4 5		24 25 26

Figure 11.1 Message segment format

format of that message segment. The first four positions follow the standard format for IMS transactions. Following the first four bytes is the message text. The message text in this case consists of a twenty-position hospital name followed by a two-position ward number.

The program will read the transaction and then retrieve the HOSPI-TAL and WARD segments from the data base corresponding to the hospital name and ward number in the transaction. The program then sends a response back to the originating terminal. Figure 11.2 shows the format of the first message segment of the response. This message segment displays the hospital name and ward number as verification to the operator. Following this header message segment, the program sends a message segment for each PATIENT segment stored under that particular WARD segment. Each PATIENT message segment should look like the one in figure 11.3.

The program will result in a complete listing of all the patients in that ward, sent to the terminal. The listing will contain the patient name and bed identifier for each PATIENT segment. Following, in figure 11.4, is the complete message processing program to produce this patient list. Let's take a look now at each part of this program to see how communication with IMS works.

Entry Coding

Notice that the entry coding in the program sets up the linkage for the I/O PCB and the data base PCB. (See figure 11.5.) As you learned in the last chapter, the I/O PCB is supplied by IMS and is not a part of your PSB. The I/O PCB is the first PCB passed to your program. In this case we don't need an alternate PCB since we're only sending messages back to the terminal that entered the transaction. The second PCB is for the data base. If our PSB had

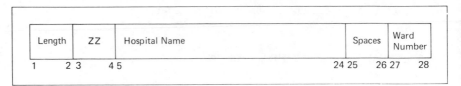

Figure 11.2 **HOSPITAL** and **WARD** message segment

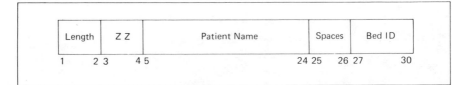

Figure 11.3 **PATIENT** message segment

Figure 11.4 Complete program

```
000100  ID DIVISION.
000200  PROGRAM-ID. CHAP11.
000300  AUTHOR. JOSEPH F. LEBEN.
000400  DATE-COMPILED.
000500
000600  REMARKS. THIS IS A VERY SIMPLE IMS/DC PROGAM. IT DOES VERY
000700           LITTLE ERROR CHECKING. IT READS AN INPUT TRANSACTION
000800           WHICH HAS THE FOLLOWING FORMAT:
000900           FORMAT.
001000              POSITIONS   1 -  2   TRANSACTION LENGTH
001100                          3 -  4   ZZ FIELD
001200                          5 - 24   HOSPITAL NAME
001300                         25 - 26   WARD NUMBER
001400
001500           FOR EACH TRANSACTION. THE PROGRAM SENDS A CONFIRMING
001600           MESSAGE BACK TO THE TERMINAL REPEATING THE HOSPITAL NAME
001700           AND WARD NUMBER, AND THEN LISTS OUT ALL THE PATIENT
001800           SEGMENTS UNDER THAT WARD AND HOSPITAL.
001900
002000  ENVIRONMENT DIVISION.
002100  CONFIGURATION SECTION.
002200  SOURCE-COMPUTER. IBM-370-168.
002300  OBJECT-COMPUTER. IBM-370-168.
002400      EJECT
002500  DATA DIVISION.
002600
002700  WORKING-STORAGE SECTION.
002800
002900  01  TERM-IN.
003000
003100      03  IN-LENGTH          PIC S9599   COMP.
003200      03  IN-ZZ              PIC XX.
003300      03  HOSPNAME-TERM      PIC X(20).
003400      03  WARDNO-TERM        PIC XX.
003500
003600  01  TERM-OUT-PATIENT-HOSPITAL.
```

179

```
003700         03  OUT-LENGTH          PIC S9999   VALUE +30 COMP.
003800         03  OUT-ZZ              PIC XX      VALUE SPACE.
004000         03  HOSPITAL-INFO       PIC X(20).
004100         03  FILLER              PIC X(4)    VALUE SPACE.
004200         03  WARD-INFO           PIC XX.
004300
004400     01  TERM-OUT-PATIENT.
004500
004600         03  OUT-LENGTH          PIC S9999   VALUE +129 COMP.
004700         03  OUT-ZZ              PIC XX.
004800         03  PATIENT-INFO        PIC X(125).
004900     01  GET-NEXT-F              PIC X(4)    VALUE 'GNP '.
005000     01  GET-UNIQUE              PIC X(4)    VALUE 'GU '.
005100     01  INSERT-FUNC             PIC X(4)    VALUE 'ISRT'.
005200     01  P-Z-D                   PIC X       VALUE SPACE.
005210     01  P-Z-D-2 REDEFINES P-Z-D.
005211         03  PACKED-ZERO         PIC S9.
005300     01  PACKED-ONE              PIC S9      VALUE +1.
005400
005500     01  HOSPITAL-SSA.
005600         03  FILLER              PIC X(21)   VALUE 'HOSPITAL*D(HOSPNAME =',
005700         03  HOSPNAME-SSA        PIC X(20)   VALUE ' '.
005800         03  FILLER              PIC X       VALUE ')'.
005900
006000     01  WARD-SSA.
006100         03  FILLER              PIC X(19)   VALUE 'WARD    (WARDNO   =',
006200         03  WARDNO-SSA          PIC X(2)    VALUE ' '.
006300         03  FILLER              PIC X       VALUE ')'.
006400
006500     01  PATIENT-SSA             PIC X(9)    VALUE 'PATIENT ',
006900     EJECT
007000     01  I-O-AREA COPY PATIENT.
007100
007200     01  HOSPITAL-INPUT.
007300         03  HOSPITAL.
007400             05  HOSPNAME        PIC X(20).
007500             05  HOSP-ADDRESS    PIC X(30).
007600             05  HOSP-PHONE      PIC X(10).
```

```
007700    03   WARD.
007800         05   WARDNO          PIC XX.
007900         05   TOT-ROOMS       PIC XXX.
008000         05   TOT-BEDS        PIC XXX.
008100         05   BEDAVAIL        PIC XXX.
008200         05   WARDTYPE        PIC X(20).
008300 LINKAGE SECTION.
008400 01   DB-PCB   COPY MASKC.
008500
008600 01   I-O-PCB.
008700      03   LTERM-NAME         PIC X(8).
008800      03   FILLER             PIC XX.
008900      03   I-O-STAT-CODE      PIC XX.
009000      03   INPUT-PREFIX.
009100         05   PREF-DATE       PIC S9(7)   COMP-3.
009200         05   PREF-TIME       PIC S9(7)   COMP-3.
009300         05   PREF-SEQ        PIC S9(7)   COMP.
009310 PROCEDURE DIVISION.
009500
009600 START-OF-PROGRAM.
009700
009800      ENTRY 'DLITCBL' USING I-O-PCB DB-PCB.
009900      PERFORM GET-MESSAGE THRU GET-MESSAGE-EXIT
010000              UNTIL I-O-STAT-CODE EQUAL 'QC' OR 'QD'.
010010      GOBACK.
010100
010200 GET-MESSAGE.
010300
010400      CALL 'CBLTDLI' USING GET-UNIQUE
010500                           I-O-PCB
010600                           TERM-IN.
010700
010800      IF I-O-STAT-CODE EQUAL 'QC'         GO TO GET-MESSAGE-EXIT.
010900      IF I-O-STAT-CODE NOT EQUAL SPACE
011000         MOVE I-O-PCB TO PATIENT-INFO
011100         PERFORM SEND-PAT-RTN
011200         MOVE SPACE TO PATIENT-INFO
011300
011400
```

```
011500          GO TO GET-MESSAGE-EXIT.
011600
011700      MOVE HOSPNAME-TERM    TO HOSPNAME-SSA.
011800      MOVE WARDNO-TERM      TO WARDNO-SSA.
011900
012000      CALL 'CBLTDLI' USING GET-UNIQUE
012100                           DB-PCB
012200                           HOSPITAL-INPUT
012300                           HOSPITAL-SSA
012400                           WARD-SSA.
012500
012600      IF STATUS-CODE NOT EQUAL SPACE
012610
012700          MOVE 'NO-HOSPITAL OR WARD' TO PATIENT-INFO
012800          PERFORM SEND-PAT-RTN
012810          MOVE SPACE TO PATIENT-INFO.
012900          GO TO GET-MESSAGE-EXIT.
013000
013100      MOVE HOSPNAME TO HOSPITAL-INFO.
013200      MOVE WARDNO   TO WARD-INFO.
013300
013400      CALL 'CBLTDLI' USING INSERT-FUNC
013500                           I-O-PCB
013600                           TERM-OUT-PATIENT-HOSPITAL.
013700
013800      IF I-O-STAT-CODE NOT EQUAL SPACE
013900          GO TO DUMP-IT.
014000      PERFORM GET-PATIENT THRU GET-PATIENT-EXIT
014010                          UNTIL STATUS-CODE EQUAL 'GE'.
014100
014200  GET-MESSAGE-EXIT.
014300      EXIT.
014500  GET-PATIENT.
014600
014700      CALL 'CBLTDLI' USING GET-NEXT-P
014800                           DB-PCB
014900                           I-O-AREA
015000                           PATIENT-SSA.
015100
```

```
015200            IF STATUS-CODE EQUAL 'GE' GO TO GET-PATIENT-EXIT.
015300            IF STATUS-CODE NOT EQUAL SPACE
015400
015500                MOVE DB-PCB TO TERM-OJT-PATIENT
015600                PERFORM SEND-PAT-RTN
015700                MOVE SPACE TO TERM-OUT-PATIENT
015800                GO TO GET-MESSAGE.
015900
016000            PERFORM SEND-PAT-RTN.
016100
016200        GET-PATIENT-EXIT.
016300            EXIT.
016400
016500        SEND-PAT-RTN.
016600
016700            CALL 'CBLTDLI' USING INSERT-FUNC
016800                                 I-O-PCB
016900                                 TERM-OUT-PATIENT.
017000
017100            IF I-O-STAT-CODE NOT EQUAL SPACE
017200                GO TO DUMP-IT.
017300
017400        DUMP-IT.
017500
017600            ADD PACKED-ONE TO PACKED-ZERO.
```

183

an alternate PCB, it would come after the I/O PCB, and before the data base PCB.

The LINKAGE SECTION

Figure 11.6 repeats the LINKAGE SECTION coding from the program. Notice that there are two PCB masks in the LINKAGE SECTION, one for the I/O PCB and one for the data base PCB. Let's look at the format of the I/O PCB.

The first eight bytes of the I/O PCB contain the logical terminal name for an input or output message. When using the I/O PCB, the input destination and the output destination are always the same.

The next field is a two-byte field reserved for IMS. You're not allowed to modify this field.

Following that is the two-byte status code. The status code field is used in much the same way as it's used in data base PCBs. We'll cover the most common status codes received by message processing programs.

Following the status code are three fields that form the *input prefix* of

```
009500 PROCEDURE DIVISION.
009600
009700 START-OF-PROGRAM.
009800
009900     ENTRY 'DLITCBL' USING I-O-PCB DB-PCB.
```

Figure 11.5 Entry coding

```
008400 LINKAGE SECTION.
008500 01  DB-PCB    COPY MASKC.
C*000010 01  DB-PCB.
C 000020     03  DBD-NAME          PIC X(8).
C 000030     03  LEVEL-NUMBER      PIC XX.
C 000040     03  STATUS-CODE       PIC XX.
C 000050     03  PROC-OPTIONS      PIC XXXX.
C 000060     03  JCB-ADDRESS       PIC XXXX.
C 000070     03  SEGMENT-NAME      PIC X(8).
C 000080     03  KEY-LENGTH        PIC S9(5) COMP.
C 000090     03  NUMBER-SEGS       PIC S9(5) COMP.
C 000100     03  KEY-FEEDBACK.
C 000110         05  HOSPNAME-KEY  PIC X(20).
C 000120         05  WARDNO-KEY    PIC XX.
C 000130         05  BEDIDENT-KEY  PIC X(4).
008600
008700 01  I-O-PCB.
008800     03  LTERM-NAME        PIC X(8).
008900     03  FILLER            PIC XX.
009000     03  I-O-STAT-CODE     PIC XX.
009100     03  INPUT-PREFIX.
009200         05  PREF-DATE     PIC S9(7)    COMP-3.
009300         05  PREF-TIME     PIC S9(7)    COMP-3.
009310         05  PREF-SEQ      PIC S9(7)    COMP.
```

Figure 11.6 Linkage section

the message. This contains the current date, the current time and an input message sequence number. The date is stored as a packed decimal number in the form 00YYDDD. The time is also a four-byte packed decimal number in the format HHMMSS.S. (Decimal point is implied.) The sequence number is a four-byte binary number.

Following the input prefix is an eight-position field that is used only when the Message Format Service facility is being used. This field gives the name of the message output descriptor, or MOD, that's to be used by this PCB.

Input and Output Message Format

The DATA DIVISION coding shows the format of the input and output messages. Notice that the COBOL coding allows for the two-position length field, and the two-position ZZ field, in both the input and output messages. A fixed-length value is stored in each of the output message types, since each message has a fixed length. This length field could be modified by the program if it were designed to send messages of varying lengths. In this simple example, the ZZ field contains binary zeros. So this program would work properly only with a very simple terminal, like a hard-copy terminal. With display terminals, the ZZ field would be used by MFS to tell IMS which line of the display screen to put each message segment on.

The PROCEDURE DIVISION

The PROCEDURE DIVISION coding shows examples of getting the first segment of a transaction with a Get-Unique call. It also shows how message segments are sent back to the originating terminal with Insert calls. Notice that both the Get-Unique and the Insert call use the I/O PCB. The Get calls to the data base use the data base PCB.

Notice that when the complete patient list has been sent back to the terminal, the program loops back on the Get-Unique call. This is a useful convention that's normally followed in MP programs. It saves IMS the trouble of loading this program back into an MP region should there be another message of the same transaction code waiting in the message queue. Most message processing programs are written to branch back on the Get-Unique call to check to see if there is another message waiting. However you should check your installation standards to see if this is a standard at your shop.

Using Alternate PCBs

The program that you just looked at shows the basics of writing an MP program that sends information back to the originating terminal. Let's look now at ways you can use alternate PCBs in MP programs. First we'll look at coding to send a message to an alternate PCB without modifying that PCB. Figure 11.7 shows the partial coding for such a program.

Alternate PCB Coding

Notice that in this case the entry coding and the LINKAGE SECTION coding are set up for three PCBs. The first one is the I/O PCB, the second one is the alternate PCB, and the third one is the data base PCB. If other alternate PCBs were used they would appear following the I/O PCB in the order they were coded in your PSB.

The Alternate PCB Mask

Let's look at the format of the PCB mask that's used for alternate PCBs. It consists of only three fields, the first three fields of the I/O PCB. Since the alternate PCB is used only for output messages and never for input, the only fields required are the name of the output destination, the two-byte reserved field, and the two-byte status code field.

The coding for an Insert call to the alternate PCB is similar to the coding for an Insert call for the I/O PCB; the only difference is the name of the PCB mask.

Modifying the Alternate PCB

In an alternate PCB, the first eight positions can contain either a logical terminal name or a transaction code. If this field contains a logical terminal name, the message will be directed to that particular logical terminal. If it contains a transaction code, the message will be stored in the appropriate

```
                .
                .
                .
        LINKAGE SECTION.
        01   ALT-PCB.
                .
                .
        01   I-O-PCB.
                .
                .
        01   DB-PCB.
                .
                .
                .
        PROCEDURE DIVISION.
            ENTRY  'DLITCBL'  USING  I-O-PCB  ALT-PCB  DB-PCB.
                .
                .
                .
            CALL   'CBLTDLI'  USING  INSERT
                                     ALT-PCB
                                     OUT-MESSAGE.
                .
                .
                .
```

Figure 11.7 Using an alternate PCB

transaction code message queue. The message will then be read later by the appropriate MP or BMP program.

If the alternate PCB has been defined in the PSB as *modifiable,* your program can store a logical terminal name or transaction code into the alternate PCB before issuing an Insert call. This allows your program to dynamically specify the destination of the output message. You don't store the destination name directly into the PCB, however. A call with the CHNG function code does this job for you. Figure 11.8 shows coding for this call.

The call uses no SSAs and the I/O area address points to an eight-position field containing the logical terminal name or transaction code. This call simply stores that eight-position field into the alternate PCB.

Message Processing Program Status Codes

There are a number of status codes that you can receive in MP programs. The most important ones are those that you'll receive when issuing Get calls to the I/O PCB. The three status codes shown in figure 11.9 are the ones that you'll use in order to control how your program reads message segments from the message queue. The status code of *blanks,* as with data base calls, indicates that your call was successful and an appropriate message segment was retrieved by the call.

The QD status code indicates that you've read all the message segments

```
           .
           .
           .
    WORKING-STORAGE SECTION.
    77  CHANGE      PIC X(4)   VALUE 'CHNG'.
    77  NEW-TERM    PIC X(8)   VALUE 'T11432  '.
           .
           .
    CALL  'CBLTDLI'  USING  CHANGE
                           I-O-PCB
                           NEW-TERM.
           .
           .
           .
```

Figure 11.8 Modifying the alternate PCB

Data Communications Status Codes

blanks	Call was successful
QD	No more segments
QC	No more messages

Figure 11.9 Message processing program status codes

associated with the particular message that you are receiving. You get it after a Get-Next call to the I/O PCB when there are no more message segments.

You'll receive the QC status code if you loop back on your Get-Unique call in order to try to retrieve another message from the message queue. The QC status code indicates that there are no more messages in the message queue for your transaction type. This tells you that you can terminate your MP program.

There are many other status codes that you can get in a message processing program, but they normally indicate various error conditions and you can look those codes up in your *Application Programming Reference Manual.*

Other Message Processing Programming Techniques

In this section we'll cover a few more programming techniques that you can use in writing MP programs. You'll learn how to use the PURG function code to send message segments to their destination at a predetermined time. Then we'll look at the format of the scratch pad area or SPA and see some programming techniques that you can use in writing conversational MP programs. Finally we'll look at a variety of techniques that you can use to increase the efficiency of MP programs.

Using the PURG Call

When you issue Insert calls, either to the I/O PCB or to an alternate PCB, the message segments that you send are held by the IMS control region in message buffers. They are not transmitted until your program finishes working with its input transaction. Normally you can indicate that you are finished with the transaction in one of two ways. You can either terminate your MP program and return control to IMS or issue another Get-Unique call to the I/O PCB. IMS then sends all the output message segments in a single transmission.

In certain circumstances it's useful to be able to explicitly tell IMS when you would like your message segments transmitted. If you would like to have your message segments grouped together as a message and transmitted before you terminate your program, or before you issue another Get-Unique call to the I/O PCB, you can issue a call with the PURG function code. This tells IMS that it's time to transmit the message segments that you've sent. The PURG call allows your message processing program to send back more than one message for each Get-Unique call to the I/O PCB. Figure 11.10 shows the coding for the PURG call.

In many installations all message processing programs are required to use the PURG call before they terminate. You should check your installation standards to see if there are any rules for using the PURG call.

Using the Scratch Pad Area

As you learned in chapter 10, the scratch pad area or SPA is a special area of either main or virtual storage, or direct access storage, that's used to save information between executions of an MP program that processes a conversational transaction. You saw in that chapter some of the differences between nonconversational and conversational MP programs. In this section we'll look at the format of the SPA to show you how conversational MP programs work. Figure 11.11 shows the format of the SPA.

SCRATCH PAD AREA FORMAT. The first two bytes give the length (in binary) of the SPA. This length is the length of the user work area plus all the control information, including the length field.

Following the length field is a four-position field reserved for IMS. This four-position field should not be modified by the MP program.

Next is an eight-position transaction code. This gives the transaction code associated with this particular conversation. When the first message segment is read in, this transaction code is the same as the transaction code associated with the input transaction. In a normal conversational MP program, the transaction code will remain unchanged throughout the conversation. This means that each new transaction sent by the operator will cause the same MP program to be scheduled again.

It is possible, however, that during the conversation, your program may determine that some other MP program should take over the next time the operator enters a transaction. If this happens, you can store a

```
            .
            .
            .
    WORKING-STORAGE SECTION.
    77  PURGE      PIC X(4)  VALUE 'PURG'.
            .
            .
            .
    CALL  'CBLTDLI' USING PURGE I-O-PCB.
            .
            .
            .
```

Figure 11.10 Using the PURG call

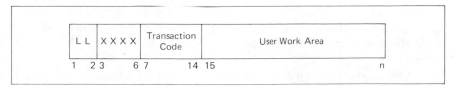

Figure 11.11. The scratch pad area

new transaction code in this field to indicate which MP program should take over.

Following the three control fields in the SPA is the *user work area*. The format of this area is determined as part of the program specifications. When the scratch pad area is read in by the first execution of the MP program, the user work area will contain binary zeros.

WORKING WITH THE SCRATCH PAD AREA. The scratch pad area appears to your program almost like an input message. In a conversational MP program you read the scratch pad area into your program with a Get-Unique call. All message segments are then gotten with Get-Next calls. This is different from a nonconversational program, in which the Get-Unique call will get the first message segment. By the same token, you return the scratch pad area to IMS with an Insert call. The first insert call to the I/O PCB will return the scratch pad area. You do this to save information for the next execution of your conversational program.

TERMINATING THE CONVERSATION. There are two ways that you can terminate a conversation. The operator can determine that the conversation is over and enter an IMS terminal command at the remote terminal. When that happens, your conversational program will not be scheduled again by IMS. Alternatively, your program can determine that the conversation is at an end. If this happens, your program stores binary zeros in the transaction code field in the scratch pad area. When the scratch pad area is then returned to IMS with an Insert call, IMS knows that the conversation has terminated. It will not schedule your MP program again.

Efficiency Techniques

The most important thing to keep in mind in writing MP programs is that program efficiency really counts. There are normally a limited number of MP regions available within the system, and each transaction code is normally assigned to a particular MP region. This means that there are normally a number of messages waiting to be scheduled into each of the MP regions. Your program must get in and out of an MP region as quickly as possible, or the entire system can bog down.

One thing that you should always do in an MP program is issue a Get-Unique call for the message as quickly as possible. There is normally no need to do any other kind of processing other than what the particular message calls for. If you find yourself doing a large amount of processing before you issue the Get-Unique call, you should reevaluate the purpose of your MP program.

One good practice that we have already mentioned is to always loop back on the Get-Unique call after you have finished processing a transaction. In case there's another message of your transaction type waiting, the message can be scheduled immediately. This saves IMS the overhead of bringing your program back into the MP region.

In order to keep your programs operating as quickly as possible, you should use whatever techniques are available to increase your program's efficiency. For example, you can avoid excessive DL/I calls, and use path calls wherever possible. Whatever you can do to avoid any excessive I/O operations will increase the efficiency of your program. If there are certain messages that will require a large amount of processing time, consider processing those messages with a BMP program. This can always be done if an immediate response back to the terminal is not required. In some cases only a portion of the processing for a particular input message needs to be done immediately. In this case the MP program can do some of the processing immediately and send a response back to the terminal. The message processing program can then take whatever information from the message is needed for later processing and send that information back to the message queue in a transaction. The transaction can then be read later by a BMP program, and the rest of the processing can be done in the batch mode. This is a good use of a program-to-program message switch.

If it's possible you should make your programs either reentrant or serially reusable. If your program is reentrant it can be made permanently resident in main or virtual storage. For some MP programs that are used very frequently this can increase the program's efficiency.

The DBA can do a lot to increase the efficiency of MP programs. For example, data bases that will be used in a data communications environment must be given extra care in their design. The segments that will be accessed by MP programs should normally be fairly high in the hierarchy to speed access to them. Also, the DL/I access method must be carefully chosen.

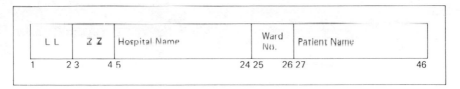

Figure 11.12 Input message segments

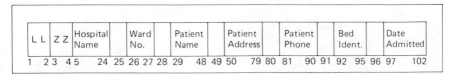

Figure 11.13 Output message format

Normally, the access method that gives quickest access to segments should be chosen, unless this conflicts with other, more important, applications that access the same data base.

CHAPTER 11 EXERCISE (CODING PROBLEM)

There is only a single exercise in this chapter. It consists of writing a complete message processing program. In this exercise you are going to take the PATIENT segment retrieval program that you saw in chapter 4 and convert it to an MP program. As you may remember, that program reads a series of cards, each containing a hospital name, a ward number, and a patient name. The program then prepares a listing of some of the information in the PATIENT segments for the patients identified in the records on the input file.

The corresponding MP program that you should write processes a message consisting of a single message segment. The format of this message segment is shown in figure 11.12. Notice that the same information is supplied to the MP program as was supplied to the batch program. Your program should send a message to the originating terminal. Its format is shown in figure 11.13.

In summary, your program reads a message consisting of one segment and sends back a single message segment to the originating terminal. This is an example of a very simple MP program. Assume that you don't know what kind of terminal will be used to receive your output message and store binary zeros in the ZZ field bytes following the length field of your output message.

12

Access Methods

Introduction

The access method chosen for a data base is not an immediate, major concern of the application programmer. Usually it's determined by the data base administrator, and is transparent to application programs. However, there are efficiency considerations that the application programmer should be aware of, and the choice of a particular access method may restrict your use of some DL/I facilities.

In this chapter, we'll try to give a brief overview of the main access methods that DL/I uses. This chapter really only scratches the surface of what can be said, but we'll try to cover those characteristics of the access methods that are of the most interest to application programmers.

Storage Organizations and Access Methods

At the heart of DL/I are the access methods that retrieve and manipulate the segments stored in a data base. DL/I supports two major methods for organizing data bases. These two storage organization methods are the *Hierarchical Sequential Organization* (HS organization) and the *Hierarchical Direct Organization* (HD organization). Each of these organizations is supported by two DL/I access methods. The Hierarchical Sequential Organization is supported by HSAM, for *Hierarchical Sequential Access Method* and HISAM, for *Hierarchical Indexed Sequential Access Method*. The Hierarchical Direct Organization is supported by HDAM, for *Hierarchical Direct Access Method,* and HIDAM, for *Hierarchical Indexed Direct Access Method.*

In addition to the two forms of storage organization and the four major access methods, DL/I supports a fifth access method called GSAM, for *Generalized Sequential Access Method.* There's an appendix at the end of this book devoted to programming with GSAM. For now, all you have to know is that

GSAM allows you to access standard sequential files using DL/I calls. GSAM is not very widely used.

The Hierarchical Sequential Organization

With the Hierarchical Sequential Organization, using either HSAM or HISAM, segments within a data base record are related to each other by physical adjacency on the storage medium. In other words, segments are arranged physically in hierarchical sequence. The major difference between HSAM and HISAM is in the way that root segments are retrieved. In HSAM data bases, no provision is made for directly accessing a particular root segment. All segments, including root segments, are stored in hierarchical sequence, and random retrieval of a root segment is performed by scanning through all the segments, up to that root. In a HISAM data base, either an ISAM or VSAM index contains pointers to all the root segments. The index is used to gain direct access to root segments.

The Hierarchical Direct Organization

In the Hierarchical Direct Organization, DL/I uses direct address pointers to chain together in hierarchical sequence all the segment occurrences in a data base record. As in the Hierarchical Sequential Organization, the main difference between HDAM and HIDAM is in the way that an individual root segment is accessed. With HDAM, a randomizing routine is used to translate a root key value into the actual physical location of that root segment. With HIDAM, DL/I uses a separate index data base to locate root segments.

The DL/I Physical Access Methods

To implement the various access methods, DL/I employs most of the standard operating system access methods. These include QSAM, BSAM, VSAM, and ISAM. DL/I also employs a special DL/I physical access method called OSAM, for *Overflow Sequential Access Method.* We'll be talking about how DL/I uses these physical access methods when we discuss each DL/I access method in detail. We should make a few comments about OSAM here, because it is a special physical access method, unique to DL/I.

In general, OSAM combines many of the good features of the sequential access methods and of BDAM. An OSAM data set looks exactly like a sequential data set to the operating system. In fact an OSAM data set can be read with BSAM or QSAM. Like the sequential access methods, OSAM allows either fixed-length, or fixed-length blocked records, and an OSAM data set does not have to be preformatted. However, like a BDAM data set, OSAM allows direct access to records. You'll see how OSAM data sets are used to implement many of the DL/I access methods when we discuss each one in more detail.

The Two Hierarchical Sequential Access Methods

As we mentioned earlier, the Hierarchical Sequential Organization supports two major access methods, HSAM and HISAM. In both access methods, the segments within each data base record are stored in hierarchical sequence on the storage medium. HISAM supports an index which DL/I uses to locate root segments for you, but HSAM does not. Let's take a look first at the physical format of segments as they are stored in either HSAM or HISAM data bases.

The Hierarchical Sequential Segment Format

HSAM and HISAM segments have the same format. Each segment consists of a segment prefix followed by data. (See figure 12.1.) In both HSAM and HISAM, the segment prefix consists of just two bytes. The first byte contains a binary number called a *segment code* which identifies the segment type. The segment codes of all the segment types are generated automatically during DBDGEN. They correspond to the hierarchical sequence of the segment types, as defined by the sequence of the SEGM statements in the DBD. For example, the root segment always has a segment code of 1. The second segment type defined has a segment code of 2, and so on.

The second byte of the prefix is the *delete byte*. This byte is maintained by DL/I and is used in handling segment deletions.

Neither of the two prefix bytes is available to the application program when retrieving or manipulating segments. The first byte of the data portion of the segment is the first byte that's stored in the application program's I/O area.

HSAM—Hierarchical Sequential Access Method

HSAM uses one of the standard operating system Sequential Access Methods, either BSAM or QSAM. HSAM is used mainly for applications that require very little random access to segments and that process segments mainly in hierarchical sequence. HSAM is generally considered to be a special-purpose

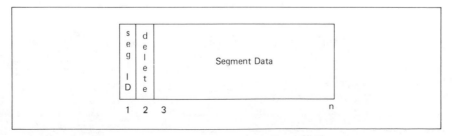

Figure 12.1 Hierarchical sequential segment format

access method because it imposes restrictions that are much too severe for most data base applications.

HSAM DATA BASE EXAMPLE. Figure 12.2 shows how segments from the HOSPITAL data base would be stored in an HSAM data base. We'll assume here that the data base consists only of HOSPITAL, WARD, and FACILITY segments. The data base consists of a standard sequential file, containing fixed-length, unblocked records. Segments are stored in hierarchical sequence, and each block contains as many segments as will fit. Segments can't span more than one block, so if a new segment won't fit at the end of the current block, that space is wasted and the segment is put at the beginning of the next block.

Notice that root segments are treated no differently than dependent segments. The root segment for the second data base record simply follows the last dependent segment occurrence of the first data base record. If there's room for it in the current block, it's placed there; if not, it's put in a new block.

Only certain DL/I calls are valid for HSAM data bases. These are: Get-Next, Get-Unique, and Insert in the load mode. HSAM segments may not be deleted, replaced, or inserted. To update an HSAM data base, an application must process the old HSAM data base as input and create a new HSAM data base using Insert Calls in the load mode.

HSAM DBD AND PSB STATEMENTS. HSAM processing will be more clear if you look at figures 12.3 and 12.4. In figure 12.3 is a possible DBD and PSB for an HSAM data base. Figure 12.4 shows parts of a sample update program using that PSB.

Notice that in the DBD two DD names are specified in the DATASET statement. One DD name, named DD1, is for the input data base, and the other, named DD2, is for the output data base. Notice that the PSB contains two PCBs. The first PCB is for the input data base and the second is for output. The update program issues a series of Get-Next calls using the first PCB and

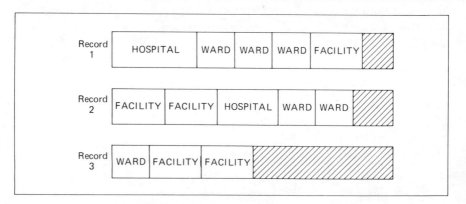

Figure 12.2 An HSAM data base

```
DBD        NAME=HOSPITAL,ACCESS=HSAM
DATASET    DD1=INPUT,DD2=OUTPUT,DEVICE=TAPE
SEGM       ...
  .
  .
  .
FIELD      ...
DBDGEN
FINISH
END



PCB        TYPE=DB,PROCOPT=G,NAME=HOSPITAL
SENSEG     ...
  .
  .
  .
SENSEG     ...
PCB        TYPE=DB,PROCOPT=LS,NAME=HOSPITAL
SENSEG     ...
  .
  .
  .
SENSEG
PSBGEN     LANG=COBOL,PSBNAME=HSAMPSB
END
```

Figure 12.3 HSAM, DBD and PSB coding


```
  .
  .
  .
LINKAGE SECTION.
01  INPUT-PCB.
  .
  .
  .
01  OUTPUT-PCB.
  .
  .
  .
PROCEDURE DIVISION.
    ENTRY 'DLITCBL' USING INPUT-PCB OUTPUT-PCB.
  .
  .
  .
    CALL    'CBLTDLI' USING GET-NEXT
                            INPUT-PCB
                            INPUT-AREA.
  .
  .
  .
    CALL    'CBLTDLI' USING INSERT
                            OUTPUT-PCB
                            OUTPUT-AREA
                            UNQUAL-SSA.
  .
  .
  .
```

Figure 12.4 An HSAM program

a series of Insert calls using the second PCB. In this way the application program reads the old version of the data base and writes out a new version, processing whatever updates are required. As you might guess, this is pretty close to the way that traditional file-oriented programs operate. It illustrates why HSAM data bases are not normally suited to general data base applications.

Since Delete calls are not allowed for HSAM data bases, DL/I does not manipulate the delete byte in the prefix of an HSAM segment. It's there for compatibility with the other access methods.

GET-UNIQUE PROCESSING WITH HSAM. A short discussion of how HSAM handles Get-Unique calls will help you see how inefficient HSAM can be for random retrieval. The first Get-Unique call that you make in your application program always causes DL/I to start at the beginning of the HSAM data base. DL/I then scans forward until the segment is located. What happens when you make subsequent Get-Unique calls depends on the answers to the following questions:

Is there a key field defined for your root segment? (HSAM is the only access method that does not require a key field for the root segment.)

Is your processing option defined as PROCOPT=G or PROCOPT= GS?

If you do have a sequence field defined for the root segment, is your root key greater than or less than the key used in the last Get-Unique call?

If there is no key field defined for your root segment, DL/I will always start at the beginning of the data base for each Get-Unique call. If your root segment has a key field defined, then DL/I attempts to make use of current position in handling Get-Unique calls. If your second Get-Unique call specifies a root key that's greater than the root key specified in the last Get-Unique call, DL/I moves forward in the data base from the current position.

When you ask DL/I to move backward in the data base by specifying a root key that is lower in value than the root key of the last segment retrieved, the search is handled differently, depending on whether a processing option of G or GS was specified in the PCB. If a processing option of G was specified, DL/I scans backward in the data base from current position in searching for your segment. If a processing option of GS was specified, DL/I starts at the beginning of the data base.

HSAM data bases are most often used when it's necessary to maintain data in the form of a DL/I data base, and the data is not used very often, such as in the case of historical data.

SHSAM—SIMPLE HSAM (IMS/VS ONLY). There is a variation of HSAM, available only with IMS/VS, that is used from time to time to gain some compatibility with standard operating system data sets. An SHSAM data base is a data base consisting of only root segments. When you load an SHSAM data base, segments are loaded without segment prefixes. This makes the segment occurrences look exactly like records in a standard operating system data set. With SHSAM, you can load a root-only data base using DL/I calls, and later process the segments with a non-DL/I program using standard operating system access methods. The applications for SHSAM are rather limited.

HISAM—Hierarchical Indexed Sequential Access Method

HISAM is a popular access method which, although still oriented to sequential processing of segments, allows you to use all the DL/I calls. The main difference between HSAM and HISAM is in the way that root segments are accessed. In HSAM no special provision is made for root segments, but in HISAM, a VSAM or ISAM index is used to locate root segments. Dependent segments within each data base record are stored sequentially, much like HSAM.

HISAM DATA SET STRUCTURE. A HISAM data base always consists of at least two data sets. In the DBD for a HISAM data base, the data base administrator can specify that either VSAM or the ISAM/OSAM combination be used to implement the data base. (See figure 12.5.) If VSAM is chosen, the data base will consist of a KSDS and an ESDS. If the ISAM/OSAM combination is chosen, an ISAM data set and an OSAM data set are used to store the segments.

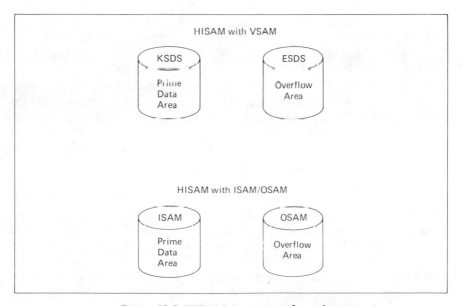

Figure 12.5 HISAM data set configurations

The KSDS or ISAM portion of a HISAM data base contains at least all of the root segments in the data base. The KSDS or ISAM index contains a pointer to each root segment within the data portion of the KSDS or ISAM data set. The ESDS or OSAM data set contains all of the dependent segments that don't fit in the KSDS or ISAM data set.

Figure 12.6 will make it more clear how this works. The example uses ISAM/OSAM, but the VSAM version is very similar. Figure 12.6 shows how a portion of a HISAM data base looks after the data base has been loaded. There is one logical record in the ISAM data set for each data base record. Each logical record contains at least a root segment for a data base record and as many of the dependent segments, in hierarchical sequence, as will fit. The segments that don't fit in the ISAM logical record are stored in one or more logical records in the OSAM data set.

Notice that each logical record in both the ISAM and the OSAM data sets has a pointer to the next record containing dependent segments for that data base record. The need for this pointer will be more clear if you look at what happens after a few segments have been added to a data base record.

ADDING SEGMENTS TO A HISAM DATA BASE. Figure 12.7 shows what can happen in the OSAM data set after a PATIENT segment is added to the first data base record. Notice that the dependent segments are maintained in *hierarchical* sequence with pointers, but they don't necessarily remain in *physical* sequence in the OSAM data set. This is quite a departure from HSAM, where segments are always maintained strictly in physical sequence.

HISAM DISADVANTAGES. Some of the drawbacks of HISAM are apparent if you examine figure 12.7 closely. Suppose you wanted to access the FACILITY segments for a particular hospital. But you aren't interested in any of the WARD, PATIENT, SYMPTOM, TREATMNT, or DOCTOR segments. Since all segments in a data base record are maintained in hierarchical sequence, it's necessary to read through all preceding segment occurrences to get to the first occurrence of the FACILITY segment. As it's likely that each data base record in the HOSPITAL data base will be quite large, HISAM would be an extremely inefficient access method to use if you were going to require random access to FACILITY segments.

In general HISAM is a good access method to use when you need random access to root segments within the data base, when data base records are fairly small, or when access to dependent segments will be sequential. Also, keep in mind that if your data base will be subject to a lot of additions and deletions, HISAM tends to be rather inefficient.

HISAM DBD STATEMENTS. Figure 12.8 shows a DBD for a HISAM data base. Notice that, as in HSAM, two DD statements are required for a HISAM data base. The first, named DD1, describes either the KSDS or the ISAM data

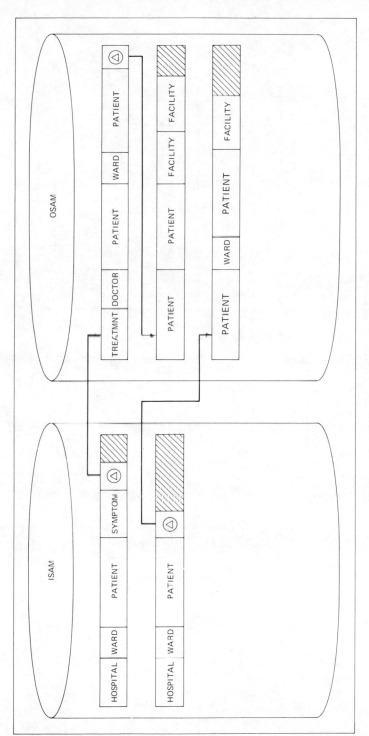

Figure 12.6 HISAM with ISAM/OSAM

201

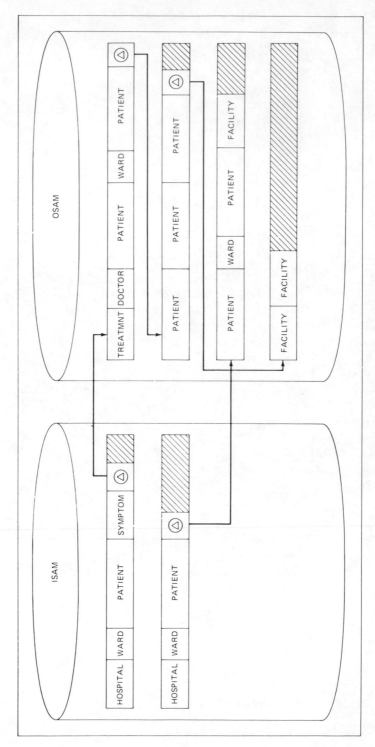

Figure 12.7 Adding a PATIENT segment to the first data base record

set. The second DD statement, named OVFLW, describes either the ESDS or the OSAM data set.

SHISAM—simple HISAM (IMS/VS ,only). As with HSAM, HISAM in IMS/VS also allows a variation which provides some compatibility with standard operating system access methods. When you load a root-only SHISAM data base, segments are loaded without prefixes. Since SHISAM allows only root segments, the ESDS or OSAM data set is not used. Root segments are always stored in the KSDS or ISAM data set in HISAM or SHISAM.

An SHISAM data base consists of a standard VSAM KSDS or an ISAM file which can be processed by non-DL/1 programs using standard VSAM or ISAM. As with SHSAM, SHISAM is available only with IMS/VS.

The Two Hierarchical Direct Access Methods

As in the hierarchical sequential storage organization, the hierarchical direct organization supports two access methods. They're called HDAM for *Hierarchical Direct Access Method* and HIDAM for *Hierarchical Indexed Direct Access Method*. With either of the hierarchical direct access methods, segments are stored in either an ESDS, if you're using VSAM, or an OSAM data set, if you're using the ISAM/OSAM combination.

HD Segment Format

As you just read, segments in a hierarchical sequential data base are related to each other by their physical sequence in the data base. The physical sequence of segments as they're stored in a hierarchical direct data base does not normally relate to hierarchical sequence. Segments in a hierarchical direct data base are related to each other by direct address pointers that are stored within each segment.

Figure 12.9 shows the format of a hierarchical direct segment. The first two bytes contain the segment code and the delete byte, as do hierarchical sequential segments. Following those two bytes is an area reserved for the direct address pointers used to chain segments together. This area varies in

```
DBD        NAME=HOSPITAL,ACCESS=(HISAM,ISAM)
DATASET    DD1=PRIME,OVFLW=OVERFLOW,DEVICE=3330
SEGM       ...
  .
  .
  .
FIELD      ...
DBDGEN
FINISH
END
```

Figure 12.8 HISAM DBD statements

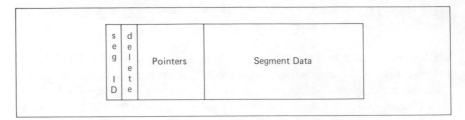

Figure 12.9 Hierarchical direct segment format

format depending on the type of pointers that have been requested in the DBD for each segment type. Following the pointer area is the data area of the segment.

HD Access Method Characteristics

HD data base performance frequently depends on the size of your data base records and the types of pointers that you specify. In general, however, access to segments within a hierarchical direct data base record can often be much faster than access in the hierarchical sequential organization. Both HDAM and HIDAM work similarly within a data base record. The difference between the two access methods is in the way that root segments are accessed.

HDAM ROOT SEGMENT ACCESS. In HDAM, a *randomizing routine,* identified in the DBD, is used to access root segments. A randomizing routine is a special program, usually written by a system programmer, that converts a root-key value into the actual location within the data base where that root segment is stored.

The biggest problem with randomizing routines is that they invariably produce *synonyms.* A synonym occurs when the randomizing routine tries to store more than one root segment in the same location in the data base. HDAM can deal with synonyms; however, they cause inefficiencies. A good randomizing routine will produce few synonyms, a bad one can create a lot. The more synonyms your randomizing routine creates, the less efficient the HDAM data base is.

After a data base has been loaded using a randomizing routine, the physical sequence of the root segment usually bears no resemblance to the logical sequence of segments based on the sequence of the root keys. This causes HDAM to be poorly suited to sequential processing. In fact, if you try to issue a series of Get-Next calls on root segments, DL/I bypasses the randomizing routine and gets you the root segments in a sequence roughly equivalent to physical sequence, not in root key sequence. This can be a problem in applications that require access to root segments in root-key sequence. You can only retrieve root segments in root-key sequence if you know what all the key values are.

HDAM DBD STATEMENTS. When the DBA codes the DBDGEN statements for both HDAM and HIDAM DBDs, there is an additional responsibility of choosing pointer types. Pointers are specified in the SEGM statements for each segment type, and the way they're chosen is identical for both HDAM and HIDAM data bases. For this reason, we'll look at pointers later in the chapter. First, we'll talk about HDAM and HIDAM differences, and we'll look at the DBDGEN statements that are different for HDAM and HIDAM. Figure 12.10 shows statements in an HDAM DBD.

We won't be going into HDAM DBD coding in detail in this book, but here's what the important operands mean. The ACCESS parameter specifies that the data base is an HDAM data base. The RMNAME operand is required for HDAM. The first subparameter gives the load module name of the randomizing routine that HDAM is to use in accessing root segments. The numbers following the randomizing module name specify information about the physical nature of the ESDS or OSAM data set that is used to store segments. Values for these parameters are chosen by the DBA, and have a big effect on the efficiency of the data base.

```
DBD       NAME=HOSPITAL,ACCESS=HDAM,RMNAME=(RANDMOD,1,125,400)
DATASET   DD1=HDAMDD,DEVICE=3330
SEGM      ...
  .
  .
  .
FIELD     ...
DBDGEN
FINISH
END
```

Figure 12.10 HDAM DBD statements

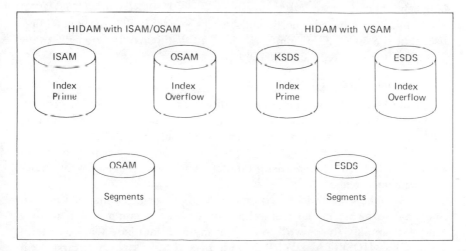

Figure 12.11 HIDAM data set configurations

HIDAM Root Segment Access

In HIDAM, a randomizing routine is not used to locate root segments. Instead, an index points to root segments that are stored in the ESDS or OSAM data set. Actually, a HIDAM data base is a combination of two data bases. Figure 12.11 shows the way a HIDAM data base would be set up using either VSAM or the ISAM/OSAM combination.

Using VSAM, a combination of a KSDS and an ESDS is used to maintain an index to root segments which are stored in a separate ESDS data set containing the segments. The index portion of the data base is actually a separate data base and can be processed apart from the data for some applications.

The ISAM/OSAM combination works in a similar manner. A combination of an ISAM data set and an OSAM data set makes up the index, which points to root segments in the separate OSAM data set.

A little used data set combination allows you to use VSAM to maintain the index portion of the data base and OSAM for the segments. This configuration might be useful in a conversion from IMS/360 to IMS/VS.

HIDAM solves both the synonym problem and the problem of retrieving root segments in key sequence. It's ideally suited to applications that require a more or less even split of sequential and random retrieval. The price you pay is that random access to roots is through an index, which requires storage space.

HIDAM DBD Statements

Figure 12.12 shows the main DBD statements for a HIDAM data base. Notice that a HIDAM data base requires two separate and distinct DBDs. The first DBD is for the HIDAM index, and the second is for the data portion.

The boxes in the diagram show how the various operands in the DBD statements hook the two DBDs together. A new DBD statement, LCHILD, is used to connect the index portion of the data base to the data portion. Notice, also, that the ACCESS operands are used to distinguish between the index portion of the data base and the data portion.

Hierarchical Direct Pointers

When the DBA sets up a hierarchical direct data base, pointers are chosen individually for each segment type. The more pointers that the DBA chooses, the faster access will be to segments within a data base record. But on the other hand, the more pointers that are specified, the more space will be taken up within each segment occurrence for pointers. Each pointer occupies four bytes in a segment's prefix.

Let's take a quick look now at the kinds of pointers that can be specified for segments in the hierarchical direct organization and how they work. To simplify things we'll look at a physical data base that consists of nothing but HOSPITAL, WARD, and FACILITY segments. First we'll

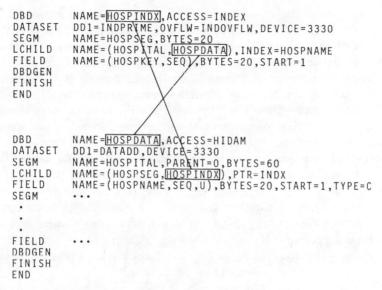

```
DBD        NAME=HOSPINDX,ACCESS=INDEX
DATASET    DD1=INDPRIME,OVFLW=INDOVFLW,DEVICE=3330
SEGM       NAME=HOSPSEG,BYTES=20
LCHILD     NAME=(HOSPITAL,HOSPDATA),INDEX=HOSPNAME
FIELD      NAME=(HOSPKEY,SEQ),BYTES=20,START=1
DBDGEN
FINISH
END


DBD        NAME=HOSPDATA,ACCESS=HIDAM
DATASET    DD1=DATADD,DEVICE=3330
SEGM       NAME=HOSPITAL,PARENT=0,BYTES=60
LCHILD     NAME=(HOSPSEG,HOSPINDX),PTR=INDX
FIELD      NAME=(HOSPNAME,SEQ,U),BYTES=20,START=1,TYPE=C
SEGM       ...
  .
  .
  .
FIELD      ...
DBDGEN
FINISH
END
```

Figure 12.12 HIDAM DBDGEN statements

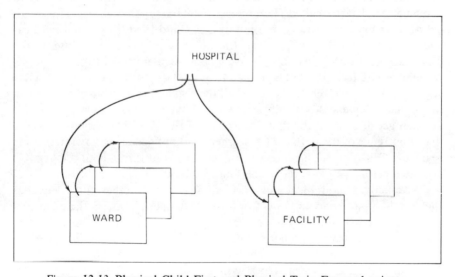

Figure 12.13 Physical Child First and Physical Twin Forward pointers

look at the kinds of pointers that the DBA gets when nothing about pointers is coded in the DBDGEN statements. These are the default pointers. They're called *Physical Child First* and *Physical Twin Forward* pointers. You can see these for the HOSPITAL, WARD, and FACILITY segments in Figure 12.13.

PHYSICAL CHILD FIRST AND PHYSICAL TWIN FORWARD POINTERS. The pointers from the HOSPITAL segment to the WARD and FACILITY segments are Physical Child First pointers. They point from a parent segment to the first occurrence of each of that parent's physical child segment types.

The other pointers are Physical Twin Forward pointers. In figure 12.13 you can see that there are three WARD segments stored under the HOSPITAL segment occurrence. The Physical Twin Forward pointers chain the three WARD segment occurrences together. The Physical Twin Forward pointers point from each occurrence of a particular segment type to the next occurrence of that same segment type, forming a *twin chain*.

You can also see Physical Twin Forward pointers for the FACILITY segment in figure 12.13. Physical Child First pointers and Physical Twin Forward pointers work together. If a particular segment type has a Physical Child First pointer pointing to it from its parent, it must also have Physical Twin Forward pointers. If there is only a single occurrence of a child segment type, space is still reserved for a Physical Twin Forward pointer. It would indicate the end of the twin chain.

HIERARCHICAL POINTERS. Figure 12.14 shows another type of pointer that can be used instead of the Physical Child First and Physical Twin Forward combination. They're called *Hierarchical* pointers. On first glance, Hierarchical pointers look very similar to the Physical Child First/Physical Twin Forward combination. The difference is that there is only a single pointer in the parent segment rather than one for each child segment type. In the example, the first FACILITY segment is pointed to by the last occurrence of the WARD segment. With Hierarchical pointers, all the segments are chained together in hierarchical sequence. With Physical Child First pointers, as in figure 12.13, you can get directly to the first occurrence of the WARD segment or to the first occurrence of the FACILITY segment without accessing any intervening segments. With Hierarchical pointers, you must read through all the WARD segments before you can get to the first FACILITY segment.

Actually, Hierarchical pointers chain segments together in the sequence they would be stored in an HSAM or HISAM data base. But, in the hierarchical direct organization they're chained together with direct address pointers and are not necessarily stored in physical sequence within the data base.

Physical Child First pointers can be used when you would like direct access to particular segment types within the data base. Hierarchical pointers can be used in portions of a data base record where access will normally be sequential. You'll see in a minute how the data base administrator can request different types of pointers in different portions of the data base record. Before we get to that, let's look at some variations of the three main pointer types.

POINTER VARIATIONS. Each of the three types of pointers, Physical Child First, Physical Twin Forward, and Hierarchical, have a second variation. With

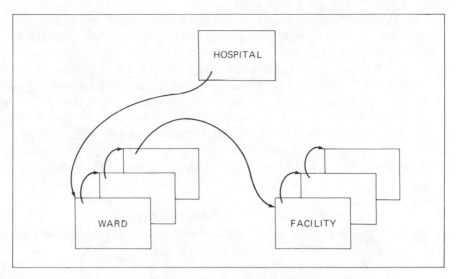

Figure 12.14 Hierarchical pointers

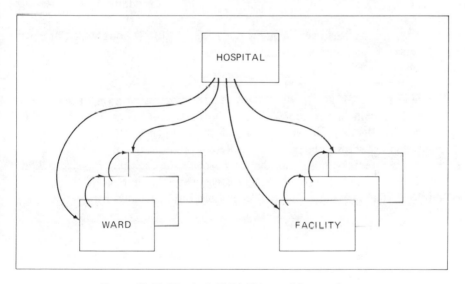

Figure 12.15 Physical Child First and Last pointers

Physical Child pointers, the DBA can specify either Physical Child First pointers, which you've already seen, or *Physical Child First and Last* pointers. Physical Child First and Last pointers are shown in figure 12.15.

As you can see, when these types of pointers are specified, each HOSPITAL segment occurrence will have four pointers in its prefix, rather than only two when Physical Child First pointers are used. There's a pointer to the first occurrence of each child segment type and also a pointer to the last occurrence of each child segment type. When physical child pointers are used, the DBA must specify either Physical Child First pointers or Physical Child First and Last pointers. The DBA cannot specify only Physical Child Last pointers. Physical Child Last pointers allow quicker access to the last occurrence of a particular segment type for ease of segment insertion at the ends of long twin chains.

Physical twin pointers also have two variations. In addition to the Physical Twin Forward pointers that you've already seen, the DBA can choose *Physical Twin Forward and Backward pointers.* Figure 12.16 shows what Physical Twin Forward and Backward pointers would look like in a chain of WARD segments. In addition to a set of pointers pointing forward along the twin chain, a second set of pointers points backward along the twin chain. The combination of Physical Twin Forward and Backward pointers can improve segment deletion performance in long twin chains.

The second variation of Hierarchical pointers is called *Hierarchical Forward and Backward.* Hierarchical Forward and Backward pointers work in a similar manner to Physical Twin Forward and Backward pointers. Figure 12.17 shows this pointer variation. In addition to a set of pointers pointing forward along the hierarchical path, there's also a set of pointers pointing backward. Again, the main use for Hierarchical Forward and Backward pointers is to improve segment deletion performance in long twin chains.

COMBINATIONS OF POINTERS. Figure 12.18 shows a portion of an entire HOSPITAL data base record. We can't show all occurrences of each segment type because the diagram would be much too confusing. The segment occurrences that are shown illustrate how different pointer types can be chosen for different segments within a data base record. In the example, Physical Child First pointers are used in the HOSPITAL segment to point to both the WARD and the FACILITY segments. However, both Physical Child First and Physi-

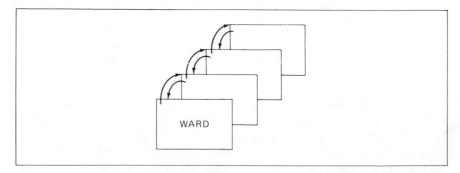

Figure 12.16 Physical Twin Forward and Backward pointers

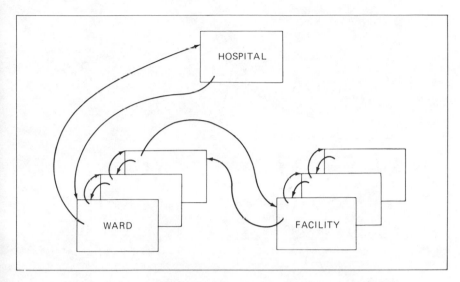

Figure 12.17 Hierarchical Forward and Backward pointers

cal Child Last pointers have been chosen to point from the WARD segment to the PATIENT segment.

Also, Physical Twin Forward and Backward pointers were chosen for the PATIENT segment, although Physical Child First pointers only are specified for the WARD and FACILITY segments. And finally, Hierarchical pointers have been chosen for the SYMPTOM, TREATMNT, and DOCTOR segments. This would be a good choice if we were always going to process those segment types sequentially, and it was a good bet that we would not process the DOCTOR segments without first processing the SYMPTOM and TREATMNT segments.

In this particular example we don't have an example of Hierarchical Forward and Backward pointers. Actually, this is a pretty rare pointer combination; you won't see it used very often.

CHOOSING POINTER TYPES. Pointer types are specified in the SEGM statements of the DBD for the data base. Figure 12.19 shows the SEGM statements for the pointer combination in figure 12.18. The PARENT and POINTER operands are used to specify pointer types for each segment in the data base.

Pointer Selection Rules

As was mentioned earlier, Physical Child First and Physical Twin Forward pointers are set up if no mention of pointers is made in the SEGM statements for an HD data base. Pointer selection is a fairly complicated subject, and we won't be going into it in any great detail here. There are a few simple rules that illustrate how pointers are chosen, however.

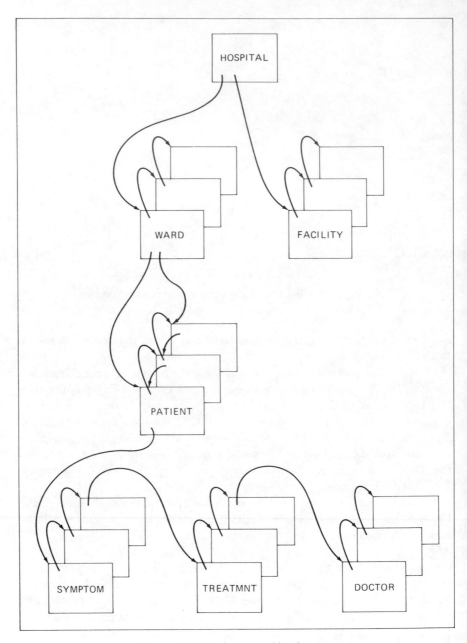

Figure 12.18 Pointer combinations

```
SEGM    NAME=HOSPITAL,PARENT=0

SEGM    NAME=WARD,PARENT=(HOSPITAL,SNGL),PTR=TWIN

SEGM    NAME=PATIENT,PARENT=(WARD,SNGL),PTR=TB

SEGM    NAME=SYMPTOM,PARENT=(PATIENT,SNGL),PTR=HIER

SEGM    NAME=TREATMNT,PARENT=PATIENT,PTR=HIER

SEGM    NAME=DOCTOR,PARENT=PATIENT,PTR=HIER

SEGM    NAME=FACILITY,PARENT=(HOSPITAL,SNGL),PTR=TWIN
```

Figure 12.19 SEGM statements for pointer combination example

Pointer Rule 1. There are two main types of pointers to choose from, the Physical Child/Physical Twin Combination, and Hierarchical pointers. For a given segment type, these are mutually exclusive.

Pointer Rule 2. When you code the POINTER operand in a SEGM statement, the pointers that you specify will reside in the segment named in that SEGM statement. You may choose either Physical Twin pointers or Hierarchical pointers in the POINTER operand.

Pointer Rule 3. The second subparameter of the PARENT operand can be used to select Physical Child pointers. When you code this subparameter, the pointers will reside in the segment's parent. This means that you cannot ask for physical child pointers in the PARENT operand if this segment's parent has hierarchical pointers specified in a POINTER operand. Physical Child pointers and Hierarchical pointers are mutually exclusive in this context.

Data Set Groups

There's one more topic to mention while we're on the subject of access methods, the concept of *data set groups*. Most access methods allow the data base administrator to separate segments into groups. Each group of segments may be stored in its own data set or group of data sets. This is done quite frequently when different segment types are subject to different maintenance requirements. For example, only a few segment types may require frequent updating, while the rest of the data base will remain fairly static. It's best to create one or more data set groups for segments that are subject to heavy maintenance requirements, because often it's possible to reorganize only a single data set group rather than the entire data base.

Data set groups have no effect on an application program, other than to sometimes increase its efficiency, so they are not normally of interest to the application programmer. However, additional DD statements are required in the JCL for an application program accessing a data base organized into data set groups. A DD statement is needed for each data set that makes up the data base.

CHAPTER 12 EXERCISES

1. Figure 12.20 shows the four major IMS access methods. Below is a list of statements. Match each statement with the access method or methods the statement best describes.

Statements

a. Access to root segments is via an index.
b. Access to all segments is sequential.
c. Dependent segments are accessed via direct address pointers.
d. Segments have a two-byte prefix area.
e. Simple root-only data bases are supported where segments have no prefix area.
f. Get-Next calls do not retrieve root segments in key sequence.
g. Dependent segments are accessed sequentially.
h. Normally the best access methods to use for a mixture of sequential and direct retrievals.
i. Segment prefix normally bigger than two bytes.
j. Normally the best access method if all or most retrievals will be random.
k. Normally used only for sequential retrieval or for historical files.
l. Best for limited random retrievals and low volume of updating.
m. Root segments are accessed via a randomizing routine.
n. Requires two separate DBDs.
o. Requires pointer in segments.

HSAM —Hierarchical Sequential Access Method

HISAM—Hierarchical Indexed Sequential Access Method

HDAM —Hierarchical Direct Access Method

HIDAM—Hierarchical Indexed Direct Access Method

Figure 12.20 The four major access methods

1. Physical Child First

2. Physical Twin Forward

3. Hierarchical

4. Physical Child First and Last

5. Physical Twin Forward and Backward

6. Hierarchical Forward and Backward

Figure 12.21 The six main pointer types

2. Figure 12.21 shows the six pointer combinations that may be specified for segments in a hierarchical direct data base. Below are six statements, each of which describes one of the pointer combinations. Match each pointer combination with the statement that best describes it.

Statements

a. Segments are chained in a forward direction in hierarchical sequence.
b. Pointers are maintained in both forward and backward directions along a twin chain.
c. A parent segment contains a pointer to the first occurrence of each of its dependent segment types on the next lowest level.
d. Segments are chained in both forward and backward directions in hierarchical sequence.
e. A parent segment contains pointers to the first and last occurrence of its dependent segment types at the next lower level.
f. Pointers are maintained in a forward direction along a twin chain.

IMS JCL Coding

JCL coding for IMS programs is very complex and involved, especially for IMS DB/DC systems. For this reason, IMS JCL is normally handled by the data base administration group, and application programmers normally gain access to IMS through cataloged procedures. Some knowledge of IMS JCL, however, can give you some insight into how the various parts of IMS relate to one another. So in this appendix, while we can't cover the subject of IMS JCL in great detail, we will hit the high points of the JCL for a few common situations.

The examples in this appendix consist of JCL that might be used in an IMS/VS shop. The main difference between IMS/VS JCL and the JCL used in an IMS/360 shop is in the names of the IMS system data sets. We won't cover DOS or DOS/VS JCL in this book. Let's start our discussion of JCL by looking at the names and uses of the most common IMS system data sets.

IMS/VS System Data Sets

There are many data sets that contain the components of IMS. The standard names for the more important of these data sets are listed in figure A.1. It's possible that your shop has changed the names of some of these data sets. If so, it's up to you to find out what the new names are. Even if your shop doesn't use the names exactly as they appear in the list, chances are they're similar. For example, many shops change the initial qualifier in the names, but retain the last qualifiers for ease of identification. This might be done in order to conform to installation naming conventions.

IMS/360 Differences

The only difference between the names of system data sets supplied with IMS/VS and IMS/360 is in the initial qualifier of each name. IMS/VS systems use an initial qualifier of IMSVS. The initial qualifier of the data sets supplied

IMSVS.RESLIB

IMSVS.PGMLIB

IMSVS.PSBLIB

IMSVS.DBDLIB

IMSVS.MACLIB

IMSVS.PROCLIB

IMSVS.ACBLIB

Figure A.1 Some IMS/VS system data sets

with IMS/360 systems is IMS2. (The "2" stands for version 2 of IMS/360.) For most of the examples in this appendix, simply substitute initial qualifiers of IMS2 for all instances of IMSVS and the JCL will be almost identical to IMS/360 JCL. We'll point out any other IMS/360 differences in each individual example.

The IMSVS.RESLIB Data Set

This system data set contains all the load modules that make up the IMS software, including both DL/I and the data communications component. The operating system must have access to this data set, or its equivalent, via a STEPLIB or JOBLIB DD statement whenever you execute an IMS program.

The IMSVS.PGMLIB Data Set

If your shop follows IBM's standard, all your IMS application program load modules are stored in this data set. The operating system must have access to this data set, as well as to IMSVS.RESLIB, whenever you execute an IMS program. Normally, the STEPLIB or JOBLIB statement specifies a concatenation of this data set with IMSVS.RESLIB. This standard is not followed in a lot of IMS shops, however, and in many cases, IMS application program load modules are stored in multiple load module libraries. The JCL that executes an IMS application must concatenate the appropriate IMS load module library with IMSVS.RESLIB, or its equivalent.

IMSVS.PSBLIB and IMSVS.DBDLIB

We've already talked about these two system data sets. They contain the DBDs and PSBs used by your installation. Again, many installations have a lot of libraries for DBDs and PSBs—often separate libraries for each application. It's important that your execution JCL references the right PSB and DBD libraries.

The IMSVS.MACLIB Data Set

This data set is normally used only by the data base administrator. It contains the definitions of the macros that are used to generate the IMS system and of other macros, such as the DBDGEN and PSBGEN macros.

The IMSVS.PROCLIB Data Set

The IMS cataloged procedures supplied with IMS are stored in this data set. Some installations store the IMS procedures used for application programs in this library. If this is the case, the reader procedure that's used to read in IMS jobs must reference this procedure library. In many cases, however, the IMS procedures are stored in the standard system procedure library, and IMSVS. PROCLIB is not used in daily production. The cataloged procedures shown in this appendix are some of the ones received from IBM in the IMSVS. PROCLIB data set.

The IMSVS.ACBLIB Data Set

The execution JCL example in chapter 3 showed that execution JCL must have access to the IMSVS.PSBLIB and IMSVS.DBDLIB data sets or their equivalents. There are exceptions to this rule. When you execute an IMS application program, IMS must combine the information in your DBD and PSB before the application program can be executed. To save IMS this trouble each time your program runs, the DBA may choose to merge the DBD and PSB information ahead of time. To do this, a procedure called ACBGEN, which stands for *Application Control Block Generation* is executed. The IMSVS.ACBLIB data set is used to store the combined DBDs and PSBs. When this is done, the execution JCL must reference IMSVS.ACBLIB rather than the PSBLIB and DBDLIB.

The use of the IMSVS.ACBLIB data set is optional for batch DL/I programs, but it is required for message processing and BMP programs. DBDs and PSBs must be merged ahead of time with an ACBGEN before MP or BMP programs can run. As with the other data sets, your shop may use other names for this data set, and you may have separate ACBLIBs for different applications.

The DBDGEN Procedure

The first set of JCL that we'll look at is the JCL in the DBDGEN procedure that's supplied with IMS/VS. The JCL that your shop uses to execute DBDGEN's may differ from the JCL in figure A.2, but it's probably quite similar. In the IMS/VS DBDGEN procedure, the two programs that are executed are the IFOX00 program and the DFSILNK0 program. These programs invoke the system assembler and linkage editor respectively. In

```
//       PROC  MBR=TEMPNAME,SOUT=A
//C      EXEC  PGM=IFOX00,REGION=120K,PARM='LOAD,NODECK'
//SYSLIB DD    DSN=IMSVS.MACLIB,DISP=SHR
//SYSGO  DD    UNIT=SYSDA,DISP=(,PASS),SPACE=(80,(100,100),RLSE),
//             DCB=(BLKSIZE=400,RECFM=FB,LRECL=80)
//SYSPRINT DD  SYSOUT=&SOUT,DCB=(LRECL=121,RECFM=FBM,BLKSIZE=605),
//             SPACE=(121,(500,500),RLSE,,ROUND)
//SYSUT1 DD    UNIT=SYSDA,DISP=(,DELETE),SPACE=(1700,(100,50))
//SYSUT2 DD    UNIT=SYSDA,DISP=(,DELETE),SPACE=(1700,(100,50))
//SYSUT3 DD    UNIT=(SYSDA,SEP=(SYSLIB,SYSUT1,SYSUT2)),
//             SPACE=(1700,(100,50))
//L      EXEC  PGM=DFSILNKO,PARM='XREF,LIST',COND=(0,LT,C),REGION=120K
//STEPLIB DD   DSN=IMSVS.RESLIB,DISP=SHR
//SYSLIN DD    DSN=*.C.SYSGO,DISP=(OLD,DELETE)
//SYSPRINT DD  SYSOUT=&SOUT,DCB=(LRECL=121,RECFM=FBA,BLKSIZE=605),
//             SPACE=(121,(100),RLSE)
//SYSLMOD DD   DSN=IMSVS.DBDLIB(&MBR),DISP=SHR
//SYSUT1 DD    UNIT=(SYSDA,SEP=(SYSLMOD,SYSLIN)),DISP=(,DELETE),
//             SPACE=(1024,(100,10),RLSE)
```

Figure A.2 The IMS/VS DBDGEN procedure

220

```
//DBD        EXEC  DBDGEN,MBR=HOSPITAL
//C.SYSIN    DD    *
             ---
             ---
             ---
        DBDGEN Cards
             ---
             ---
             ---
```

Figure A.3 Executing the DBDGEN procedure

IMS/360 JCL, the assembler and linkage editor are usually referenced directly in the JCL with the names IEUASM and IEWL.

The DBDGEN statements that define a DBD actually consist of Assembler Language macros. The DBDGEN procedure first invokes the assembler to process the DBDGEN macros producing an object module. The second step invokes the Linkage Editor which processes the object module passed from the first step. The Linkage Editor produces a DBD in load module form and stores it in DBDLIB.

The most useful symbolic parameter in this procedure is the MBR parameter. It allows you to substitute your own member name when you use the procedure. Figure A.3 shows the JCL you might use to invoke this procedure for a DBD named HOSPITAL. The MBR=HOSPITAL parameter causes the procedure to store the DBD into DBDLIB under the member name HOSPITAL.

The PSBGEN Procedure

We have not included a copy of the PSBGEN procedure here because it's almost identical to the DBDGEN procedure. Its name is PBSGEN instead of DBDGEN, and the SYSLMOD data set in the linkage editor step is IMSVS.PSBLIB instead of IMSVS.DBDLIB. It uses the MBR symbolic parameter to assign a member name to the resulting PSB.

The IMSCOBOL Procedure

This procedure is very similar to the standard procedure used to execute a COBOL compile and link edit job. The main differences are in the data sets used within the procedures. Let's look at the major differences between an IMS compile and link edit, and a normal one. The IMSCOBOL procedure for IMS/VS is shown in figure A.4.

The COBOL compile step is similar to any other COBOL compile. The main differences appear in the linkage editor step. The program being executed is DFSILNK0 instead of the normal IEWL. This program invokes the linkage

```
//C        PROC  MBR=,PAGES=60,SOUT=A
//C        EXEC  PGM=IKFCBL00,PARM='SIZE=130K,BUF=10K,LINECNT=50',REGION=150K
//SYSLIN   DD    DSN=&&LIN,DISP=(MOD,PASS),UNIT=SYSDA,
//               DCB=(LRECL=80,RECFM=FB,BLKSIZE=400),
//               SPACE=(CYL,(4,1),RLSE
//SYSPRINT DD    SYSOUT=&SOUT,DCB=(LRECL=121,BLKSIZE=605,RECFM=FBA),
//               SPACE=(605,(&PAGES,0,&PAGES),RLSE,,ROUND)
//SYSUT1   DD    UNIT=SYSDA,DISP=(DELETE),SPACE=(CYL,(10,1),RLSE)
//SYSUT2   DD    UNIT=SYSDA,DISP=(DELETE),SPACE=(CYL,(10,1),RLSE)
//SYSUT3   DD    UNIT=SYSDA,DISP=(DELETE),SPACE=(CYL,(10,1),RLSE)
//SYSUT4   DD    UNIT=SYSDA,DISP=(DELETE),SPACE=(CYL,(10,1),RLSE)
//L        EXEC  PGM=DFSILNK0,REGION=120K,PARM='XREF,LET,LIST',
//               COND=(4,LT,C)
//STEPLIB  DD    DSN=IMSVS.RESLIB,DISP=SHR
//SYSLIB   DD    DSN=SYS1.COBLIB,DISP=SHR
//         DD    DSN=SYS1.PL1LIB,DISP=SHR
//RESLIB   DD    DSN=IMSVS.RESLIB,DISP=SHR
//SYSLIN   DD    DSN=&&LIN,DISP=(OLD,DELETE),VOL=REF=*.C.SYSLIN
//         DD    DSN=IMSVS.PROCLIB(CBLTDLI),DISP=SHR
//         DD    DDNAME=SYSIN
//SYSLMOD  DD    DSN=IMSVS.PGMLIB(&MBR),DISP=SHR
//SYSPRINT DD    SYSOUT=&SOUT,DCB=(RECFM=FBA,LRECL=121,BLKSIZE=605),
//               SPACE=(605,(&PAGES,&PAGES),RLSE,,ROUND)
//SYSUT1   DD    UNIT=(SYSDA,SEP=(SYSLMOD,SYSLIN)),DISP=(,DELETE),
//               SPACE=(CYL,(10,1),RLSE)
```

Figure A.4 The IMS/VS IMSCOBOL procedure

editor. In IMS/360 JCL, the linkage editor is normally invoked directly by the JCL.

Notice the RESLIB DD statement. It gives the linkage editor access to the IMSVS.RESLIB data set or its equivalent. The SYSLIN DD statement concatenates three data sets. The first one is the temporary object module passed by the COBOL compile step. The second one is a member of the IMSVS.PROCLIB data set. This member contains a few linkage editor control statements that, among other things, causes a load module in IMSVS.RESLIB to be combined with the object module passed by the compiler. This sets up the required linkages between your program and DL/I. The third data set is the standard DDNAME=SYSIN that allows you to bring in additional input from the input stream.

The rest of the JCL is similar to other linkage editor JCLs. Notice that the SYSLMOD DD statement references the IMSVS.PGMLIB data set, and the MBR symbolic parameter assigns the load module name to the program.

Figure A.5 shows the JCL you might use to compile and link edit the

```
//COMP        EXEC  IMSCOBOL,MBR=HOSPLOAD
//C.SYSIN     DD    *
             ---
             ---
             ---
         COBOL Source Program
             ---
             ---
             ---
```

Figure A.5 Executing the IMSCOBOL procedure

```
//LOAD        EXEC  PGM=DFSRRC00,PARM='DLI,HOSPLOAD'
//STEPLIB     DD    DSN=IMSVS.RESLIB,DISP=SHR
//            DD    DSN=IMSVS.PGMLIB,DISP=SHR
//IMS         DD    DSN=IMSVS.PSBLIB,DISP=SHR
//            DD    DSN=IMSVS.DBDLIB,DISP=SHR
//SYSUDUMP    DD    SYSOUT=A
//PRIME       DD    DSN=IMSVS.PRIME(PRIME),DISP=(,KEEP),
//                  SPACE=(CYL,3,,CONTIG),VOL=SER=123456,
//                  UNIT=3330,DCB=DSORG=IS
//OVERFLOW    DD    DSN=IMSVS.OVFLW,DISP-(,KEEP),
//                  SPACE=(CYL,3,,CONTIG),VOL=SER=654321,
//                  UNIT=3330
//OUTPUT      DD    SYSOUT=A,DCB-BLKSIZE=1330
//INPUT       DD    *
             ---
             ---
             ---
      input data base load cards
             ---
             ---
             ---
```

Figure A.6 Executing the HOSPLOAD IMS batch program

HOSPLOAD program. Notice the MBR symbolic parameter is used to assign the name HOSPLOAD to the resulting load module.

IMS Execution JCL

Execution JCL for IMS programs is normally pretty complex. We'll look at three JCL examples to show the basics of execution JCL for batch DL/I programs. IMS DB/DC JCL is beyond the scope of this appendix. The thing to keep in mind here is that execution JCL is almost always supplied to the application programmer in the form of precoded cataloged procedures.

The first JCL example, in figure A.6, shows JCL to execute a single DL/I batch application program. In this case it's a data base load program called HOSPLOAD. This program reads an input file via a DD statement named INPUT and produces a report via a DD statement named OUTPUT. The data base is a HISAM data base that requires two DD statements named PRIME and OVERFLOW. These DD names are defined in the DATASET statement in the DBD for the data base.

In addition to the PRIME, OVERFLOW, INPUT, and OUTPUT DD statements, two other DD statements are required by IMS. These are the STEPLIB and IMS DD statements. The STEPLIB DD statement tells the operating system where the program libraries for this program are stored. For batch DL/I programs, the system must have access to the IMSVS.RESLIB and IMSVS.PGMLIB data sets or their equivalents. (A JOBLIB statement can, of course, take the place of the STEPLIB card.)

The IMS DD statement is used to tell IMS where the DBD and PSB for this program are stored. This is the place where you would substitute the IMSVS.ACBLIB data set for the DBDLIB and PSBLIB concatenation if the DBA combined the DBD and PSB by means of an ACBGEN.

The EXEC statement has the name of the DL/I region controller in the PGM= parameter. The characters "DLI" in the first three positions of the PARM field tell IMS that this is a DL/I batch application program. The second subparameter of the PARM operand specifies the name of the application load module being executed. Since only one name is specified, the name of the application program load module and the name of the PSB must be the same. Additional information can be specified in the PARM operand. You'll see what some of it is in the DLIBATCH procedure.

The DLIBATCH Procedure

IMS programs are seldom executed directly, as in the last example. They are usually invoked through the use of cataloged procedures. The DLIBATCH procedure is one of the ones supplied with IMS. It can be used to execute a batch DL/I program. Figure A.7 shows the DLIBATCH procedure. This is

```
//       PROC  MBR=TEMPNAME,SOUT=A,PSB=,BUF=,
//       SPIE=0,TEST=0,EXCPVR=0,RST=0,
//       PRLD=,SRCH=0,CKPTID=,MON=N
//G      EXEC  PGM=DFSRRC00,REGION=190K,
//       PARM=(DLI,&MBR,&PSB,&BUF,
//       &SPIE&TEST&EXCPVR&RST,&PRLD,&SRCH,&CKPTID,&MON)
//STEPLIB  DD  DSN=IMSVS.RESLIB,DISP=SHR
//         DD  DSN=IMSVS.PGMLIB,DISP=SHR
//IMS      DD  DSN=IMSVS.PSBLIB,DISP=SHR
//         DD  DSN=IMSVS.DBDLIB,DISP=SHR
//PROCLIB  DD  DSN=IMSVS.PROCLIB,DISP=SHR
//IEFRDER  DD  DSN=IMSLOG,DISP=(,KEEP),VOL=(,,,99),
//       UNIT=(2400,,DEFER),
//       DCB=(RECFM=VBS,BLKSIZE=1920,LRECL=1916,BUFNO=2)
//IEFRDER2 DD  DSN=IMSLOG2,DISP=(,KEEP),VOL=(,,,99),
//       UNIT=(2400,,DEFER,SEP=IEFRDER),
//       DCB=(RECFM=VBS,BLKSIZE=1920,LRECL=1916,BUFNO=2)
//SYSUDUMP DD  SYSOUT=&SOUT,DCB=(RECFM=FBA,LRECL=121,BLKSIZE=605),
//       SPACE=(605,(500,500),RLSE,,ROUND)
//IMSMON   DD  DUMMY
```

Figure A.7 The IMS/VS DLIBATCH procedure

225

```
//LOAD          EXEC  DLIBATCH,MBR=HOSPLOAD
//G.PRIME       DD    DSN=IMSVS.PRIME(PRIME),DISP=(,KEEP),
//                    SPACE=(CYL,3,,CONTIG),VOL=SER=123456,
//                    UNIT=3330,DCB=DSORG=IS
//G.OVERFLOW    DD    DSN=IMSVS.OVFLW,DISP=(,KEEP),
//                    SPACE=(CYL,3,,CONTIG),VOL=SER=654321,
//                    UNIT=3330
//G.OUTPUT      DD    SYSOUT=A,DCB=BLKSIZE=1330
//G.INPUT       DD    *
                ---
                ---
                ---
        input data base load cards
                ---
                ---
                ---
```

Figure A.8 Executing the DLIBATCH procedure for HOSPLOAD

the one that's supplied by IBM with IMS/VS. It's unlikely that your installation uses this procedure as is, however. A look at your version of the DLIBATCH procedure can tell you a lot about your installation's standards with respect to execution JCL.

Notice that a number of parameters are provided for specifying additional information in the PARM operand of the EXEC statement. If you're interested in what some of these values are used for, you can look them up in your *System Programming Reference Manual.* You should also check your own installation standards to see how to code these values.

The three extra DD statements included in DLIBATCH are the IEFRDER, IEFRDER2, and IMSMON DD statements. These are used for various logging and monitoring functions. Your installation standards are the best place to look to find out how these DD statements are used in your shop.

Figure A.8 shows an example of how the DLIBATCH procedure is invoked. Notice that the only additional DD statements required are the ones for your data base and your input and output files. The DD statements in the DLIBATCH procedure take care of all the standard IMS requirements.

B

IMS Debugging Hints

This appendix will give you some tools that you can use when one of your IMS application programs terminates abnormally and gives you a dump. These hints apply to IMS/VS and IMS/360 programs running under MFT, MVT, VS1, VS2 rel. 1 (SVS), or VS2 rel. 2 or later (MVS). We won't cover debugging for DOS/VS DL/I systems.

In general, the hints in this appendix will allow you to find your CALL statement parameter list, your PCBs, and a data area that will give you information about the last few DL/I calls that your program issued. Finding these areas in your dump will usually give you a big head start in diagnosing and fixing the problem.

In this appendix, we assume that you have a basic knowledge of the dump format for your operating system version, and are able to find your way around in a dump.

Locating Your Parameter List

The way that you locate the parameter list for your last DL/I Call depends on whether your program is a batch DL/I program, or a message processing or BMP program. If your program is a batch program the technique that you use is also slightly different for IMS/VS than it is for IMS/360. We'll show you all three techniques.

DL/I Batch Programs

To locate your parameter list in a batch DL/I program, you must first locate a particular DL/I load module in your dump. For IMS/VS, the name of the load module that you're looking for is DFSPRPX0; for IMS/360, it's DFSPRPL0. Figure B.1 summarizes this procedure for IMS/VS, and figure B.2 summarizes it for IMS/360.

The way that you locate the appropriate load module depends upon the particular operating system version your shop uses. But after you've located

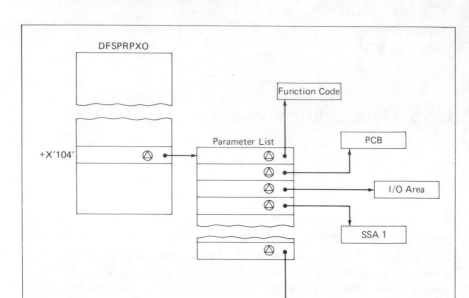

Figure B.1 Locating the parameter list (IMS/VS batch)

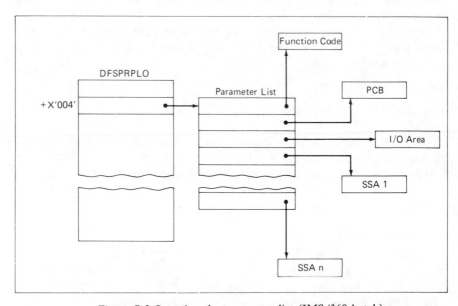

Figure B.2 Locating the parameter list (IMS/360 batch)

the load module, an address within that load module points directly to the first word of your parameter list. For IMS/VS, add hex "104" to the entry point address (EPA) of DFSPRPX0. For IMS/360, add hex "004" to the EPA of DFSPRPL0.

This points you to a fullword address that points directly to the first word of your parameter list. After you locate your parameter list, you can use the addresses in that list to find all the DL/I-related data areas in your program. You can also find your PCB. This often gives you all the information that you need to identify the problem and correct it.

MP and BMP Programs

When you're working with a message processing or BMP program, the technique that you use to find the parameter list for your last call is even easier than it is for a batch program. However, the technique varies slightly depending on the version of IMS you're using. The technique for the latest releases of IMS/VS (Version 1, Release 1.1 and later) is different from the technique that you use for IMS/360 and IMS/VS releases prior to 1.1.1. We'll show both techniques here.

IMS/VS VERSION 1, RELEASE 1.1 AND LATER. If you're using IMS/VS version 1 at Release 1.1 or later look for the *save area trace* portion of your dump. Then locate the register printout corresponding to the first occurrence of DFSPR020 WAS ENTERED VIA CALL in the PROCEEDING BACK VIA REG 13 portion of the save area trace. Register 1 in that register printout points directly to your CALL statement parameter list. Figure B.3 summarizes this procedure for all releases of IMS.

IMS/360 AND EARLY IMS/VS RELEASES. If you're using IMS/360 or a release of IMS/VS prior to Version 1 release 1.1, simply look for the portion of the dump that lists the contents of the REGS AT ENTRY TO ABEND. This will

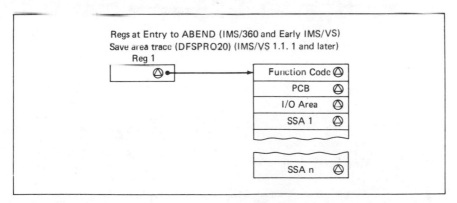

Figure B.3 Locating the parameter list (MP or BMP programs)

appear immediately before the main or virtual storage printout. Register 1 in that register printout points directly to your parameter list.

Locating Your PCBs

By locating the parameter list for your last DL/I call, you also find the PCB used by that call. That's because one of the addresses in the parameter list points to your PCB. If your program uses more than one PCB, it's often useful to locate one or more of the other PCBs. This is especially true for MP or BMP programs.

Figure B.4 summarizes the technique that you can use to locate all of your PCBs. Again, the contents of register one is the key. This time, however, locate the *save area trace* portion of the dump. The particular save area that you're looking for is the one for the first time that your program's load module was entered via a LINK. Register one within that save area points to a list of addresses of your PCBs. (Note that it does not point to a PCB, but to a list of addresses of your PCBs.) The addresses will be in the same order as the PCB mask names in your entry coding.

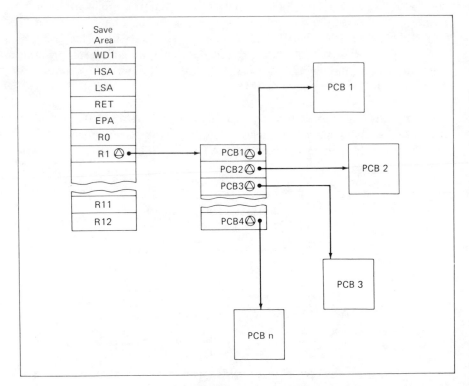

Figure B.4 Locating the PCBs

Locating Information about Recent DL/I Calls

IMS saves two bytes of information about the most recent DL/I calls that you made. In the latest releases of IMS/VS (IMS/VS Version 1 release 1.1 and later) IMS stores information about your last six calls. In earlier versions of IMS/VS and in IMS/360, information about your last eight calls is kept.

Figure B.5 summarizes the procedure that you can use in finding the information about recent calls. The fifth word in your PCB contains a pointer

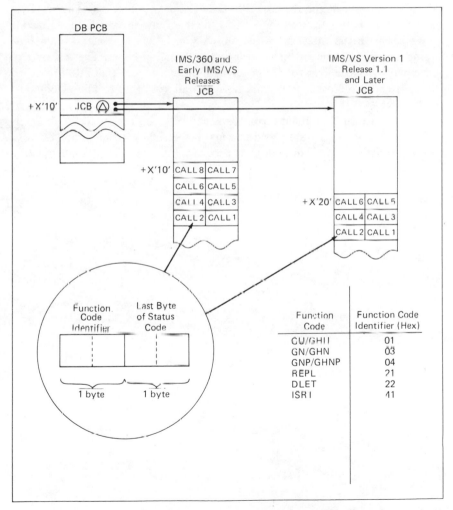

Figure B.5 Finding information about recent calls

to a system control block called the JCB. An area within the JCB keeps track of your most recent calls.

To locate this area, find your PCB by one of the methods already covered. Then if your system is IMS/VS Version 1, Release 1.1 or later, add hex '20' to the beginning address of your PCB. That gets you to a twelve byte area that tells you about your last six calls. If your system is an earlier release of IMS/VS, or a release of IMS/360, add hex '10' to the beginning address of your PCB. This gets you to a sixteen byte area that tells you about your last eight calls.

Information about each of your most recent calls is contained in a two-byte area. The first of each of these two-byte areas within the JCB tells about the oldest call and the last tells about the most recent one. The first byte of each of the two-byte areas contains a code that tells you which function code was used with the call. Figure B.5 shows you how you can translate these hexadecimal codes into their corresponding function codes. The last byte of each two-byte area gives you the last byte of the status code that DL/I returned for that call. The last byte usually tells you all you need to know about the status code.

The information about recent calls can often be very valuable in determining what your program was doing just before you got the dump. You can usually trace your way through your program logic by using the information in this area.

C

GSAM Programming (IMS/VS Only)

GSAM

The *Generalized Sequential Access Method,* or GSAM for short, is a feature unique to IMS/VS. The main purpose of GSAM is to allow you to access either a standard sequential data set or a VSAM ESDS through DL/I calls. As you'll see later, these DL/I calls are similar to standard data base calls; however, the GSAM parameter list is a little different.

Access Methods Used with GSAM

The access method used by GSAM depends on the type of data set you're working with. If you're using a standard sequential data set, GSAM uses BSAM. If you're accessing a VSAM ESDS, GSAM will use VSAM.

GSAM Record Formats

One of the unique features of GSAM is that it allows you to access files that use any of the standard operating system record formats. By using GSAM, you can access files that are organized with fixed-length records, fixed-length blocked records, variable-length records, variable-length blocked records, and undefined records.

GSAM Functions Supported

Only a few of the normal data base function codes are supported with GSAM. A few additional function codes are unique to GSAM. We'll go into those unique to GSAM in more detail later. You're allowed to sequentially load a data base from scratch, and you're allowed to retrieve a segment sequentially from a GSAM data base. You can also add records to a GSAM data base. However, you are limited to adding records to the end. You are allowed to randomly retrieve segments from the data base, but as you'll see later, random retrieval capabilities are somewhat limited.

GSAM Differences from Standard Data Bases

A GSAM data base actually consists of a standard operating system sequential data set or a VSAM ESDS. No provision is made in GSAM to define different segment types, nor is a hierarchical structure defined. The units of data that you retrieve when you use GSAM are *records,* just as with normal operating system data sets. Since the concept of *segment* does not exist in GSAM data bases, there are no search fields or key fields defined in GSAM records. You'll see later how you are able to access individual records in a GSAM data base.

GSAM DBD and PSB Statements

Figure C.1 shows an example of a DBD and PSB for a GSAM data base and a portion of a related application program. Notice that in some ways the GSAM DBD and PSB statements are similar to those for HSAM. Because there's no concept of segments in GSAM, there are no SEGM or FIELD macros in the DBD, and no SENSEG statements in the PSB. Notice that in the DATASET statement in the DBD statements, two DD names are specified. These DD names are used in a similar manner to the DD names in an HSAM DBD. One DD name specifies an input GSAM data base for retrieval and the other DD name specifies an output GSAM data base for sequential loading. In this way you can process an old version of the GSAM data base, process updates to it, and load a new version using the output DD statement.

Notice in the PSB statements, that there are two PCB statements. One PCB statement is used to retrieve segments from the old GSAM data base and the other is used to load segments into a new GSAM data base. A PSB for a GSAM data base can consist of only a single PCB statement if all you're going to do is either retrieve or load segments.

```
DBD       NAME=GSAMDBD,ACCESS=(GSAM,VSAM)
DATASET   DD1=INPUT,DD2=OUTPUT,
          RECFM=F,RECORD=80
DBDGEN
FINISH
END


PCB       TYPE=GSAM,PROCOPT=G,DBDNAME=GSAMDBD
PCB       TYPE=GSAM,PROCOPT=L,DBDNAME=GSAMDBD
PSBGEN    LANG=COBOL,PSBNAME=GSAMPSB
END
```

Figure C.1 GSAM, DBD and PSB Coding

GSAM DL/I Calls

Figure C.2 shows the COBOL coding for a typical GSAM CALL statement and its associated parameter list. The first parameter specifies the function codes that you'll be using with this GSAM call, and the second parameter specifies the PCB mask. The third parameter, as in standard DL/I calls, specifies the I/O area that you're using in this call. The fourth parameter in the list differs from the fourth parameter in a normal DL/I call. This parameter specifies the address of a *record search argument,* abbreviated RSA. This is not a segment search argument, since GSAM doesn't work with segments. The RSA is optional for all but Get-Unique calls.

The Record Search Argument

The RSA is the means of finding your way around in a GSAM data base. It consists of a double word whose format depends on the type of device used to store the GSAM data base. Because the format of the RSA varies, it's not recommended that your program actually work with the data in the RSA. If you're interested in the actual format of the RSA, you can look it up in your *Application Programming Reference Manual.* Now let's see how the RSA is used in the different types of calls that you can issue with GSAM. We'll look at the different function codes that can be specified in GSAM calls, and we'll see how the RSA is used for each.

GSAM Function Codes

Figure C.3 shows the function codes that you can use with GSAM calls. We'll go into detail on three of those function codes: GU, GN, and ISRT. The OPEN and CLSE function codes are optional and are used to explicitly open or close the GSAM data base. These are not normally used because opens and closes will automatically be issued when they're required. The CHKP and XRST function codes are used in conjunction with the DL/I checkpoint/restart

```
              .
              .
              .
    WORKING-STORAGE SECTION.
    01   GSAM-RSA.
         03   RSA-WORD1    PIC S9(5) COMP.
         03   RSA-WORD2    PIC S9(5) COMP.
              .
              .
              .
         CALL   'CBLTDLI'   USING   GET-NEXT
                                    GSAM-PCB
                                    I-O-AREA
                                    GSAM-RSA
              .
              .
              .
```

Figure C.2 A GSAM CALL statement

facilities. The DUMP or SNAP function codes are used to send GSAM control blocks to special DL/I data sets for debugging purposes.

THE GN FUNCTION CODE. Get-Next calls are used with GSAM to sequentially retrieve records. The use of the RSA in a Get-Next call parameter list is optional. If you include an RSA in your parameter list, the GSAM routines will store information in it about the location of the record just retrieved. After a Get-Next call, you can move the contents of the RSA to some other area for future use.

THE GU FUNCTION CODE. A Get-Unique call can be used to retrieve segments randomly from a GSAM data base. The Get-Unique call is the only call that requires you to use an RSA in your parameter list. The normal way that you use a Get-Unique call with GSAM is to save the value that was stored in the RSA field from a previous Get-Next or Insert call. You then use the contents of the saved RSA field in a Get-Unique call.

There is one instance where you can code an explicit value in the double-word RSA field. That's when you would like to access the first record of the GSAM data base. An RSA that contains a binary 1 in the first fullword and a binary 0 in the second full word always refers to the first record in the GSAM data base, no matter what type of device it's stored on. An RSA with this value can be used in a Get-Unique call to retrieve the first record in a GSAM data base.

THE ISRT FUNCTION CODE. The Insert call can be used in two ways: to load a GSAM data base from scratch or to add segments to the end of an existing GSAM data base. The DISP= parameter that you code in your output data set DD statement determines which of these functions will be performed by the Insert call. DISP=NEW or DISP=OLD says that you will load the data

---

GSAM Function Codes

GU   —Retrieve a unique record

GN   —Retrieve next sequential record

ISRT —Add a record to the end

OPEN —Open a GSAM data base

CLSE —Close a GSAM data base

CHKP —Checkpoint/Restart

XRST —Checkpoint/Restart

DUMP—For debugging

SNAP —For debugging

Figure C.3 GSAM function codes

base from scratch, and DISP=MOD says that you will be adding segments to the end of an existing GSAM data base.

As with Get-Next calls, the RSA is optional when used with the Insert call. If you specify an RSA, DL/I will return information in the double word RSA field about the location of the segment that was just inserted. You can then save this RSA value for future use in Get-Unique calls.

D

The HOSPITAL Data Base

This appendix summarizes information that you need to know about the HOSPITAL data base to complete the coding problems in chapters 5, 7, and 9. Figure D.1 is a copy of the HOSPITAL data base hierarchy chart. Figure D.2 shows the segment description coding, in COBOL, that you should assume is stored in a source statement library when you code your solutions. Figures D.3 and D.4 repeat that coding in PL/I and Assembler Language. Figure D.5

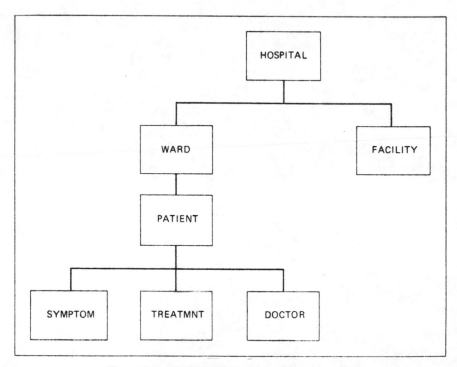

Figure D.1 HOSPITAL data base hierarchy chart

shows the DBD coding for the HOSPITAL data base. You can assume that
this is the DBD in effect for the data base that the sample solutions will access.
Each exercise has its own PSB, but a sample PSB, allowing all calls but Insert
in the load mode for all seven segment types, is shown in figure D.6.

```
000010 01   HOSPITAL.
000020      03   HOSPNAME              PIC X(20).
000030      03   HOSP-ADDRESS          PIC X(30).
000040      03   HOSP-PHONE            PIC X(10).

000010 01   WARD.
000020      03   WARDNO                PIC XX.
000030      03   TOT-ROOMS             PIC XXX.
000040      03   TOT-BEDS              PIC XXX.
000050      03   BEDAVAIL              PIC XXX.
000060      03   WARDTYPE              PIC X(20).

000010 01   PATIENT.
000020      03   PATNAME               PIC X(20).
000030      03   PAT-ADDRESS           PIC X(30).
000040      03   PAT-PHONE             PIC X(10).
000050      03   BEDIDENT              PIC X(4).
000060      03   DATEADMT              PIC X(6).
000070      03   PREV-STAY-FLAG        PIC X.
000080      03   PREV-HOSP             PIC X(20).
000090      03   PREV-DATE             PIC X(4).
000100      03   PREV-REASON           PIC X(30).

000010 01   SYMPTOM.
000020      03   DIAGNOSE              PIC X(20).
000030      03   SYMPDATE              PIC X(6).
000040      03   PREV-TREAT-FLAG       PIC X.
000050      03   TREAT-DESC            PIC X(20).
000060      03   SYMP-DOCTOR           PIC X(20).
000070      03   SYMP-DOCT-PHONE       PIC X(10).

000010 01   TREATMNT.
000020      03   TRTYPE                PIC X(20).
000030      03   TRDATE                PIC X(6).
000040      03   MEDICATION-TYPE       PIC X(20).
000050      03   DIET-COMMENT          PIC X(30).
000060      03   SURGERY-FLAG          PIC X.
000070      03   SURGERY-DATE          PIC X(6).
000080      03   SURGERY-COMMENT       PIC X(30).

000010 01   DOCTOR.
000020      03   DOCTNAME              PIC X(20).
000030      03   DOCT-ADDRESS          PIC X(30).
000040      03   DOCT-PHONE            PIC X(10).
000050      03   SPECIALT              PIC X(20).

000010 01   FACILITY.
000020      03   FACTYPE               PIC X(20).
000030      03   TOT-FACIL             PIC XXX.
000040      03   FACAVAIL              PIC XXX.
```

Figure D.2 COBOL segment description coding

```
DCL       HOSPITAL_PTR   POINTER;                          00000005
DCL    1  HOSPITAL       BASED (HOSPITAL_PTR),             00000010
          3   HOSPNAME            CHAR (20),               00000020
          3   HOSP_ADDRESS        CHAR (30),               00000030
          3   HOSP_PHONE          CHAR (10);               00000040
                                                           00000050
          HOSPITAL_PTR = ADDR (HOSPITAL);                  00000051

DCL       WARD_PTR   POINTER;                              00000005
DCL    1  WARD BASED (WARD_PTR),                           00000010
          3   WARDNO              CHAR (2),                00000020
          3   TOT_ROOMS           CHAR (3),                00000030
          3   TOT_BEDS            CHAR (3),                00000040
          3   BEDAVAIL            CHAR (3),                00000050
          3   WARDTYPE            CHAR (20);               00000060
                                                           00000061
          WARD_PTR = ADDR (WARD);                          00000062

DCL       PATIENT_PTR   POINTER;                           00000005
DCL    1  PATIENT        BASED (PATIENT_PTR),              00000010
          3   PATNAME             CHAR (20),               00000020
          3   PAT_ADDRESS         CHAR (30),               00000030
          3   PAT_PHONE           CHAR (10),               00000040
          3   BEDIDENT            CHAR (4),                00000050
          3   DATEADMT            CHAR (6),                00000060
          3   PREV_STAY_FLAG      CHAR (1),                00000070
          3   PREV_HOSP           CHAR (20),               00000080
          3   PREV_DATE           CHAR (4),                00000090
          3   PREV_REASON         CHAR (30);               00000100
                                                           00000110
          PATIENT_PTR = ADDR (PATIENT);                    00000111

DCL    1  SYMPTOM,                                         00000010
          3   DIAGNOSE            CHAR (20),               00000020
          3   SYMPDATE            CHAR (6),                00000030
          3   PREV-TREAT-FLAG     CHAR (1),                00000040
          3   TREAT-DESC          CHAR (20),               00000050
          3   SYMP-DOCTOR         CHAR (20),               00000060
          3   SYMP-DOCT-PHONE     CHAR (10);               00000070

DCL    1  TREATMNT,                                        00000010
          3   TRTYPE          CHAR  (20),                  00000020
          3   TRDATE          CHAR  (6),                   00000030
          3   MEDICATION_TYPE CHAR  (20),                  00000040
          3   DIET_COMMENT    CHAR  (30),                  00000050
          3   SURGERY_FLAG    CHAR  (1),                   00000060
          3   SURGERY_DATE    CHAR  (6),                   00000070
          3   SURGERY_COMMENT CHAR  (30);                  00000080

DCL    1  DOCTOR,                                          00000010
          3   DOCTNAME            CHAR (20),               00000020
          3   DOCT_ADDRESS        CHAR (30),               00000030
          3   DOCT_PHONE          CHAR (10),               00000040
          3   SPECIALT            CHAR (20);               00000050

DCL    1  FACILITY,                                        00000010
          3   FACTYPE             CHAR (20),               00000020
          3   TOT_FACIL           CHAR (3),                00000030
          3   FACAVAIL            CHAR (3);                00000040
```

Figure D.3 PL/I segment description coding

```
HOSPITAL  DS      OCL60           HOSPITAL  SEGMENT        00000010
*                                                          00000020
HOSPNAME  DS      CL20            UNIQUE KEY               00000030
HOSPADDR  DS      CL30                                     00000040
HOSPPHON  DS      CL10                                     00000050

WARD      DS      OCL31           WARD  SEGMENT          - 00000010
*                                                          00000020
WARDNO    DS      CL2             UNIQUE KEY               00000030
TOTROOMS  DS      CL3                                      00000040
TOTBEDS   DS      CL3                                      00000050
BEDAVAIL  DS      CL3             SEARCH                   00000060
WARDTYPE  DS      CL20            SEARCH                   00000070

PATIENT   DS      OCL125          PATIENT SEGMENT          00000010
*                                                          00000020
PATNAME   DS      CL20            SEARCH                   00000030
PATADDR   DS      CL30                                     00000040
PATPHONE  DS      CL10                                     00000050
BEDIDENT  DS      CL4             UNIQUE KEY               00000060
DATEADMT  DS      CL6             SEARCH                   00000070
PREVSTAY  DS      C                                        00000080
PREVHOSP  DS      CL20                                     00000090
PREVDATE  DS      CL4                                      00000100
PREVREAS  DS      CL30                                     00000110

SYMPTOM   DS      OCL77           SYMPTOM  SEGMENT         00000010
*                                                          00000020
DIAGNOSE  DS      CL20            SEARCH                   00000030
SYMPDATE  DS      CL6             KEY                      00000040
PREVTRT   DS      C                                        00000050
TREATDES  DS      CL20                                     00000060
SYMPDOCT  DS      CL20                                     00000070
SYMPPHON  DS      CL10                                     00000080

TREATMNT  DS      OCL113          TREATMNT SEGMENT         00000010
*                                                          00000020
TRTYPE    DS      CL20            SEARCH                   00000030
TRDATE    DS      CL6             KEY                      00000040
MEDICAT   DS      CL20                                     00000050
DIETCOMM  DS      CL30                                     00000060
SURGFLAG  DS      C                                        00000070
SURGDATE  DS      CL6                                      00000080
SURGCOMM  DS      CL30                                     00000090

DOCTOR    DS      OCL80           DOCTOR SEGMENT           00000010
*                                                          00000020
DOCTNAME  DS      CL20            SEARCH                   00000030
DOCTADDR  DS      CL30                                     00000040
DOCTPHON  DS      CL10                                     00000050
SPECIALT  DS      CL20            SEARCH                   00000060

FACILITY  DS      OCL26           FACILITY SEGMENT         00000010
*                                                          00000020
FACTYPE   DS      CL20            SEARCH                   00000030
TOTFACIL  DS      CL3                                      00000040
FACAVAIL  DS      CL3             SEARCH                   00000050
```

Figure D.4 Assembler language segment description coding

```
       PRINT NOGEN
DBD    NAME=HOSFIBD,ACCESS=(HISAM,ISAM)                            00000010
       DATASET DD1=PRIME,OVFLW=OVERFLW,DEVICE=3330                 00000020
                                                                   00000030
*                                                                  00000040
       SEGM  NAME=HOSPITAL,PARENT=0,BYTES=60                       00000050
       FIELD NAME=(HOSPNAME,SEQ,U),BYTES=20,START=1,TYPE=C         00000052
*                                                                  00000060
       SEGM  NAME=WARD,PARENT=HOSPITAL,BYTES=31                    00000070
       FIELD NAME=(WARDNO,SEQ,U),BYTES=2,START=1,TYPE=C            00000080
       FIELD NAME=BEDAVAIL,BYTES=3,START=9,TYPE=C                  00000090
       FIELD NAME=WARDTYPE,BYTES=20,START=12,TYPE=C                00000092
*                                                                  00000100
       SEGM  NAME=PATIENT,PARENT=WARD,BYTES=125                    00000110
       FIELD NAME=(BEDIDENT,SEQ,U),BYTES=4,START=61,TYPE=C         00000120
       FIELD NAME=PATNAME,BYTES=20,START=1,TYPE=C                  00000130
       FIELD NAME=DATEADMT,BYTES=6,START=65,TYPE=C                 00000132
*                                                                  00000140
       SEGM  NAME=SYMPTOM,PARENT=PATIENT,BYTES=77                  00000150
       FIELD NAME=(SYMPDATE,SEQ),BYTES=6,START=21,TYPE=C           00000160
       FIELD NAME=DIAGNOSE,BYTES=20,START=1,TYPE=C                 00000162
*                                                                  00000170
       SEGM  NAME=TREATMNT,PARENT=PATIENT,BYTES=113                00000180
       FIELD NAME=(TRDATE,SEQ),BYTES=6,START=21,TYPE=C             00000190
       FIELD NAME=TRTYPE,BYTES=20,START=1,TYPE=C                   00000192
*                                                                  00000200
       SEGM  NAME=DOCTOR,PARENT=PATIENT,BYTES=80                   00000210
       FIELD NAME=DOCTNAME,BYTES=20,START=1,TYPE=C                 00000220
       FIELD NAME=SPECIALT,BYTES=20,START=61,TYPE=C                00000222
*                                                                  00000230
       SEGM  NAME=FACILITY,PARENT=HOSPITAL,BYTES=26                00000240
       FIELD NAME=FACTYPE,BYTES=20,START=1,TYPE=C                  00000250
       FIELD NAME=FACAVAIL,BYTES=3,START=24,TYPE=C                 00000252
*                                                                  00000260
       DBDGEN                                                      00000270
       FINISH                                                      00000280
       END
```

Figure D.5 HOSPITAL data base DBD coding

```
PRINT    NOGEN                                                          00000010
PCB      TYPE=DB,DBDNAME=HOSPDBD,PROCOPT=A,KEYLEN=32                     00000020
                                                                        00000030
SENSEG   NAME=HOSPITAL,PARENT=0                                         00000040
SENSEG   NAME=WARD,PARENT=HOSPITAL                                      00000050
SENSEG   NAME=PATIENT,PARENT=WARD                                       00000060
SENSEG   NAME=SYMPTOM,PARENT=PATIENT                                    00000070
SENSEG   NAME=TREATMNT,PARENT=PATIENT                                   00000080
SENSEG   NAME=DOCTOR,PARENT=PATIENT                                     00000090
SENSEG   NAME=FACILITY,PARENT=HOSPITAL                                  00000100
                                                                        00000110
PSBGEN   LANG=COBOL,PSBNAME=SAMPLE                                      00000120
END                                                                     00000130
```

Figure D.6 HOSPITAL data base PSB coding

243

E

Exercise Answers

This appendix contains the answers to all of the exercises found at the end of each chapter. All answers that require actual coding are given here in COBOL. In addition to these COBOL solutions, a solution to the coding problem in chapter 5 may be found in PL/I in appendix F, and in Assembler Language in appendix G.

ANSWERS TO CHAPTER 1 EXERCISES

1. Increase data dependence, reduce data redundancy, and provide facilities for data communications.

2. The answer to this exercise depends upon a knowledge of the characteristics of your installation.

3. a-1, b-5, c-3, d-2, e-4, f-4.

ANSWERS TO CHAPTER 2 EXERCISES

1. a-12, b-7, c-3, d-8, e-11, f-9, g-1, h-10, i-6, j-5, k-2, l-4.

2. a. A, B, C, D, E, and F.
   b. A.
   c. A—B—C; A—B—D; A—E—F.
   d. E.
   e. C and D.
   f. Three.
   g. Six.

3. a. 255.
   b. 15.

ANSWERS TO CHAPTER 3 EXERCISES

1. a-11, b-3, c-1, d-2 & 5, e-9, f-12, g-8, h-10, i-7, j-4, k-6.

2. a. EMPLOYEE, 100 bytes.
   TASK, 42 bytes.
   TIME, 20 bytes.
   PERSONNL, 56 bytes.

   b. EMPNO, 8 bytes long, starting in position 1, unique.
   TASKNO, 6 bytes long, starting in position 1, unique.
   DATA, 6 bytes long, starting in position 15, nonunique.

   c. EMPNAME, 25 bytes long, starting in position 30.
   TASKNAME, 25 bytes long, starting in position 7.

   d. PAYROLL.

   e. Figure E.1 shows the solution to 2e.

3. a. EMPLOYEE, TASK, TIME.
   b. Figure E.2 shows the solution to 3b.
   c. One.
   d. HOURCALC.
   e. PAYROLL.
   f. TASK, TIME.

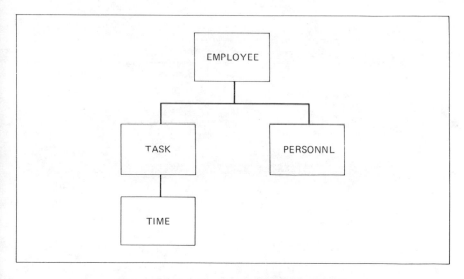

Figure E.1 Solution to chapter 3—exercise 2e

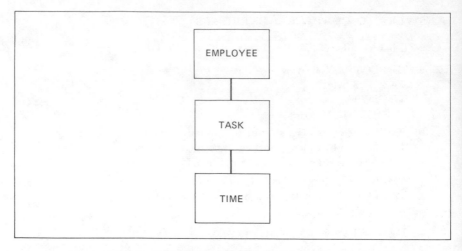

Figure E.2 Solution to chapter 3—exercise 3b

```
a.  GU      HOSPITAL(HOSPNAME =MAC NEAL              )
    ^^^^    ^^^^^^^^^^^^^^^^^^^^^^^^^^^^^^^^^^^^^^^^^^^^
            WARD    (WARDTYPE =INTENSIVE            )
            ^^^^^^^^^^^^^^^^^^^^^^^^^^^^^^^^^^^^^^^^^^^^^
            PATIENT (PATNAME  =WHEELER              )
            ^^^^^^^^^^^^^^^^^^^^^^^^^^^^^^^^^^^^^^^^^^^^^


b.  GU      HOSPITAL
    ^^^^    ^^^^^^^^^^
            WARD    (BEDAVAIL >100)
            ^^^^^^^^^^^^^^^^^^^^^^^^^

    GU      WARD    (BEDAVAIL >100)
    ^^^^    ^^^^^^^^^^^^^^^^^^^^^^^^^


c.  GU      PATIENT (PATNAME  =BAILEY               )
    ^^^^    ^^^^^^^^^^^^^^^^^^^^^^^^^^^^^^^^^^^^^^^^^^^^^
            DOCTOR  (DOCTNAME =ROGERS               )
            ^^^^^^^^^^^^^^^^^^^^^^^^^^^^^^^^^^^^^^^^^^^^^


d.  GU      HOSPITAL(HOSPNAME =MAC NEAL             )
    ^^^^    ^^^^^^^^^^^^^^^^^^^^^^^^^^^^^^^^^^^^^^^^^^^^
            FACILITY(FACTYPE  =COBALT               )
            ^^^^^^^^^^^^^^^^^^^^^^^^^^^^^^^^^^^^^^^^^^^^
```

Figure E.3 Answers to chapter 4—exercise 3

ANSWERS TO CHAPTER 4 EXERCISES

1. a-5, b-1, c-4, d-3, e-2.

2. a—3, blanks; b—10, blanks; c—none, GE; d—21, blanks.

3. Figure E.3 shows the answer to exercise 3.

4. The Blank status code means that the segment was retrieved successfully. The GE status code means that the segment could not be found.

ANSWER TO CHAPTER 5 EXERCISE (CODING PROBLEM)

The listing in figure E.4 shows a possible COBOL solution to the chapter 5 coding problem. If you would like to see a PL/I or Assembler Language solution, see either appendix F or G. The thing to keep in mind about these sample solutions is that they are not the only correct solutions. Evaluate your solution against the ones shown for reasonableness in determining if your solution is correct.

ANSWERS TO CHAPTER 6 EXERCISES

1. a-1, b-4, c-6, d-2, e-3, f-5.

2 and 3. Figure E.5 shows the solutions to these exercises.

4. a. Insert Rule FIRST—11.
   Insert Rule LAST—14.
   Insert Rule HERE—11.
   b. Insert Rule FIRST—15.
   Insert Rule LAST—18.
   Insert Rule HERE—15.

ANSWERS TO CHAPTER 8 EXERCISES

1. a-6, b-1, c-5, d-10, e-7, f-3, g-4, h-8, i-2, j-9.

2, 3, and **4.** Figure E.7 shows the solutions to exercises 2, 3, and 4.

ANSWERS TO CHAPTER 10 EXERCISES

1. IMS Control Region, Message Processing Region, Batch Message Processing Region.

2. Data Base PCB, used for accessing a DL/I data base; I/O PCB, used to receive messages and send messages back to the originating terminal; Alternate PCB, used to send messages to terminals other than the originating terminal, or to the message queues.

3. a-4; b-3; c-6; d-7; e-9; f-5; g-8; h-10; i-2; j-1

Figure E.4 COBOL solution to the chapter 5 coding problem

```
000100   ID DIVISION.
000200   PROGRAM-ID. CHAP5C.
000300   AUTHOR. DKAPP.
000400   DATE-WRITTEN.   APRIL 26 1977.
000500   DATE-COMPILED.
000600
000610   REMARKS.     THE OUTPUT OF THIS PROGRAM IS A LIST OF PATIENTS WHO
000700                ARE IN QUARANTINE WARDS PRESENTLY BUT ALSO HAVE
000800                BEEN IN A HOSPITAL WITHIN THE PAST YEAR.
000900
001000
001100
001200   ENVIRONMENT DIVISION.
001300
001400   CONFIGURATION SECTION.
001500
001600   SOURCE-COMPUTER.   IBM-370-158.
001700   OBJECT-COMPUTER.   IBM-370-158.
001800
001900   INPUT-OUTPUT SECTION.
002000   FILE-CONTROL.
002100
002200       SELECT   PARMETER   ASSIGN TO UT-S-INPUT.
002300       SELECT   PRNTER     ASSIGN TO UT-S-OUTPUT.
002400       EJECT
002500   DATA DIVISION.
002600
002700
002800   FILE SECTION.
002900
003000   FD   PARMETER
003100
003200       BLOCK CONTAINS O RECORDS
003300       RECORDING MODE IS F
003400       LABEL RECORDS ARE OMITTED
003500       DATA RECORD IS PARM-CARD.
```

```
003600 01  PARM-CARD.
003700     05  HOSPCONST    PIC XX.
003800     05  IHDSPNAM     PIC X(20).
003900     05  FILLER       PIC X(58).
004000
004100
004200 FD  PRNTER
004300
004400     BLOCK CONTAINS 0 RECORDS
004500     RECORDING MODE IS F
004600     LABEL RECORDS ARE OMITTED
004700     DATA RECORD IS A-LINE.
004800
004900
005000 01  A-LINE.
005100     05  PRINT-CTL    PIC X.
005200     05  PRINT-AREA   PIC X(132).
005400 WORKING-STORAGE SECTION.
005500
005600 77  NO-HOSPITAL      PIC X      VALUE '0'.
005700 77  NO-WARDS         PIC X      VALUE '0'.
005800 77  NO-PATIENTS      PIC X      VALUE '0'.
005900 77  TOP-PAGE         PIC X      VALUE '1'.
006000 77  DOUBLE-SPACE     PIC X      VALUE '0'.
006100 77  SINGLE-SPACE     PIC X      VALUE ' '.
006200 77  TRIPLE-SPACE     PIC X      VALUE '-'.
006300 77  END-DATABASE     PIC XX     VALUE 'GB'.
006400 77  SEG-NOT-FOUND    PIC XX     VALUE 'GE'.
006500 77  GET-UNIQUE       PIC XXXX   VALUE 'GU  '.
006600 77  GET-NEXT         PIC XXXX   VALUE 'GN  '.
006700 77  GET-NEXT-P       PIC XXXX   VALUE 'GNP '.
006800 77  LINE-CNT         PIC 99     VALUE 52.
006900 77  PAGE-CNT         PIC 9(4)   VALUE ZERO.
007000 77  CALL-SUCCESSFUL  PIC XX     VALUE ZERO.
007100 77  END-HOSP-DATA    PIC X      VALUE SPACE.
007200 77  HOSP-NOT-FOUND   PIC X(20)  VALUE SPACE.
007300 77  NEW-MONTH        PIC S99.
007400 77  NEW-YEAR         PIC S99.
007500 77  WRDTYPE          PIC X(20)  VALUE SPACE.
```

```
007600
007700 01  CURR-DATE.
007800     05  CURRMO        PIC S99.
007900     05  FILLER        PIC X      VALUE '/'.
008000     05  CURRDAY       PIC S99.
008100     05  FILLER        PIC X      VALUE '/'.
008200     05  CURRYR        PIC S99.
008300
008400 01  WS-PREV-DATE.
008500     05  PREVMO        PIC S99.
008600     05  PREVYR        PIC S99.
008700     EJECT
008800 HOSP-I-O-AREA COPY HOSPITAL.
008900
009000 01  WARD-I-O-AREA COPY WARD.
009100
009200 01  PAT-I-O-AREA COPY PATIENT.
009300
009400 01  SSA-HOSP.
009500     05  HOSPSEG         PIC X(8)   VALUE 'HOSPITAL'.
009600     05  FILLER          PIC X      VALUE '('.
009700     05  SEG-SEARCH-NAM  PIC X(8)   VALUE 'HOSPNAME'.
009800     05  HOSP-REL-OP     PIC XX     VALUE 'EQ'.
009900     05  HOSP-NAME       PIC X(20).
010000     05  FILLER          PIC X      VALUE ')'.
010100
010200 01  SSA-WARD.
010300     05  WARDSEG         PIC X(8)   VALUE 'WARD'
010400     05  FILLER          PIC X      VALUE '('.
010500     05  SEG-SEARCH-NAME PIC X(8)   VALUE 'WARDTYPE'.
010600     05  WARD-REL-OP     PIC XX     VALUE 'EQ'.
010700     05  WARD-TYPE       PIC X(20)  VALUE 'QUARANTINE
010800     05  FILLER          PIC X      VALUE ')'.
010900
010905
010910 01  SSA-PATIENT        PIC   X(9)  VALUE 'PATIENT
011000 01  HEAD-1.
011100
011200     05  FILLER               PIC X(26) VALUE SPACES.
011300
```

```
011400          05  TITLE           PIC X(106) VALUE
011500              'PREVIOUS STAY REPORT'.
011700
011800      01  HEAD-2.
011900
012100          05  FILLER          PIC X(5)    VALUE 'PAGE'.
012200          05  HPAGE-CTR       PIC ZZZ9.
012300          05  FILLER          PIC X(123)  VALUE SPACES.
012400
012500      01  HEAD-3.
012600
012800          05  HHOSPNAM        PIC X(25)   VALUE 'HOSPITAL NAME'.
013000          05  HHOSPADR        PIC X(35)   VALUE 'HOSPITAL ADDRESS'.
013200          05  HHOSPHON        PIC X(10)   VALUE 'HOSP PHONE'.
013300          05  FILLER          PIC X(62)   VALUE SPACE.
013400
013500      01  HEAD-4.
013600
013800          05  HWARDNO         PIC X(12)   VALUE 'WARD NO'.
013900          05  HTOTRMS         PIC X(14)   VALUE 'TOT ROOMS'.
014000          05  HTOTBDS         PIC X(13)   VALUE 'TOT BEDS'.
014100          05  HBDSAVAI        PIC X(15)   VALUE 'BEDS AVAIL'.
014200          05  HBDAVAIL        PIC X(20)   VALUE 'WARD TYPE'.
014300          05  FILLER          PIC X(53)   VALUE SPACE.
014400
014500      01  HEAD-5.
014600
014800          05  HPATNAM         PIC X(21)   VALUE 'PATIENT NAME'.
014900          05  HBDID           PIC X(6)    VALUE 'BED'.
015000          05  HDATADMIT       PIC X(12)   VALUE 'ADMIT DATE'.
015100          05  HPREVDAT        PIC X(11)   VALUE 'PREV DATE'.
015200          05  HPREVHOS        PIC X(21)   VALUE 'PREVIOUS HOSPITAL'.
015400          05  HFREV-REASON    PIC X(31)   VALUE 'PREVIOUS REASON'.
015500          05  FILLER          PIC X(31)   VALUE SPACE.
015700      01  DETAIL-1.
015800
016000          05  DHOSPNAM        PIC X(20).
016100          05  FILLER          PIC X(5)    VALUE SPACE.
```

```
016200          05  DHOSP-ADDRESS    PIC  X(30).   VALUE  SPACE.
016300          05  FILLER           PIC  X(5).    VALUE  SPACE.
016400          05  DHOSPHON         PIC  X(10).   VALUE  SPACE.
016500          05  FILLER           PIC  X(62)    VALUE  SPACE.
016600
016700      01  DETAIL-2.
016800
016900          05  FILLER           PIC  X(3)     VALUE  SPACE.
017000          05  DWARDNO          PIC  99.      VALUE  SPACE.
017100          05  FILLER           PIC  X(10)    VALUE  SPACE.
017200          05  DTOTRMS          PIC  999.     VALUE  SPACE.
017300          05  FILLER           PIC  X(11)    VALUE  SPACE.
017400          05  DTOT-BEDS        PIC  999.     VALUE  SPACE.
017500          05  FILLER           PIC  X(10)    VALUE  SPACE.
017600          05  DBDSAVAIL        PIC  999.     VALUE  SPACE.
017700          05  FILLER           PIC  X(9)     VALUE  SPACE.
017800          05  DWARDTYPE        PIC  X(20)    VALUE  SPACE.
017900          05  FILLER           PIC  X(58)    VALUE  SPACE.
018000
018100      01  DETAIL-3.
018200
018400          05  DFATNAM          PIC  X(20).   VALUE  SPACE.
018500          05  FILLER           PIC  X        VALUE  SPACE.
018600          05  DBEDID           PIC  9999.    VALUE  SPACE.
018700          05  FILLER           PIC  X(4)     VALUE  SPACE.
018800          05  DDATADMIT        PIC  X(6).    VALUE  SPACE.
018900          05  FILLER           PIC  X(6)     VALUE  SPACE.
019000          05  DPREV-DATE       PIC  X(4).    VALUE  SPACE.
019100          05  FILLER           PIC  X(5)     VALUE  SPACE.
019200          05  DPREV-HOSP       PIC  X(20).   VALUE  SPACE.
019300          05  FILLER           PIC  X        VALUE  SPACE.
019400          05  DPREV-REASONN    PIC  X(30)    VALUE  SPACE.
019500          05  FILLER           PIC  X(31).   VALUE  SPACE.
019600
019700      01  NO-HOSP-LINE.
019800
020100          05  ERR-HOSPNAM      PIC  X(20).   VALUE  SPACE.
020110          05  FILLER           PIC  X(5)     VALUE  SPACE.
020200          05  FILLER           PIC  X(107)   VALUE
```

```
020300                          '**** HOSPITAL NOT FOUND ****'.
020310
020311  01  NO-WARD-LINE        PIC X(132)  VALUE
020312                          '**** NO QUARANTINE WARDS ****'.
020313
020314  01  NO-PAT-LINE         PIC X(132)  VALUE
020315                          '**** NO PATIENTS WITH PREVIOUS STAY ****'.
020500  LINKAGE SECTION.
020600  01  DB-PCB-HOSP COPY MASKC.
020800  PROCEDURE DIVISION.
021000  ENTRY-POINT.
021200      ENTRY 'DLITCBL' USING DB-PCB-HOSP.
021300      OPEN INPUT PARMETER  OUTPUT PRNTER.
021500      MOVE CURRENT-DATE TO CURR-DATE.
021600
021700  READ-CARD.
021900      READ PARMETER AT END GO TO END-JOB.
022000      MOVE IHOSPNAM TO HOSP-NAME.
022100      MOVE 45 TO LINE-CNT.
022200
022300      CALL 'CBLTDLI' USING GET-UNIQUE
022400                           DB-PCB-HOSP
022500                           HOSP-I-O-AREA
022600                           SSA-HOSP.
022700
022800      IF STATUS-CODE NOT EQUAL ' '
022900          PERFORM HOSPITAL-NOT-FOUND
023000          GO TO READ-CARD.
023100
023200      MOVE HOSPNAME    TO  IHOSPNA1.
023300      MOVE HOSP-ADDRESS TO  IHOSP-ADDRESS.
023400      MOVE HOSP-PHONE  TO  IHOSPHON.
023500
023700      CALL 'CBLTDLI' USING GET-UNIQUE
023800                           DB-PCB-HOSP
023900                           WARD-I-O-AREA
024000                           SSA-HOSP.
```

253

```
                                                           SSA-WARD

024100
024200          IF STATUS-CODE NOT EQUAL ' '
024300
024400
024500              PERFORM WARD-NOT-FOUND
024600              GO TO READ-CARD.
024700
024710          MOVE WARDNO       TO    DWARDNO.
024800          MOVE TOT-ROOMS    TO    DTOTRMS.
024900          MOVE TOT-BEDS     TO    DTOT-BEDS.
025000          MOVE BEDAVAIL     TO    DBDSAVAIL.
025100          MOVE WARDTYPE     TO    DWARDTYPE.
025200          MOVE '0' TO NO-PATIENTS.
025300
025400          PERFORM CALL-PATIENT THRU CALL-PATIENT-EXIT
025600                               UNTIL STATUS-CODE = 'GE'.
025610
025700          IF NO-PATIENTS EQUAL '0'
025800
025900              MOVE NO-PAT-LINE TO DETAIL-3
026000              PERFORM WRITE-RTN THRU WRITE-RTN-EXIT
026100              MOVE SPACE TO DETAIL-3.
026200
026300          MOVE '0' TO NO-PATIENTS.
026400          GO TO READ-CARD.
026600      CALL-PATIENT.
026700
026800          CALL 'CBLTDLI' USING GET-NEXT-P
026900                               DB-PCB-HOSP
027000                               PAT-I-O-AREA
027010                               SSA-PATIENT.
027100
027200          IF STATUS-CODE EQUAL 'GE' GO TO CALL-PATIENT-EXIT.
027300          IF STATUS-CODE NOT EQUAL ' '
027400
027500              MOVE DB-PCB-HOSP TO DETAIL-3
027600              PERFORM WRITE-RTN THRU WRITE-RTN-EXIT
027700              MOVE SPACE TO DETAIL-3
027800              GO TO READ-CARD.
```

254

```
027900
028000     IF  PREV-STAY-FLAG NOT EQUAL '1' GO TO CALL-PATIENT-EXIT.
028100
028200         MOVE PREV-DATE TO WS-PREV-DATE.
028300         SUBTRACT PREVMO FROM CURRMO GIVING NEW-MONTH.
028500         SUBTRACT PREVYR FROM CURRYR GIVING NEW-YEAR.
028700
029000     IF  NEW-YEAR GREATER THAN 1 GO TO CALL-PATIENT-EXIT.
029100     IF  NEW-YEAR EQUAL 0
029200
029300              PERFORM WRITE-PAT-DATA
029400              MOVE '1' TO NO-PATIENTS
029500              GO TO CALL-PATIENT-EXIT.
029600
029700     IF  NEW-YEAR   EQUAL   1
029800     AND NEW-MONTH LESS THAN 1
029900
030000              PERFORM WRITE-PAT-DATA
030100              MOVE '1' TO NO-PATIENTS.
030110
030200 CALL-PATIENT-EXIT.
030300     EXIT.
030500 WRITE-RTN.
030600     IF LINE-CNT LESS THAN 44 GO TO WRITE-PAT-LINE.
030700
030800     MOVE 1 TO LINE-CNT.
030900     MOVE HEAD-1 TO PRINT-AREA.
031000     WRITE A-LINE AFTER POSITIONING TOP-PAGE.
031010
031100     ADD 1 TO PAGE-CNT.
031200     MOVE PAGE-CNT TO HPAGE-CTR.
031300     MOVE HEAD-2 TO PRINT-AREA.
031400     WRITE A-LINE AFTER POSITIONING DOUBLE-SPACE.
031410
031500     MOVE HEAD-3  TO PRINT-AREA.
031600     WRITE A-LINE AFTER POSITIONING DOUBLE-SPACE.
031610
031700     MOVE DETAIL-1    TO PRINT-AREA.
031800     WRITE A-LINE AFTER POSITIONING DOUBLE-SPACE.
```

```
031900 IF NO-HOSPITAL EQUAL '1' GO TO WRITE-RTN-EXIT.
032000
032010     MOVE HEAD-4 TO PRINT-AREA.
032200     WRITE A-LINE AFTER POSITIONING DOUBLE-SPACE.
032300
032310     MOVE DETAIL-2 TO PRINT-AREA.
032400     WRITE A-LINE AFTER POSITIONING DOUBLE-SPACE.
032500
032600
032700 IF NO-WARDS EQUAL '1' GO TO WRITE-RTN-EXIT.
032710
032900     MOVE HEAD-5 TO PRINT-AREA.
033000     WRITE A-LINE AFTER POSITIONING DOUBLE-SPACE.
033010
033100     MOVE SPACE TO PRINT-AREA.
033200     WRITE A-LINE AFTER POSITIONING SINGLE-SPACE.
033210
033220 WRITE-PAT-LINE.
033230
033300
033400     MOVE DETAIL-3 TO PRINT-AREA.
033500     WRITE A-LINE AFTER POSITIONING SINGLE-SPACE.
033600     ADD 1 TO LINE-CNT.
033700
033800 WRITE-RTN-EXIT.
033900     EXIT.
034100 WRITE-PAY-DATA.
034200
034300     MOVE PATNAME TO DPATNAM.
034400     MOVE BEDIDENT TO DBEDID.
034500     MOVE DATEADMT TO DDATADMIT.
034600     MOVE PREV-HOSP TO DPREV-HOSP.
034700     MOVE PREV-DATE TO DPREV-DATE.
034800     MOVE PREV-REASON TO DPREV-REASONN.
034900     PERFORM WRITE-RTN THRU WRITE-RTN-EXIT.
035000
035100 HOSPITAL-NOT-FOUND.
035200
035300     MOVE '1' TO NO-HOSPITAL.
```

```
035310        MOVE IHOSPNAM TO ERR-HOSPNAM.
035400        MOVE NO-HOSP-LINE TO DETAIL-1.
035500        PERFORM WRITE-RTN THRU WRITE-RTN-EXIT.
035510        MOVE SPACE TO DETAIL-1.
035600        MOVE '0' TO NO-HOSPITAL.
035700
035800    WARD-NOT-FOUND.
035900        MOVE '1' TO NO-WARDS.
036000        MOVE NO-WARD-LINE TO DETAIL-2.
036100        PERFORM WRITE-RTN THRU WRITE-RTN-EXIT.
036200        MOVE SPACE TO DETAIL-2.
036210        MOVE '0' TO NO-WARDS.
036300
036400    END-JOB.
036500        CLOSE PARMETER FRNTER.
036600        GOBACK.
036700
036800
```

```
a.   ISRT    PATIENT
     ~~~~    ~~~~~~~~~
```

```
b.   ISRT    HOSPITAL(HOSPNAME =MAC NEAL                    )
     ~~~~    ~~~~~~~~~~~~~~~~~~~~~~~~~~~~~~~~~~~~~~~~~~~~~~~~~~
             WARD     (WARDNO   =04)
             ~~~~~~~~~~~~~~~~~~~~~~~~~
             PATIENT
             ~~~~~~~~~
```

Figure E.5 Answers to chapter 6—exercises 2 and 3

```
2.   GHU     HOSPITAL*DN(HOSPNAME =MAC NEAL                  )
     ~~~~    ~~~~~~~~~~~~~~~~~~~~~~~~~~~~~~~~~~~~~~~~~~~~~~~~~~~~
             WARD     *D-(WARDNO   =02)
             ~~~~~~~~~~~~~~~~~~~~~~~~~~~~
             PATIENT *N(BEDIDENT =0002)
             ~~~~~~~~~~~~~~~~~~~~~~~~~~~~
```

```
3.   GU      WARD     *C(RIVEREDGE              08)
     ~~~~    ~~~~~~~~~~~~~~~~~~~~~~~~~~~~~~~~~~~~~~~
```

```
4.   GU      HOSPITAL*P(HOSPNAME =MAC NEAL                  )
     ~~~~    ~~~~~~~~~~~~~~~~~~~~~~~~~~~~~~~~~~~~~~~~~~~~~~~~~~~
             WARD     (WARDTYPE =RECOVERY                   )
             ~~~~~~~~~~~~~~~~~~~~~~~~~~~~~~~~~~~~~~~~~~~~~~~~~~~
             PATIENT *L
             ~~~~~~~~~~~
```

Figure E.7 Answer to chapter 8—exercises 2, 3, and 4

ANSWER TO CHAPTER 11 EXERCISE (CODING PROBLEM)

The listing in figure E.9 shows a possible COBOL solution to the chapter 11 coding problem. The thing to keep in mind about this solution is that it is not the only possible correct solution. Evaluate your solution against this one for reasonableness in determining if your solution is correct.

ANSWERS TO CHAPTER 12 EXERCISES

1. a—HISAM, HIDAM; b—HSAM; c—HDAM, HIDAM; d—HSAM, HISAM;
   e—HSAM, HISAM; f—HDAM; g—HSAM, HISAM; h—HIDAM;
   i—HDAM, HIDAM; j—HDAM; k—HSAM; l—HISAM; m—HDAM;
   n—HIDAM; o—HDAM, HIDAM.

2. a-3, b-5, c-1, d-6, e-4, f-2.

Figure E.9 COBOL solution to the chapter 11 coding problem

```
000100 ID DIVISION.
000200 PROGRAM-ID. CHAP11C.
000300 AUTHOR. JOSEPH F. LEBEN.
000400 DATE-COMPILED.
000500
000600 REMARKS. THIS IS A VERY SIMPLE IMS/DC PROGAM. IT DOES VERY
000700          LITTLE ERROR CHECKING. IT READS AN INPUT TRANSACTION
000800          WHICH HAS THE FOLLOWING FORMAT:
000900          FORMAT.
001000          POSITIONS  1 -  2  TRANSACTION LENGTH
001100                     3 -  4  ZZ FIELD
001200                     5 - 24  HOSPITAL NAME
001300                    25 - 26  WARD NUMBER
001400                    27 - 46  PATIENT NAME
001500
001600          FOR EACH TRANSACTION, THE PROGRAM ISSUES A DL/I CALL
001700          FOR THE PATIENT SEGMENT IDENTIFIED IN THAT TRANSACTION.
001800          IT THEN SENDS A COPY OF THAT PATIENT SEGMENT TO THE
001900          I/O PCB.
002000
002100 ENVIRONMENT DIVISION.
002200 CONFIGURATION SECTION.
002300 SOURCE-COMPUTER. IBM-370-168.
002400 OBJECT-COMPUTER. IBM-370-168.
002600 DATA DIVISION.
002700
002800 WORKING-STORAGE SECTION.
002900
003000 01 TERM-IN.
003100
003200    03 IN-LENGTH        PIC S9999    COMP.
003300    03 IN-ZZ            PIC XX.
003400    03 HOSPNAME-TERM    PIC X(20).
003500    03 WARDNO-TERM      PIC X(2).
003600    03 PATNAME-TERM     PIC X(20).
003700
```

```
003800 01  TERM-OUT.
003900
004000     03  OUT-LENGTH          PIC S9999    VALUE +129   COMP.
004100     03  OUT-ZZ              PIC XX.
004200     03  PATIENT-INFO        PIC X(125).
004300
004400 01  GET-UNIQUE              PIC X(4)     VALUE 'GU  '.
004500 01  INSERT-FUNC             PIC X(4)     VALUE 'ISRT'.
004600 01  P-Z-D                   PIC X        VALUE SPACE.
004610 01  P-Z-D-2 REDEFINES P-Z-D.
004620     03  PACKED-ZERO         PIC S9.
004700 01  PACKED-ONE             PIC S9       VALUE +1.
004800
004900 01  HOSPITAL-SSA.
005000     03  FILLER              PIC X(19)    VALUE 'HOSPITAL(HOSPNAME  ='.
005100     03  HOSPNAME-SSA        PIC X(20).
005200     03  FILLER              PIC X        VALUE ')'.
005300
005400 01  WARD-SSA.
005500     03  FILLER              PIC X(19)    VALUE 'WARD      (WARDNO   ='.
005600     03  WARDNO-SSA          PIC X(2).
005700     03  FILLER              PIC X        VALUE ')'.
005800
005900 01  PATIENT-SSA.
006000     03  FILLER              PIC X(19)    VALUE 'PATIENT (PATNAME   ='.
006100     03  PATNAME-SSA         PIC X(20).
006200     03  FILLER              PIC X        VALUE ')'.
006300
006400 01  I-O-AREA COPY PATIENT.
006500     EJECT
006600 LINKAGE SECTION.
006700 01  DB-PCB  COPY MASKC.
006800
006900 01  I-O-PCB.
007000     03  LTERM-NAME          PIC X(8).
007100     03  FILLER              PIC XX.
007200     03  I-O-STAT-CODE       PIC XX.
007300     03  INPUT-PREFIX.
```

```
007400           05  PREF-DATE           PIC S9(7)      COMP-3.
007500           05  PREF-TIME           PIC S9(7)      COMP-3.
007510           05  PREF-SEQ            PIC S9(7)      COMP.
007700  PROCEDURE DIVISION.
007800
007900  START-OF-PROGRAM.
008000
008100      ENTRY 'DLITCBL' USING I-O-PCB DB-PCB.
008200      PERFORM GET-MESSAGE  THRU GET-MESSAGE-EXIT
008210                 UNTIL I-O-STAT-CODE EQUAL 'QC' OR 'QD'.
008300      GOBACK.
008400
008500  GET-MESSAGE.
008600
008700      CALL 'CBLTDLI' USING GET-UNIQUE
008800                           I-O-PCB
008900                           TERM-IN.
008910
009000      IF I-O-STAT-CODE EQUAL 'QC'           GO TO GET-MESSAGE-EXIT.
009100      IF I-O-STAT-CODE NOT EQUAL SPACE
009110
009200          MOVE I-O-PCB TO PATIENT-INFO
009300          PERFORM SEND-MESSAGE
009400          GO TO GET-MESSAGE-EXIT.
009410
009500      MOVE HOSPNAME-TERM TO HOSPNAME-SSA.
009600      MOVE WARDNO-TERM   TO WARDNO-SSA.
009700      MOVE PATNAME-TERM  TO PATNAME-SSA.
009710
009800      CALL 'CBLTDLI' USING GET-UNIQUE
009900                           DB-PCB
010000                           I-O-AREA
010100                           HOSPITAL-SSA
010200                           WARD-SSA
010300                           PATIENT-SSA.
010310
010400      IF STATUS-CODE NOT EQUAL SPACE
010410
010500          MOVE DB-PCB TO PATIENT-INFO
```

261

```cobol
010600         PERFORM SEND-MESSAGE
010700         GO TO GET-MESSAGE-EXIT.
010710
010800     MOVE I-O-AREA TO PATIENT-INFO.
010900     PERFORM SEND-MESSAGE.
011000
011100 GET-MESSAGE-EXIT.
011200     EXIT.
011300
011400 SEND-MESSAGE.
011500
011600     CALL 'CBLTDLI' USING INSERT-FUNC
011700                         I-O-PCB
011800                         TERM-OUT.
011810
011900     IF I-O-STAT-CODE NOT EQUAL SPACE
011910
012100        ADD PACKED-ONE TO PACKED-ZERO.
```

F

PL/I Coding Examples

This appendix contains information that will allow you to code DL/I programs in PL/I. Figure F.1 summarizes the PL/I conventions that you must follow for entry linkage, PCB masks, and CALL statements. Notice that the PCB mask must be set up as a based variable, and the name that you use in the entry linkage is the pointer name that you declare in the PCB mask coding.

We don't show any SSA examples, because any type of PL/I structure can be used to set up SSAs. You can define an SSA as a major structure, an array, a fixed-character string, an adjustable character string, a pointer to any of these, or a pointer to a minor structure.

There is one major difference between the CALL statement parameter list in PL/I and the parameter list in COBOL. In PL/I, the function code is the second parameter in the list rather than the first. In a PL/I parameter list, the first parameter must point to a full-word binary number that gives the number of parameters that follow the first one in the list. You can use this parameter-count field in COBOL and Assembler Language programs, but in those languages it's optional. In PL/I programs, this parameter count field is required.

This appendix also contains two complete PL/I programs. Figure F.2 is a PL/I version of the PATIENT segment retrieval program from chapter 4. Figure F.3 is a PL/I solution to the coding problem in chapter 5. The COBOL version of this program is shown in appendix E.

```
/*                                                            */
/*   PL/I  ENTRY  LINKAGE                                      */
/*                                                            */
     DLITPLI:  PROC  (PCB_MASK)  OPTIONS  (MAIN);
/*                                                            */
/*   PL/I PCB MASK CODING                                     */
/*                                                            */
     DCL   1   PCB_NAME            BASED  (PCB_MASK),
               2   DBD_NAME         CHAR  (8),
               2   LEVEL_NUMBER     CHAR  (2),
               2   STATUS_CODE      CHAR  (2),
               2   PROC_OPTIONS     CHAR  (4),
               2   JCB_ADDRESS      FIXED BIN (31,0),
               2   SEGMENT_NAME     CHAR  (8),
               2   KEY_LENGTH       FIXED BIN (31,0),
               2   NUMBER_SEGS      FIXED BIN (31,0),
               2   KEY              CHAR  (42);
     DCL       KEY_PTR   POINTER;
     DCL   1   KEY_FEEDBACK         BASED  (KEY_PTR),
               2   HOSPNAME_KEY     CHAR  (20),
               2   WARDNO_KEY       CHAR  (2),
               2   PATNAME_KEY      CHAR  (20);
     KEY_PTR = ADDR (KEY);
/*                                                            */
/*   FUNCTION CODE, PARM COUNT, I/O AREA                      */
/*                                                            */
     DCL       GET_UNIQUE          CHAR (4) INIT ('GU  ');
     DCL       PARMCNT             FIXED BIN (31,0) INIT (6);
     DCL       I_O_AREA            CHAR (200);
/*                                                            */
/*   PL/I CALL STATEMENT                                      */
/*                                                            */
     CALL   PLITDLI   (PARMCNT,
                       GET_UNIQUE,
                       PCB_MASK,
                       I_O_AREA,
                       SSA_ONE,
                       SSA_TWO,
                       SSA_THREE);
```

Figure F.1 PL/I coding conventions

Figure F.2 PATIENT segment retrieval program in PL/I

```
DLITPLI: PROC (PCB_MASK) OPTIONS (MAIN);                                 00000100
                                                                        00000200
    /*      THIS IS A VERY SIMPLE LIST PROGRAM,  IT DOES VERY           00000300
            LITTLE ERROR CHECKING,  IT READS AN INPUT CARD              00000400
            IMAGE DATA SET WHOSE RECORDS HAVE THE FOLLOWING             00000500
            FORMAT:                                                     00000600
                                                                        00000700
            COLUMNS   1 - 20   HOSPITAL NAME                            00000800
                     21 - 22   WARD NUMBER                              00000900
                     23 - 42   PATIENT NAME                             00001000
                                                                        00001100
            FOR EACH CARD READ, THE PROGRAM ISSUES A DL/I CALL          00001200
            FOR THE PATIENT SEGMENT IDENTIFIED IN THAT CARD.            00001300
            IT THEN PRINTS OUT THAT PATIENT SEGMENT.          */        00001400
                                                                        00001500
                                                                        00001600
DCL INPUT FILE RECORD SEQUENTIAL;                                       00001700
                                                                        00001800
DCL OUTPUT FILE RECORD SEQUENTIAL;                                      00001900
                                                                        00002000
DCL PLITDLI ENTRY;                                                      00002100
                                                                        00002200
DCL 1 CARD_AREA,                                                        00002300
      3 HOSPNAME_CARD          CHAR (20),                               00002400
      3 WARDNO_CARD            CHAR (2),                                 00002500
      3 PATNAME_CARD           CHAR (20),                               00002600
      3 CARD_AREA_PAD          CHAR (38);                               00002700
                                                                        00002800
DCL 1 PRINT_LINE,                                                       00002900
      3 CARR_CNTL              CHAR (1),                                 00003000
      3 PATIENT_INFO           CHAR (125),                              00003100
      3 PRINT_LINE_PAD         CHAR (7);                                00003200
                                                                        00003300
DCL TOP_PAGE             CHAR (1)          INIT ('1');                  00003400
DCL SINGLE_SPACE         CHAR (1)          INIT (' ');                  00003500
DCL GET_UNIQUE           CHAR (4)          INIT ('GU  ');               00003600
DCL LINE_COUNT           FIXED BIN (31)    INIT (50);
```

265

```
DCL      SIX                       FIXED BIN (31)  INIT (6);         00003700
                                                                    00003800
DCL   1  HOSPITAL_SSA,                                               00003900
      3  ST_HOSP_SSA     CHAR (19)  INIT ('HOSPITAL(HOSPNAME ='),    00004000
      3  HOSPNAME_SSA    CHAR (20),                                  00004100
      3  END_HOSP_SSA    CHAR (1)   INIT (')');                      00004200
                                                                    00004300
DCL   1  WARD_SSA,                                                   00004400
      3  ST_WARD_SSA     CHAR (19)  INIT ('WARD    (WARDNO ='),      00004500
      3  WARDNO_SSA      CHAR (2),                                   00004600
      3  END_WARD_SSA    CHAR (1)   INIT (')');                      00004700
                                                                    00004800
DCL   1  PATIENT_SSA,                                                00004900
      3  ST_PAT_SSA      CHAR (19)  INIT ('PATIENT (PATNAME ='),     00005000
      3  PATNAME_SSA     CHAR (20),                                  00005100
      3  END_PAT_SSA     CHAR (1)   INIT (')');                      00005200
                                                                    00005300
DCL PATIENT_STRING BASED (PATIENT_PTR) CHAR (125);                  00005400
%INCLUDE PPATIENT;                                                  00005500
                                                                    00005600
DCL PCB_STRING BASED (PCB_MASK)  CHAR (62);                         00005700
%INCLUDE MASKP;                                                     00005800
                                                                    00005900
DCL ADDR BUILTIN;                                                   00006000
START_OF_PROGRAM:                                                  00006100
                                                                    00006200
   OPEN FILE (INPUT)  INPUT;                                        00006300
   OPEN FILE (OUTPUT) OUTPUT;                                       00006400
   ON ENDFILE (INPUT) GO TO END_OF_JOB;                            00006500
   PATIENT_PTR = ADDR (PATIENT);                                   00006600
                                                                    00006700
READ_CARD:                                                         00006800
                                                                    00006900
   READ FILE (INPUT) INTO (CARD_AREA);                             00007000
   HOSPNAME_SSA = HOSPNAME_CARD;                                   00007100
   WARDNO_SSA  = WARDNO_CARD;                                      00007200
   PATNAME_SSA = PATNAME_CARD;                                     00007300
                                                                    00007400
   CALL   PLITDLI   (SIX,                                          00007500
                                                                    00007600
```

```
            GET_UNIQUE,
            PCB_MASK,
            PATIENT:
            HOSPITAL_SSA,
            WARD_SSA,
            PATIENT_SSA);

    IF STATUS_CODE ^= ' '
    THEN DO;

        CALL BAD_STATUS;
        GO TO READ_CARD;
        END;

    CALL PRINT_ROUTINE;
    GO TO READ_CARD;

BAD_STATUS: PROC;

    PATIENT_STRING = PCB_STRING;
    CALL PRINT_ROUTINE;
    RETURN;
    END;
PRINT_ROUTINE: PROC;

    IF LINE_COUNT = 50
    THEN DO;

        LINE_COUNT = 0;
        PATIENT_INFO = '                P A T I E N T   L I S T';
        CARR_CNTL = TOP_PAGE;
        WRITE FILE (OUTPUT) FROM (PATIENT_INFO);
        PATIENT_INFO = ' ';
        CARR_CNTL = SINGLE_SPACE;
        WRITE FILE (OUTPUT) FROM (PRINT_LINE);
        END;
```

```
00007700
00007800
00007900
00008000
00008100
00008200
00008300
00008400
00008500
00008600
00008700
00008800
00008900
00009000
00009100
00009200
00009300
00009400
00009500
00009600
00009700
00009800
00009900
00010000
00010100
00010200
00010300
00010400
00010500
00010600
00010700
00010800
00010900
00011000
00011100
00011200
00011300
00011400
00011500
```

```
00011600
00011700
00011800
00011900
00012000
00012100
00012200
00012300
00012400
00012500
00012600
```

```
          PATIENT_INFO = PATIENT_STRING;
          WRITE FILE (OUTPUT) FROM (PRINT_LINE);
          LINE_COUNT = 1;
          RETURN;
          END;

END_OF_JOB:

          CLOSE FILE (INPUT), FILE (OUTPUT);
          RETURN;
          END;
```

Figure F.3 Chapter 5 coding problem solution in PL/I

```
ILITPLI: PROC (PCB_MASK) OPTIONS (MAIN);                          00000100
                                                                 00000200
/*    THE OUTPUT OF THIS PROGRAM IS A LIST OF PATIENTS WHO       00000300
      ARE IN QUARANTINE WARDS PRESENTLY BUT ALSO HAVE            00000400
      BEEN IN A HOSPITAL WITHIN THE PAST YEAR.       */          00000500
                                                                 00000600
DCL PARMETER FILE RECORD SEQUENTIAL;                             00000700
                                                                 00000800
DCL 1 PARM_CARD,                                                 00000900
      5 HOSPCONST   CHAR (2),                                    00001000
      5 IHOSPNAM    CHAR (20),                                   00001100
      5 PAD1        CHAR (58);                                   00001200
                                                                 00001300
DCL PRNTER FILE RECORD SEQUENTIAL;                              00001400
                                                                 00001500
DCL 1 A_LINE,                                                    00001600
      5 PRINT_CTL    CHAR (1),                                   00001700
      5 PRINT_AREA   CHAR (132);                                 00001800
                                                                 00001900
DCL FLITDLI          ENTRY;                                      00002000
DCL ADDR             BUILTIN;                                    00002100
DCL THREE            FIXED BIN (31) INIT (3);                    00002200
DCL FOUR             FIXED BIN (31) INIT (4);                    00002300
DCL FIVE             FIXED BIN (31) INIT (5);                    00002400
DCL NO_HOSPITAL      CHAR (1)  INIT ('0');                       00002500
DCL NO_WARDS         CHAR (1)  INIT ('0');                       00002600
DCL NO_PATIENTS      CHAR (1)  INIT ('0');                       00002700
DCL TOP_PAGE         CHAR (1)  INIT ('1');                       00002800
DCL DOUBLE_SPACE     CHAR (1)  INIT ('0');                       00002900
DCL SINGLE_SPACE     CHAR (1)  INIT (' ');                       00003000
DCL TRIPLE_SPACE     CHAR (1)  INIT ('-');                       00003100
DCL END_DATABASE     CHAR (2)  INIT ('GB');                      00003200
DCL SEG_NC_FOUND     CHAR (2)  INIT ('GE');                      00003300
DCL GET_UNIQUE       CHAR (2)  INIT ('GU  ');                    00003400
DCL GET_NEXT         CHAR (4)  INIT ('GN  ');                    00003500
DCL GET_NEXT_P       CHAR (4)  INIT ('GNP ');                    00003600
```

```
DCL  LINE_CNT            FIXED BIN (31) INIT (52);        00003700
DCL  PAGE_CNT            FIXED BIN (31) INIT (0);         00003800
DCL  CALL_SUCCESSFUL     CHAR (2)   INIT ('  ');          00003900
DCL  END_HOSP_DATA       CHAR (1)   INIT (' ');           00004000
DCL  HOSP_NOT_FOUND      CHAR (20)  INIT (' ');           00004100
DCL  NEW_MONTH           DECIMAL FIXED (2,0);             00004200
DCL  NEW_YEAR            DECIMAL FIXED (2,0);             00004300
DCL  WRDTYPE             CHAR (20)  INIT (' ');           00004400
DCL  1  CURR_DATE,                                        00004600
     5  CURRMO           PIC '99',                        00004700
     5  PAD2             CHAR (1)     INIT ('/'),          00004800
     5  CURRDAY          PIC '99',                        00004900
     5  PAD3             CHAR (1)     INIT ('/'),          00005000
     5  CURRYR           PIC '99';                        00005100
                                                          00005200
DCL  DATE_PTR POINTER;                                    00005300
DCL  DATE_STRING  BASED (DATE_PTR)    CHAR (4);           00005400
DCL  1  WS_PREV_DATE BASED (DATE_PTR),                    00005500
     5  PREVMO         PIC '99',                          00005600
     5  PREVYR         PIC '99';                          00005700
                                                          00005800
DATE_PTR = ADDR (WS_PREV_DATE);                           00005900
                                                          00006000
%INCLUDE PHOSPITA;                                        00006100
                                                          00006200
%INCLUDE PWARD;                                           00006300
                                                          00006400
%INCLUDE PPATIENT;                                        00006500
                                                          00006600
DCL  1  SSA_HOSP,                                         00006700
                                                          00006800
     5  HOSPSEG          CHAR (8)    INIT ('HOSPITAL'),    00006900
     5  PAD4             CHAR (1)    INIT ('('),           00007000
     5  SEG_SEARCH_NAM   CHAR (8)    INIT ('HOSPNAME'),    00007100
     5  HOSP_REL_OP      CHAR (1)    INIT ('EQ'),          00007200
     5  HOSP_NAME        CHAR (20),  INIT ('  '),          00007300
     5  PAD5             CHAR (1)    INIT (')');           00007400
                                                          00007500
DCL  1  SSA_WARD,                                         00007600
```

```
5  WARDSEG          CHAR (8)    INIT ('WARD      '),
5  PAI6             CHAR (1)    INIT ('( '),                        00007700
5  SEC_SEARCH_NAME  CHAR (8)    INIT ('WARDTYPE'),                  00007800
5  WARD_REL_OP      CHAR (1)    INIT ('EQ'),                       00007900
5  WARD_TYPE        CHAR (20)   INIT ('QUARANTINE'),               00008000
5  FAD7             CHAR (1)    INIT (')');                        00008100
                                                                   00008200
DCL SSA_PATIENT         CHAR (7)    INIT ('PATIENT');              00008300
DCL HEAD1_PTR      POINTER;                                        00008400
DCL HEAD1_STRING   BASED (HEAD1_PTR) CHAR (132);                   00008500
DCL 1 HEAD_1       BASED (HEAD1_PTR),                              00008600
                                                                   00008700
5  FAD8    CHAR (26) INIT ('  '),                                  00008800
5  TITLE   CHAR (106)                                              00008900
   INIT ('P R E V I O U S   S T A Y   R E P O R T');               00009000
                                                                   00009100
HEAD1_PTR = ADDR (HEAD_1);                                         00009200
                                                                   00009300
DCL HEAD2_PTR      POINTER;                                        00009400
DCL HEAD2_STRING   BASED (HEAD2_PTR) CHAR (132);                   00009500
DCL 1 HEAD_2       BASED (HEAD2_PTR),                              00009600
                                                                   00009700
5  FAD11       CHAR (5)   INIT ('FAGE'),                           00009800
5  HPAGE_CTR   PIC 'ZZZ9',                                         00009900
5  FAD12       CHAR (123) INIT ('  ');                             00010000
                                                                   00010100
HEAD2_PTR = ADDR (HEAD_2);                                         00010200
                                                                   00010300
DCL HEAD3_PTR      POINTER;                                        00010400
DCL HEAD3_STRING   BASED (HEAD3_PTR) CHAR (132);                   00010500
DCL 1 HEAD_3       BASED (HEAD3_PTR),                              00010600
                                                                   00010700
5  HHOSPNAM    CHAR (25) INIT ('HOSPITAL NAME'),                   00010800
5  HHOSPADR    CHAR (35) INIT ('HOSPITAL ADDRESS'),                00010900
5  HHOSPHON    CHAR (10) INIT ('HOSPITAL PHONE'),                  00011000
5  FAD16       CHAR (62) INIT ('  ');                              00011100
                                                                   00011200
HEAD3_PTR = ADDR (HEAD_3);                                         00011300
                                                                   00011400
                                                                   00011500
                                                                   00011600
                                                                   00011700
```

271

```
DCL     HEAD4_PTR         POINTER;                                        00011800
DCL     HEAD4_STRING      BASED (HEAD4_PTR) CHAR (132);                   00011900
DCL  1  HEAD_4            BASED (HEAD4_PTR),                              00012000
                                                                         00012100
        5 HWARDNO         CHAR (12) INIT ('WARD NO'),                     00012200
        5 HTOTRMS         CHAR (14) INIT ('TOT ROOMS'),                   00012300
        5 HTOTBDS         CHAR (13) INIT ('TOT BEDS'),                    00012400
        5 HBDSAVAI        CHAR (15) INIT ('BEDS AVAIL'),                  00012500
        5 HWARDTP         CHAR (20) INIT ('WARD TYPE'),                   00012600
        5 FAD19           CHAR (58) INIT (' ');                           00012700
                                                                         00012800
HEAD4_PTR = ADDR (HEAD_4);                                                00012900
                                                                         00013000
DCL     HEAD5_PTR         POINTER;                                        00013100
DCL     HEAD5_STRING      BASED (HEAD5_PTR);                              00013200
DCL  1  HEAD_5            BASED (HEAD5_PTR),                              00013300
                                                                         00013400
        5 HPATNAM         CHAR (21) INIT ('PATIENT NAME'),                00013500
        5 HBDID           CHAR (6)  INIT ('BED'),                         00013600
        5 HDATADMIT       CHAR (12) INIT ('ADMIT DATE'),                  00013700
        5 HPREVDAT        CHAR (11) INIT ('PREV DATE'),                   00013800
        5 HPREVHOS        CHAR (21) INIT ('PREVIOUS HOSPITAL'),           00013900
        5 HPREV_REASON    CHAR (30) INIT ('PREVIOUS REASON'),             00014000
        5 FAD21           CHAR (31) INIT (' ');                           00014100
                                                                         00014200
HEAD5_PTR = ADDR (HEAD_5);                                                00014300
DCL     DETAIL1_PTR       POINTER;                                        00014400
DCL     DETAIL1_STRING    BASED (DETAIL1_PTR) CHAR (132);                 00014800
DCL  1  DETAIL_1          BASED (DETAIL1_PTR),                            00014900
                                                                         00015000
        5 DHOSPNAM        CHAR (20),                                      00015100
        5 FAD23           CHAR (5)  INIT (' '),                           00015200
        5 DHOSP_ADDRESS   CHAR (30),                                      00015300
        5 FAD24           CHAR (5)  INIT (' '),                           00015400
        5 DHOSPHON        CHAR (10),                                      00015500
        5 FAD25           CHAR (62) INIT (' ');                           00015600
                                                                         00015700
DETAIL1_PTR = ADDR (DETAIL_1);                                           00015800
                                                                         00015900
```

272

```
DCL    DETAIL2_PTR         POINTER;                                    00016000
DCL    DETAIL2_STRING   BASED (DETAIL2_PTR)  CHAR (132);               00016100
DCL 1  DETAIL_2         BASED (DETAIL2_PTR),                           00016200
                                                                       00016300
       5  FAD26            CHAR (3)    INIT (' '),                     00016400
       5  DWARDNO          CHAR (2),                                   00016500
       5  FAD27            CHAR (10)   INIT (' '),                     00016600
       5  DTOTRMS          CHAR (3),                                   00016700
       5  FAD28            CHAR (11)   INIT (' '),                     00016800
       5  DTOT_BEDS        CHAR (3),                                   00016900
       5  FAD29            CHAR (10)   INIT (' '),                     00017000
       5  DBEDSAVAIL       CHAR (3),                                   00017100
       5  FAD30            CHAR (9)    INIT (' '),                     00017200
       5  DWARDTYPE        CHAR (20),                                  00017300
       5  FAD31            CHAR (58)   INIT (' ');                     00017400
                                                                       00017500
                                                                       00017600
DETAIL_2_PTR = ADDR (DETAIL_2);                                        00017700
DCL    DETAIL3_PTR         POINTER;                                    00017800
DCL    DETAIL3_STRING   BASED (DETAIL3_PTR);                           00017900
DCL 1  DETAIL_3         BASED (DETAIL3_PTR),                           00018000
                                                                       00018100
       5  DFATNAM          CHAR (20),                                  00018200
       5  FAD33            CHAR (1)    INIT (' '),                     00018300
       5  DBEDID           CHAR (4),                                   00018400
       5  FAD34            CHAR (4)    INIT (' '),                     00018500
       5  DDATADMIT        CHAR (6),                                   00018600
       5  FAD35            CHAR (4)    INIT (' '),                     00018700
       5  DFREV_DATE       CHAR (4),                                   00018800
       5  FAD36            CHAR (5)    INIT (' '),                     00018900
       5  DFREV_HOSP       CHAR (29),                                  00019000
       5  FAD37            CHAR (1)    INIT (' '),                     00019100
       5  DFREV_REASONN    CHAR (30),                                  00019200
       5  FAD38            CHAR (31)   INIT (' ');                     00019300
                                                                       00019400
                                                                       00019500
DETAIL3_PTR = ADDR (DETAIL_3);                                         00019600
DCL    ERROR_PTR           POINTER;                                    00020000
DCL    ERROR_STRING     BASED (ERROR_PTR)  CHAR (132);                 00020100
```

273

```
DCL 1  NO_HOSP_LINE    BASED (ERROR_PTR),                              00020200
                                                                       00020300
       5  ERR_HOSPNAM  CHAR (20),                                      00020600
       5  PAD39        CHAR (5) INIT (' '),                            00020610
       5  PAD41        CHAR (107)                                      00020700
                       INIT ('**** HOSPITAL NOT FOUND ****');          00020800
                                                                       00021300
DCL    NO_WARD_LINE    CHAR (132)                                      00021400
                       INIT ('*** NO QUALRANTINE WARDS ***');          00021410
                                                                       00021600
DCL    NO_PAT_LINE     CHAR (132)                                      00021700
                       INIT ('*** NO PATIENTS WITH RECENT STAY ***');  00021800
                                                                       00021900
DCL    PCB_STRING BASED (PCB_MASK)  CHAR (62);                         00022000
%INCLUDE MASKP;                                                        00022100
                                                                       00022300
ENTRY_POINT:                                                           00022400
                                                                       00022500
       OPEN FILE  (PARMETER)  INPUT;                                   00022600
       OPEN FILE  (PRNTER)    OUTPUT;                                  00022700
       ON ENDFILE (PARMETER) GO TO END_JOB;                            00022800
       CALL DATE;                                                      00022900
                                                                       00023000
                                                                       00023100
READ_CARD:                                                             00023200
                                                                       00023300
       READ FILE (PARMETER) INTO (PARM_CARD);                          00023400
       HOSP_NAME = IHOSPNAM;                                           00023500
       LINE_CNT = 45;                                                  00023600
                                                                       00023700
       CALL  PLITDLI    (FOUR,                                         00023800
                         GET_UNIQUE,                                   00023900
                         PCB_MASK,                                     00024000
                         HOSPITAL,                                     00024100
                         SSA_HOSP);                                    00024200
                                                                       00024300
       IF STATUS_CODE ^= ' ' THEN                                      00024400
                                                                       00024500
           DO;   CALL   HOSPITAL_NOT_FOUND;                            00024600
```

274

```
                        END;
            GO TO READ_CARD;

DHOSPNAM      = HOSPNAME;
DHOSP_ADDRESS = HOSP_ADDRESS;
DHOSPHON      = HOSP_PHONE;

CALL  FLITDLI     (FIVE,
                   GET_UNIQUE,
                   PCB_MASK,
                   WARD,
                   SSA_HOSP,
                   SSA_WARD);

IF STATUS_CODE ^= ' ' THEN

   DO;
      CALL WARD_NOT_FOUND;
      GO TO READ_CARD;
   END;

DWARDNO    = WARDNO;
DTOTRMS    = TOT_ROOMS;
DTOT_BEDS  = TOT_BEDS;
DBDSAVAIL  = BEDAVAIL;
DWARDTYPE  = WARDTYPE;
NO_PATIENTS = '0';

DO WHILE (STATUS_CODE ^= 'GE');

   CALL CALL_PATIENT;

END;

IF NO_PATIENTS = '0' THEN

   DO;
      DETAIL3_STRING = NO_PAT_LINE;
```

                                                                    00024700
                                                                    00024800
                                                                    00024900
                                                                    00025000
                                                                    00025100
                                                                    00025200
                                                                    00025300
                                                                    00025400
                                                                    00025500
                                                                    00025600
                                                                    00025700
                                                                    00025800
                                                                    00025900
                                                                    00026000
                                                                    00026100
                                                                    00026200
                                                                    00026300
                                                                    00026400
                                                                    00026500
                                                                    00026600
                                                                    00026710
                                                                    00026800
                                                                    00026900
                                                                    00027000
                                                                    00027100
                                                                    00027200
                                                                    00027300
                                                                    00027400
                                                                    00027500
                                                                    00027600
                                                                    00027700
                                                                    00027800
                                                                    00027900
                                                                    00028000
                                                                    00028100
                                                                    00028200
                                                                    00028400

```
              CALL   WRITE_RTN;                                            00028500
              DETAIL3_STRING = '  ';                                       00028600
                                                                           00028700
          END;                                                             00028800
                                                                           00028900
      NO_PATIENTS = 'O';                                                   00029000
      GO TO READ_CARD;                                                     00029100
                                                                           00029200
  CALL_PATIENT:   PROC;                                                    00029300
                                                                           00029400
      CALL   PLITDLI          (FOUR,                                       00029500
                               GET_NEXT_F,                                 00029600
                               PCB_MASK,                                   00029700
                               PATIENT,                                    00029800
                               SSA_PATIENT);                               00029900
                                                                           00030000
      IF STATUS_CODE = 'GE' THEN RETURN;                                   00030100
      IF STATUS_CODE ^= ' ' THEN                                           00030200
                                                                           00030300
          DO;                                                              00030500
              DETAIL3_STRING = PCB_STRING;                                 00030600
              CALL WRITE_RTN;                                              00030700
              DETAIL3_STRING = '  ';                                       00030800
              GO TO READ_CARD;                                             00030900
          END;                                                             00031000
                                                                           00031100
      IF   PREV_STAY_FLAG ^= '1'   THEN   RETURN;                          00031200
                                                                           00031400
          DATE_STRING = PREV_DATE;                                         00031500
          NEW_MONTH = CURRMO - PREVMO;                                     00031600
          NEW_YEAR  = CURRYR - PREVYR;                                     00031700
                                                                           00031800
      IF   NEW_YEAR > 1 THEN RETURN;                                       00031900
      IF   NEW_YEAR = O THEN                                               00032100
                                                                           00032200
          DO;                                                              00032300
              CALL WRITE_PAT_DATA;                                         00032400
              NO_PATIENTS = '1';
              RETURN;
```

276

```
        END;

IF   NEW_YEAR = 1 & NEW_MONTH < 1 THEN
     DO;
        CALL WRITE_PAT_DATA;
        NO_PATIENTS = '1';
     END;

RETURN;

END;

WRITE_RTN: PROC;

IF LINE_CNT > 44 THEN
     DO;
        LINE_CNT = 1;
        PRINT_AREA = HEAD1_STRING;
        PRINT_CTL = TOP_PAGE;
        WRITE FILE (PRNTER) FROM (A_LINE);

        PAGE_CNT = PAGE_CNT + 1;
        HPAGE_CTR = PAGE_CNT;
        PRINT_AREA = HEAD2_STRING;
        PRINT_CTL = DOUBLE_SPACE;
        WRITE FILE (PRNTER) FROM (A_LINE);

        PRINT_AREA = HEAD3_STRING;
        PRINT_CTL = DOUBLE_SPACE;
        WRITE FILE (PRNTER) FROM (A_LINE);

        PRINT_AREA = DETAIL1_STRING;
        PRINT_CTL = DOUBLE_SPACE;
        WRITE FILE (PRNTER) FROM (A_LINE);

        IF NO_HOSPITAL = '1' THEN RETURN;

        PRINT_AREA = HEAD4_STRING;
```

```
                    PRINT_CTL = DOUBLE_SPACE;                  00036900
                    WRITE FILE (PRNTER) FROM (A_LINE);         00037000
                                                               00037100
                    PRINT_AREA = DETAIL2_STRING;               00037300
                    PRINT_CTL = DOUBLE_SPACE;                  00037400
                    WRITE FILE (PRNTER) FROM (A_LINE);         00037500
                                                               00037600
          IF NO_WARDS = '1' THEN RETURN;                       00037700
                                                               00037800
                    PRINT_AREA = HEAD5_STRING;                 00038000
                    PRINT_CTL = DOUBLE_SPACE;                  00038100
                    WRITE FILE (PRNTER) FROM (A_LINE);         00038200
                                                               00038300
                    PRINT_AREA = ' ';                          00038400
                    PRINT_CTL = SINGLE_SPACE;                  00038500
                    WRITE FILE (PRNTER) FROM (A_LINE);         00038600
                                                               00038700
          END;                                                 00038800
                                                               00039000
          PRINT_AREA = DETAIL3_STRING;                         00039100
          PRINT_CTL = SINGLE_SPACE;                            00039200
          WRITE FILE (PRNTER) FROM (A_LINE);                   00039300
                                                               00039400
          LINE_CNT = LINE_CNT + 1;                             00039500
                                                               00039600
RETURN;                                                        00039700
                                                               00039800
END;                                                           00039900
                                                               00040000
WRITE_PAT_DATA:    PROC;                                       00040100
                                                               00040200
          DPATNAM    = PATNAME;                                00040300
          DBEDID     = BEDIDENT;                               00040400
          DDATADMIT  = DATEADMT;                               00040500
          DPREV_HOSP = PREV_HOSP;                              00040600
          DPREV_DATE = PREV_DATE;                              00040700
          DPREV_REASONN = PREV_REASON;                         00040800
          CALL    WRITE_RTN;                                   00040900
                                                               00041000
RETURN;
```

278

```
END;

HOSPITAL_NOT_FOUND:    PROC;

    NO_HOSPITAL = '1';
    ERR_HOSPNAM = IHOSPNAM;
    ERROR_PTR = ADDR (NO_HOSP_LINE);
    DETAIL1_STRING = ERROR_STRING;
    CALL WRITE_RTN;
    DETAIL1_STRING = ' ';
    NO_HOSPITAL = 'O';

RETURN;

END;

WARD_NOT_FOUND:    PROC;

    NO_WARDS = '1';
    ERROR_PTR = ADDR (NO_WARD_LINE);
    DETAIL2_STRING = ERROR_STRING;
    CALL WRITE_RTN;
    DETAIL2_STRING = ' ';
    NO_WARDS = 'O';

RETURN;

END;

DATE: PROC;

    CURRMO  = 06;
    CURRDAY = 27;
    CURRYR  = 77;

RETURN;
```

```
                                                           00045100
                                                           00045200
                                                           00045300
                                                           00045400
                                                           00045500
                                                           00045600
                                                           00045700
                                                           00045800
                                                           00045900

      END;
      END_JOB:
           CLOSE FILE (PARMETER), FILE (PRNTER);

      RETURN;

      END;
```

G

Assembler Language Coding Examples

This appendix contains information that will allow you to code DL/I programs in Assembler Language. Figure G.1 summarizes the Assembler Language Conventions that must be followed for entry coding, CALL statements, and PCB masks. Following that figure are two complete Assembler Language programs. Figure G.2 shows the Assembler Language version of the PATIENT segment retrieval program from chapter 4. Figure G.3 shows the Assembler Language version of a sample solution to the coding problem in chapter 5. The COBOL version of this program is shown in appendix E.

```
*
*            ASSEMBLER LANGUAGE ENTRY LINKAGE
*
DLITASM   CSECT
          SAVE  (14,12)
          BALR  12,0              REG 12 -- PROG BASE REGISTER
          USING *,12
          LA    11,SAVE
          ST    11,8(0,13)
          ST    13,SAVE+4
          LR    13,11
          L     11,0(0,1)         REG 11 -- PCB BASE REGISTER
          USING PCBMASK,11
            .
*
*            ASSEMBLER CALL STATEMENT
*
          CALL  ASMTDLI,(GU,(11),IOAREA,SSA1,SSA2,SSA3),VL
            .
            .
            .
*
*            FUNCTION CODE, I/O AREA
*
GU        DC    CL4'GU  '
IOAREA    DC    CL200' '
            .
            .
            .
*
*            PCB MASK
*
PCBMASK   DSECT
DBDNAME   DS    CL8
LEVELNO   DS    CL2
STATCODE  DS    CL2
PROCOPT   DS    CL4
JCBADDR   DS    F
SEGNAME   DS    CL8
KEYLNGTH  DS    F
NOSEGS    DS    F
KEYFEED   DS    OCL42
HOSPKEY   DS    CL20
WARDKEY   DS    CL2
PATKEY    DS    CL20
          END   DLITASM
```

Figure G.1 Assembler language coding conventions

Figure G.2 PATIENT segment retrieval program in assembler language

```
         PRINT NOGEN                                                  00000100
CHAP4A   START 0                                                      00000200
DLITCBL  EQU   *                                                      00000210
         ENTRY DLITCBL                                                00000211
         SAVE  (14,12)                                                00000300
         BALR  12,0                                                   00000400
         USING *,12                                                   00000500
         LA    2,SAVE                                                 00000600
         ST    2,SAVE+8                                               00000700
         ST    13,SAVE+4                                              00000800
         LR    13,2                                                   00000900
         MVC   REGSAVE,0(1)                                           00000910
         MVI   REGSAVE,X'00'                                          00000920
         L     3,REGSAVE                                              00000930
         USING FCBMASK,3                                              00001100
         OPEN  (INPUT,(INPUT),OUTPUT,(OUTPUT))                        00001300
*                                                                    00001400
READCARD GET   INPUT,CARDDATA                                         00001500
         MVC   HNAMSSA,FNAMCARD                                       00001600
         MVC   WNOSSA,WNOCARD                                         00001700
         MVC   FNAMSSA,FNAMCARD                                       00001800
*                                                                    00001900
         CALL  CBLTDLI,(GU,(3),IOAREA,HOSPSSA,WARDSSA,FATSSA),VL      00002000
*                                                                    00002100
*                                                                    00002200
         CLC   STATCODE,=C' '                                         00002300
         BNE   BADSTAT                                                00002400
         MVC   PATINFO,IOAREA                                         00002500
*                                                                    00002500
PRINT    LH    2,LINECNT                                              00002600
         CH    2,=H'50'                                               00002700
         BL    NOHEAD                                                 00002800
         LA    2,0                                                    00002900
         STH   2,LINECNT                                              00003000
         MVC   PRNTLINE(33),=C'1          PATIENT LIST '              00003100
         PUT   OUTPUT,PRNTLINE                                        00003200
         MVI   PRNTLINE,C' '                                          00003300
```

283

```
         MVC   PRNTLINE+1(132),PRNTLINE                    00003400
         PUT   OUTPUT,PRNTLINE                             00003500
*                                                          00003600
NOHEAD   MVC   PATINFO,IOAREA                              00003700
         PUT   OUTPUT,PRNTLINE                             00003800
         LH    2,LINECNT                                   00003900
         AH    2,=H'1'                                     00004000
         STH   2,LINECNT                                   00004100
         B     READCARD                                    00004200
*                                                          00004300
EOFCARD  CLOSE (INPUT)                                     00004400
         CLOSE (OUTPUT)                                    00004410
         L     13,SAVE+4                                   00004500
         RETURN (14,12),RC=0                               00004600
*                                                          00004700
BADSTAT  MVI   IOAREA,C' '                                 00004800
         MVC   IOAREA+1(124),IOAREA                        00004900
         MVC   IOAREA(62),PCBMASK                          00005000
         B     PRINT                                       00005100
INPUT    DCB   DSORG=PS,MACRF=GM,EODAD=EOFCARD,LRECL=80,RECFM=FB,  *00005300
               DDNAME=INPUT                                00005310
*                                                          00005400
OUTPUT   DCB   DSORG=PS,MACRF=PM,LRECL=133,RECFM=FBA,      *00005500
               DDNAME=OUTPUT                               00005510
*                                                          00005600
CARDDATA DS    OCL80                                       00005700
HNAMCARD DS    CL20                                        00005800
WNOCARD  DS    CL2                                         00005900
FNAMCARD DS    CL20                                        00006000
         DS    CL38                                        00006100
*                                                          00006200
PRNTLINE DS    OCL133                                      00006300
CARRCNTL DS    C                                           00006400
PATINFO  DS    CL125                                       00006500
         DS    CL7                                         00006600
*                                                          00006700
TOFPAGE  DC    C'1'                                        00006800
SNGLSPCE DC    C' '                                        00006900
```

```
GU        DC    CL4'GU '                      00007000
LINECNT   DC    H'60'                         00007100
*                                             00007200
HOSPSSA   DS    0CL40                         00007300
          DC    CL19'HOSPITAL(HOSPNAME ='     00007400
HNAMSSA   DS    CL20                          00007500
          DC    C')'                          00007600
*                                             00007700
WARDSSA   DS    0CL22                         00007800
          DC    CL19'WARD   (WARDNO  ='       00007900
WNOSSA    DS    CL2                           00008000
          DC    C')'                          00008100
*                                             00008200
PATSSA    DS    0CL40                         00008300
          DC    CL19'PATIENT (PATNAME ='      00008400
PNAMSSA   DS    CL20                          00008500
          DC    C')'                          00008600
SAVE      DS    18F                           00008610
*                                             00008700
IOAREA    DS    0CL125                        00008800
REGSAVE   DS    F                             00008810
          COPY  APATIENT                      00008900
*                                             00009000
PC3MASK   DSECT MASKA                         00009100
          COPY  CHAP4A                        00009200
          END                                 00009300
```

Figure G.3 Chapter 5 coding problem in assembler language

```
              PRINT  NOGEN                                              00000100
CHAP5A        START  0                                                 00000200
DLITCBL       EQU    *                                                 00000300
              ENTRY  DLITCBL                                           00000400
              SAVE   (14,12)                                           00000500
              BALR   12,0                                              00000600
              USING  *,12                                              00000700
              LA     2,SAVE                                            00000800
              ST     2,8(0,13)                                         00000900
              ST     13,SAVE+4                                         00001000
              LR     13,2                                              00001100
              MVC    FULL,0(1)                                         00001200
              MVI    FULL,X'00'                                        00001300
              L      2,FULL                                            00001400
              USING  PCBMASK,2                                         00001500
*                                                                     00001600
START         OPEN   (PARMETER,(INPUT),PRNTER,(OUTPUT))                00001700
              BAL    11,DATE                                           00001800
              EJECT                                                   00001900
READCARD      GET    PARMETER,PARMCARD                                 00002000
              MVC    SSAHNAME,IHOSPNAM                                 00002100
              MVC    LINECNT,=H'45'                                    00002200
*                                                                     00002300
              CALL   CBLTDLI,(GU,(2),HOSPITAL,SSAHOSP),VL              00002400
*                                                                     00002500
              CLC    STATCODE,=C' '                                    00002600
              BE     AHEAD1                                            00002700
              BAL    11,HOSPNFND                                       00002800
              B      READCARD                                          00002900
*                                                                     00003000
AHEAD1        MVC    DHOSPNAM,HOSPNAME                                 00003100
              MVC    DHOSPADR,HOSPADDR                                 00003200
              MVC    DHOSPHON,HOSPFHON                                 00003300
              CALL   CBLTDLI,(GU,(2),WARD,SSAHOSP,SSAWARD),VL          00003400
*                                                                     00003500
*                                                                     00003600
```

```
         CLC   STATCODE,=C' '                                  00003700
         BE    AHEAD2                                          00003800
         BAL   11,WARINFND                                     00003900
         B     READCARD                                        00004000
*                                                              00004100
AHEAD2   MVC   DWARDNO,WARDNO                                  00004200
         MVC   DTOTRMS,TOTROOMS                                00004300
         MVC   DTOTBEDS,TOTBEDS                                00004400
         MVC   DBDSAVAI,BEDAVAIL                               00004500
         MVC   DWARDTYP,WARDTYPE                               00004600
         MVI   NOPAT,C'C'                                      00004700
LOOP1    CLC   STATCODE,=C'GE'                                 00004800
         BE    AHEAD3                                          00004900
         BAL   11,CALLPAT                                      00005000
         B     LOOP1                                           00005100
*                                                              00005200
AHEAD3   CLI   NOPAT,C'C'                                      00005300
         BNE   AHEAD4                                          00005400
         MVC   DETAIL3,NOPATLN                                 00005500
         BAL   11,WRITERTN                                     00005600
         MVI   DETAIL3,C' '                                    00005700
         MVC   DETAIL3+1(131),DETAIL3                          00005800
*                                                              00005900
AHEAD4   MVI   NOPAT,C'C'                                      00006000
         B     READCARD                                        00006100
CALLPAT  ST    11,PATSAVE                                      00006300
*                                                              00006400
         CALL  CBLTDLI,=GNP,(2),PATIENT,SSAPAT),VL            00006500
*                                                              00006600
         CLC   STATCODE =C'GE'                                 00006700
         BE    PATEXIT                                         00006800
*                                                              00006900
         CLC   STATCODE =C' '                                  00007000
         BE    AHEAD5                                          00007100
*                                                              00007200
         MVI   DETAIL3+1,C' '                                  00007300
         MVC   DETAIL3+2(69),DETAIL3+61                        00007400
         MVC   DETAIL3(2),PCBMASK                              00007500
         BAL   11,WRITERTN                                     00007600
```

287

```
        MVI   DETAIL3,C' '                        00007700
        MVC   DETAIL3+1(131),DETAIL3              00007800
        B     READCARD                            00007900
*                                                 00008000
AHEAD5  CLI   PREVSTAY,C'1'                        00008100
        BNE   FATEXIT                             00008200
*                                                 00008300
        MVC   WSPREVDT,PREVDATE                   00008400
        PACK  DATEWK1,CURRMO                      00008500
        PACK  DATEWK2,PREVMO                      00008600
        ZAP   NEWMONTH,DATEWK1                    00008700
        SP    NEWMONTH,DATEWK2                    00008800
        PACK  DATEWK1,CURRYR                      00008900
        PACK  DATEWK2,PREVYR                      00009000
        ZAP   NEWYEAR,DATEWK1                     00009100
        SP    NEWYEAR,DATEWK2                     00009200
*                                                 00009300
        CP    NEWYEAR,=P'1'                       00009400
        BH    FATEXIT                             00009500
        BE    CHKMO                               00009600
        BL    WFAT                                00009700
*                                                 00009800
CHKMO   CP    NEWMONTH,=P'1'                      00009900
        BNL   FATEXIT                             00010000
WFAT    BAL   11,WFATDATA                         00010100
        MVI   NOFAT,C'1'                          00010200
*                                                 00010300
FATEXIT L     11,FATSAVE                          00010400
        BR    11                                  00010500
*                                                 00010600
FATSAVE DS    F                                   00010700
        EJECT                                     00010800
WFATDATA ST   11,WFATSAVE                         00010900
        MVC   DFATNAM,FATNAME                     00011000
        MVC   DBEDID,BEDIDENT                     00011100
        MVC   DDATADMI,DATEADMT                   00011200
        MVC   DFREHOSP,FREVHOSP                   00011300
        MVC   DPREVDTE,PREVDATE                   00011400
                                                  00011500
```

```
          MVC   DPREVREA,PREVREAS                          00011600
          BAL   11,WRITERTN                                00011700
          L     11,WFATSAVE                                00011800
          BR    11                                         00011900
*                                                          00012000
WFATSAVE  DS    F                                          00012100
HOSPNFND  ST    11,HOSPSAVE                                00012400
          MVI   NOHOSP,C'1'                                00012500
          MVC   ERRNAM,HOSPNAM                             00012600
          MVC   DETAIL1,NOHOSPLN                           00012700
          BAL   11,WRITERTN                                00012800
          MVI   NOHOSP,C'0'                                00012900
          MVI   DETAIL1,C' '                               00013000
          MVC   DETAIL1+1(131),DETAIL1                     00013100
          L     11,HOSPSAVE                                00013200
          BR    11                                         00013300
*                                                          00013400
HOSPSAVE  DS    F                                          00013500
*                                                          00013600
*                                                          00013700
WARDNFND  ST    11,WARDSAVE                                00013800
          MVI   NOWARD,C'1'                                00013900
          MVC   DETAIL2,NOWARDLN                           00014000
          BAL   11,WRITERTN                                00014100
          MVI   NOWARD,C'0'                                00014200
          MVI   DETAIL2,C' '                               00014300
          MVC   DETAIL2+1(131),DETAIL2                     00014400
          L     11,WARDSAVE                                00014500
          BR    11                                         00014600
*                                                          00014700
WARDSAVE  DS    F                                          00014800
*                                                          00014900
*                                                          00015000
ENDJOB    CLOSE (PARMETER)                                 00015100
          CLOSE (PRNTER)                                   00015200
          L     13,SAVE+4                                  00015300
          RETURN (14,12),RC=0                              00015400
*                                                          00015500
DATE      MVC   CURRDATE,=C'06/26/77'                      00015600
```

289

```
WRITERTN  BR    11                         00015700
          ST    11,WRITSAVE                 00016000
          LH    10,LINECNT                  00016100
          CH    10,=H'45'                   00016200
          BL    AHEAD6                      00016300
*                                           00016400
          MVC   LINECNT,=H'1'               00016500
          MVC   PRAREA,HEAD1                00016600
          MVC   PRCTL,TOPPAGE               00016700
          PUT   PRNTER,ALINE                00016800
*                                           00016900
          MVC   PRAREA,HEAD2                00017000
          MVC   PRCTL,DOUBSPC               00017100
          PUT   PRNTER,ALINE                00017200
*                                           00017300
          MVC   PRAREA,HEAD3                00017400
          PUT   PRNTER,ALINE                00017500
          MVC   PRAREA,DETAIL1              00017600
          PUT   PRNTER,ALINE                00017700
*                                           00017800
          CLI   NOHOSP,C'1'                 00017900
          BE    WRITEXIT                    00018000
*                                           00018100
          MVC   PRAREA,HEAD4                00018200
          PUT   PRNTER,ALINE                00018300
*                                           00018400
          MVC   PRAREA,DETAIL2              00018500
          PUT   PRNTER,ALINE                00018600
*                                           00018700
          CLI   NOWARD,C'1'                 00018800
          BE    WRITEXIT                    00018900
*                                           00019000
          MVC   PRAREA,HEAD5                00019100
          PUT   PRNTER,ALINE                00019200
*                                           00019300
          MVC   PRCTL,SINGSPC               00019400
          MVI   PRAREA,C' '                 00019500
          MVC   PRAREA+1(131),PRAREA        00019600
```

```
         PUT   PRNTER,ALINE                                       00019700
*                                                                 00019800
AHEAD6   MVC   PRAREA,DETAIL3                                     00019900
         MVC   PRCTL,SINGSPC                                      00020000
         PUT   PRNTER,ALINE                                       00020100
*                                                                 00020200
         LH    10,LINECNT                                         00020300
         LA    10,1(0,10)                                         00020400
         STH   10,LINECNT                                         00020500
*                                                                 00020600
WRITEXIT L     11,WRITSAVE                                        00020700
         BR    11                                                 00020800
*                                                                 00020900
WRITSAVE DS    ::                                                 00021000
SAVE     DS    18F               SAVE AREA                        00021200
*                                                                 00021300
PARMETER DCB   DSORG=PS,MACRF=GM,EODAD=ENDJOB,RECFM=FB,LRECL=80,  00021400
               DDNAME=INPUT                                       00021500
*                                                                 00021600
PRNTER   DCB   DSORG=PS,MACRF=PM,RECFM=FBA,LRECL=133,             00021700
               DDNAME=OUTPUT                                      00021800
*                                                                 00021900
*                                                                 00022000
PARMCARD DS    OCL133                                             00022100
         DS    CL2                                                00022200
IHOSPNAM DS    CL20                                               00022300
         DS    CL58                                               00022400
*                                                                 00022500
ALINE    DS    OCL133                                             00022600
PRCTL    DS    C                                                  00022700
PRAREA   DS    CL132                                              00022800
*                                                                 00022900
FULL     DS    F                                                  00023000
NOHOSP   DC    C'0'                                               00023100
NOWARD   DC    C'0'                                               00023200
NOPAT    DC    C'0'                                               00023300
TOPPAGE  DC    C'1'                                               00023400
DOUBSPC  DC    C'0'                                               00023500
TRIPSPC  DC    C'-'                                               00023600
```

```
SINGSPC  DC    C' '                                    00023700
GU       DC    CL4'GU  '                               00023800
GN       DC    CL4'GN  '                               00023900
GNP      DC    CL4'GNP '                               00024000
LINECNT  DC    H'52'                                   00024100
PAGECNT  DC    H'0'                                    00024200
NEWMONTH DS    PL2                                     00024300
NEWYEAR  DS    PL2                                     00024400
WRDTYPE  DS    CL20'  '                                00024500
DATEWK1  DS    PL2                                     00024600
DATEWK2  DS    PL2                                     00024700
*                                                      00024800
CURRDATE DS    OCL8                                    00024900
CURRMO   DS    CL2                                     00025000
         DC    C'/'                                    00025100
CURRDAY  DS    CL2                                     00025200
         DC    C'/'                                    00025300
CURRYR   DS    CL2                                     00025400
*                                                      00025500
WSFREVDT DS    OCL4                                    00025600
FREVMO   DS    CL2                                     00025700
FREVYR   DS    CL2                                     00025800
         COPY  AHOSPITA                                00026000
*                                                      00026100
         COPY  AWARD                                   00026200
*                                                      00026300
         COPY  AFATIENT                                00026400
*                                                      00026500
SSAHOSP  DC    C'HOSPITAL(HOSFNAME ='                  00026600
*                                                      00026700
SSAHNAME DS    CL20                                    00026800
         DC    C')'                                    00026900
*                                                      00027000
SSAWARD  DC    C'WARD   (WARDTYPE =QUARANTINE          00027100
*                                                      00027200
SSAFAT   DC    CL9'FATIENT  '                          00027300
         EJECT                                         00027400
HEAD1    DS    OCL132                                  00027500
```

```
        DC   CL26' '                              00027600
        DC   CL106' P R E V I O U S   S T A Y   R E P O R T'  00027700
*                                                00027800
HEAD2   DS   CL132' '                            00027900
*                                                00028000
HEAD3   DS   OCL132                              00028100
        DC   CL25'HOSPITAL NAME'                 00028200
        DC   CL35'HOSPITAL ADDRESS'              00028300
        DC   CL10'HOSP PHONE'                    00028400
        DC   CL62' '                             00028500
*                                                00028600
HEAD4   DS   OCL132                              00028700
        DC   CL12'WARD NO'                       00028800
        DC   CL14'TOT ROOMS'                     00028900
        DC   CL13'TOT BEDS'                      00029000
        DC   CL15'BEDS AVAIL '                   00029100
        DC   CL20'WARD TYPE'                     00029200
        DC   CL58' '                             00029300
*                                                00029400
HEAD5   DS   OCL132                              00029500
        DC   CL21'PATIENT NAME'                  00029600
        DC   CL6'BED'                            00029700
        DC   CL12'ADMIT DATE'                    00029800
        DC   CL11'PREV DATE'                     00029900
        DC   CL21'PREVIOUS HOSPITAL'             00030000
        DC   CL30'PREVIOUS REASON'               00030100
        DC   CL31' '                             00030200
DETAIL1 DS   OCL132                              00030400
DHOSPNAM DS  CL20                                00030500
        DC   CL5' '                              00030600
DHOSPADR DS  CL30                                00030700
        DC   CL5' '                              00030800
DHOSPHON DS  CL10                                00030900
        DC   CL62' '                             00031000
*                                                00031100
DETAIL2 DS   OCL132                              00031200
        DC   CL3' '                              00031300
DWARDNO DS   CL2                                 00031400
        DC   CL10' '                             00031500
```

293

```
DTOTRMS   DS   CL3                                        00031600
          DC   CL11' '                                    00031700
DTOTBEDS  DS   CL3                                        00031800
          DC   CL10' '                                    00031900
DBDSAVAI  DS   CL3                                        00032000
          DC   CL9' '                                     00032100
DWARDTYP  DS   CL20                                       00032200
          DC   CL58' '                                    00032300
*                                                         00032400
DETAIL3   DS   0CL132                                     00032500
DPATNAM   DS   CL20                                       00032600
          DC   C' '                                       00032700
DBEDID    DS   CL4                                        00032800
          DC   CL4' '                                     00032900
DDATADMI  DS   CL6                                        00033000
          DC   CL6' '                                     00033100
DPREVDTE  DS   CL4                                        00033200
          DC   CL5' '                                     00033300
DPREHOSP  DS   CL20                                       00033400
          DC   C' '                                       00033500
DPREVREA  DS   CL30                                       00033600
          DC   CL31' '                                    00033700
*                                                         00033800
NOHOSPLN  DS   0CL132                                     00033900
ERRHNAM   DS   CL20                                       00034000
          DC   CL5' '                                     00034100
          DC   CL107'**** HOSPITAL NOT FOUND ****'        00034200
*                                                         00034300
NOWARDLN  DC   CL132'**** NO QUARANTINE WARDS ****'       00034400
*                                                         00034500
NOPATLN   DC   CL132'**** NO PATIENTS WITH PREVIOUS STAY ****'  00034600
          EJECT                                           00034700
PCBMASK   DSECT                                           00034800
          COPY MASKA                                      00034900
          END  DLITCBL                                    00035000
```

The IMS Reference Manuals

There are a number of manuals that you should become familiar with if you're going to be working in an IMS environment. There are different manuals for DL/I DOS/VS, IMS/360 and IMS/VS. Figure H.1 shows the manuals that you'll use most often in an IMS/360 shop, figure H.2 shows the manuals that you'll use in an IMS/VS shop and figure II.3 shows the DL/I DOS/VS manuals. There are other manuals that apply to IMS and DL/I, but they describe special features that not all shops use. You can check your latest IBM manual bibliography to get the names and form numbers of all the available IMS and DL/I reference manuals. It's a good to check your IBM manual bibliography before you order any of these manuals since manual names and form numbers are changed from time to time.

The following sections contain brief descriptions of each of the manuals listed in figures H.1, H.2, and H.3.

The General Information Manual

This manual can be used to get an overall picture of IMS facilities. All IMS features are covered in an introductory manner. This manual can be read by programmers, analysts, data base administrators, operators, and managers.

The System/Application Design Guide

This manual is of most use to the Analyst or Data Base Administrator charged with the design or implementation of an IMS system. It includes extensive sections on data communications systems. This book is of use to any application programmer who wants to carry his or her knowledge of IMS further than the ability to write application programs.

The Application Programming Reference Manual

This manual is of the most use to the application programmer. It contains instructions on the use of all the DL/I Calls. Some of the more useful parts of the book include a complete listing of all the status codes that can be returned for all Calls and of complete sample programs that use IMS facilities.

GH20–0765   IMS/360 General Information Manual

SH20–0910   IMS/360 System/Application Design Guide

SH20–0911   IMS/360 System Programming Reference Manual

SH20–0912   IMS/360 Application Programming Reference Manual

SH20–0913   IMS/360 Operator's Reference Manual

SH20–0914   IMS/360 Messages and Codes Reference Manual

SH20–0915   IMS/360 Utilities Reference Manual

Figure H.1 IMS/360 reference manuals

GH20–1260   IMS/VS General Information Manual

SH20–9025   IMS/VS System/Application Design Guide

✓ SH20–9026   IMS/VS Application Programming Reference Manual

✓ SH20–9027   IMS/VS System Programming Reference Manual

SH20–9028   IMS/VS Operator's Reference Manual

✓ SH20–9029   IMS/VS Utilities Reference Manual

SH20–9030   IMS/VS Messages and Codes Reference Manual

SH20–9053   IMS/VS Message Format Service User's Guide

SH20–9054   IMS/VS Advanced Function for Communications

SH20–9081   IMS/VS Installation Guide

Figure H.2 IMS/VS reference manuals

GH20–1246   DL/I DOS/VS General Information Manual

SH12–5411   DL/I DOS/VS Application Programming Reference Manual

SH12–5412   DL/I DOS/VS Utilities and Guide for the System Programmer

SH12–5413   DL/I DOS/VS System/Application Design Guide

SH12–5414   DL/I DOS/VS Operator's Reference Manual and Messages and Codes

Figure H.3 DL/I DOS/VS reference manuals

The System Programming Reference Manual

Most of this manual is at level of detail that most application people will find
too deep. Its main orientation is to the system programmer who installs and
maintains the IMS system. One useful part of the book for the application
programmer is listing of the cataloged procedures that are supplied by IBM
with the IMS system. A lot can be learned about how the various parts of IMS
fit together from a study of these procedures.

After release 1.1.2 of IMS/VS, this manual was broken into two manuals. The first one has this same name, and the second one is called the *IMS/VS Installation Guide*. The information covered in the *IMS/VS Installation Guide* is described in a later section.

The Operator's Reference Manual

This manual is of the most use to people who operate remote terminals under the control of IMS. Terminal operating procedures and IMS terminal commands are covered in great detail. The introductory chapters are of interest, however, to anyone who will be working in the IMS DB/DC environment. The manual does a good job of explaining the resources that are under the control of IMS in a DB/DC environment, and the facilities that you have for working with those resources.

The Utilities Reference Manual

This manual is of the most use to data base administrators and IMS system programmers. The manual covers the utility programs that are used to reorganize and maintain DL/I data bases. The most useful part of the manual for application programmers is the section covering the DBDGEN and PSBGEN utilities. The descriptions of the operands that can be coded in the DBDGEN and PSBGEN statements often contain more information about some key IMS features than all of the other manuals combined. When in doubt about how a particular feature works, look up the appropriate DBDGEN or PSBGEN parameters that are used to implement the feature. They can often tell you a lot about how the feature works.

The Messages and Codes Reference Manual

This manual covers the messages and completion codes that can be returned by the various parts of the IMS software. It is of the most use to terminal operators, data base administrators, and IMS system programmers. The status codes that application programmers are interested in are covered in the *Application Programming Reference Manual*.

Message Format Service User's Guide (IMS/VS Only)

This manual is of interest only to people who work directly with the Message Format Service Feature. It explains, in great detail, how to set up the MIDs, MODs, DIFs, and DOFs to control the use of MFS. This manual applies to IMS/VS only. IMS/360 users will find information about MFS in the *IMS/360 Application Programming Reference Manual* and in the *IMS/360 System/Application Design Guide*.

Advanced Function for Communications (IMS/VS Only)

This manual covers some special data communications features that are available only to IMS/VS users. This manual is normally only of interest to IMS system programmers who use these special data communications features.

The Installation Guide (IMS/VS Only)

In IMS/360 installations, and for IMS/VS systems before version 1.1.2, the information in this manual is covered in the *System Programming Reference Manual*. With version 1.1.2 and later, IBM improved on the material relating to the installation of IMS and put it in its own manual. This manual covers the entire process of installing an IMS system and performing an IMS system definition.

DL/I DOS/VS Reference Manuals

Notice that there are fewer manuals listed for DL/I DOS/VS than there are for IMS/360 and IMS/VS. Some of the DL/I DOS/VS manuals combine information found in more than one IMS manual. The names are pretty self-explanatory where information is combined.

Index